Pitt Series in Composition, Literacy, and Culture

Academic Discourse and

Critical Consciousness

Patricia Bizzell

UNIVERSITY OF PITTSBURGH PRESS

Pittsburgh and London

Published by the University of Pittsburgh Press, Pittsburgh, Pa., 15260

Copyright © 1992, University of Pittsburgh Press

Manufactured in the United States of America

Printed on acid-free paper

Library of Congress Cataloging-in-Publication Data

Bizzell, Patricia.
    Academic discourse and critical consciousness / Patricia Bizzell.
        p.   cm.—(Pittsburgh series in composition, literacy, and culture)
        ISBN 0-8229-3730-1. —ISBN 0-8229-5485-0 (pbk.)
        1. English language—Rhetoric—Study and teaching.   2. Criticism—
    Authorship.   3. Critical thinking.   I. Title.   II. Series.
    PE1404.B585   1992
    808'.042'07—dc20   92-11967
                                                                              CIP

A CIP catalogue record for this book is available from the British Library.

Eurospan, London

Contents

Academic Discourse and Critical Consciousness

Introduction

I have been teaching first-year college composition since 1971. I mention the date only to locate the historical period in which I began to form and theorize my teaching practices. I have experienced this period as a time in which my skepticism has gradually increased concerning the American promise that education leads up from poverty and political oppression, a promise that seemed on the verge of realization during the campus social activism of the 1960s, and one that initially motivated my choice of teaching as a career.

The essays collected here represent attempts to understand what I was doing as a teacher of writing during this period. Looking back on them now, I would say that they chart a change in my thinking about academic discourse and critical consciousness. "Critical consciousness," a term I learned from the work of Paulo Freire, once meant for me something like an awareness of the injustices of social inequality in America, coupled with a commitment to rectifying those injustices. "Academic discourse" comprised the ways of thinking and using language that prevail in the academy. I once hoped to inculcate critical consciousness in my students through teaching them academic discourse. Now I am not only skeptical about the potential causal relationship between academic discourse and critical consciousness, but I am also dissatisfied with "critical consciousness" as a name for the goal of my teaching. But I have retained the name *Academic Discourse and Critical Consciousness* for this collection precisely because the linkage signified by the "and" is what I am grappling with in the essays included here.

I realize that assembling these essays retrospectively tends to give them a narrative coherence they did not have when I was writing them. I don't want to imply that I knew in 1971 how my thinking was going to evolve or even that there was any inner necessity for it to evolve as it has: the process has been too collaborative for that. I also don't want to imply that I now understand fully everything that is going on in these essays and exactly how they all fit together. Given these hesitations, I have found the process of constructing this introductory narrative very difficult. But I offer it diffidently with the idea that it provides one example of development in the still relatively new field of composition studies.

I graduated from Wellesley College in 1970 and went directly on to graduate school in English at Rutgers, the State University of New Jersey. I remember deciding to go to graduate school, rather than to New York City to be a poet with some of my friends, because I really didn't like my poetry very much, and I thought society could be asked to support only good poets. Others, like me, ought to find something more socially useful to do. I was defining "socially useful" in the vaguely left-liberal terms that seemed to characterize the politics of every student I knew in those days: one had to fight racism, sexism, and the economic and political oppression enforced by the military-industrial complex.

I was hoping to use teaching to act on my left-liberal values in these ways: by teaching the close analysis of texts, I would equip my students to see through the discriminatory and oppressive messages flooding the media from the dominant culture. They would learn to see that racism is wrong, for example, and that those protesting it are right. Moreover, they would learn to thread their way through the maze of daunting academic texts they had to master in order to get their degrees, and helping them do this would further my values because it would give right-thinking people access to the avenues to power. Teaching the production of a variety of written genres, and especially the genres of academic prose, would accomplish similar beneficial political goals.

I felt, too, that simply to assist any student of color to graduate, whatever he or she intended to do afterward, struck a blow for freedom. Thus as a graduate student, I volunteered to teach remedial writing rather than one of the more advanced courses in Rutgers's multiple-requirement sequence, because here seemed to be concentrated the largest numbers of students from socially disenfranchised and marginalized groups.

I taught remedial writing at Rutgers from 1971 to 1978—long enough for the course name to change from "remedial" to "developmental" to "basic." Taking my Ph.D. in English literature in 1975, I stayed on in a full-time non-tenure-track position to direct the basic writing program from 1975 to 1977, and to direct a training program for all the composition teachers in 1977–78. Also in that school year, I taught what I believe to have been the first graduate course at Rutgers in composition studies.

Teaching basic writing gradually changed many of the attitudes I brought into my work, indeed, began to make these attitudes seem woefully naive. My simple assumption that my own values would be ratified by reality, once the textual underbrush had been cleared by close reading, received repeated rude shocks from students who were willing to misread, as I thought, with great creativity in order to vigorously support what I took to be an oppressive status quo, even when it seemed that they had the most to lose from the present social arrangements. My glib assurance that students could adapt academic writing to their own purposes, that they could be "in it but not of it," could master it well enough to graduate without having their native values threatened or altered in any way, was repeatedly shaken by what seemed to be unreasoning resistance to academic ways of arguing and organizing, even from students who seemed to have the most to gain by learning them. My officious confidence that I could "help" these students, could "give" them what they needed, was constantly undermined by the frustrations they and I experienced in their work for me and for their other courses.

I kept trying to teach Standard English and academic forms of prose. I knew that in the composition classes after basic writing, my students would be expected to relish belletristic essays and produce their own memoirs and graceful speculations. But I was looking for clues. Surely there were ways to do better what I was doing, or better yet, to find something different to do, something more appropriate to everyone's circumstances. I got a wealth of practical advice from George Kearns, then director of writing programs at

Rutgers, and from my fellow graduate students, but being so text-oriented already, I wondered if I couldn't find out more from books. Were there books on the teaching of writing: not textbooks for undergraduates, but scholarly books for teachers?

If such books existed, my graduate professors had not mentioned them. My teachers were well published, indeed renowned critics, who trained us to take our own academic writing seriously, and yet no one seemed to think that writing itself was a serious object of study. This attitude is typified by the fact that no one thought it worth mentioning that Janet Emig, author of the seminal study *The Composing Processes of Twelfth-Graders* and a nationally known composition scholar, was teaching in the Education Department at Rutgers when I was a graduate student in English. I did not find out about her work until after taking my degree. To treat composition theory and pedagogy seriously was to define oneself as more student oriented, more pedagogy oriented, than those who aimed at careers in literary theory or criticism, and thus to depict oneself as somehow a less professional scholar. This is the only way I can now attempt to explain my not knowing, until several years after I started teaching, that there even existed a body of scholarship on the teaching of writing, and such journals as *College English* and *College Composition and Communication*.

At that time, Rutgers University consisted of a collection of separate colleges, each with a special defining mission. Livingston College was the "experimental" school, which in those days meant the place where the most left-oriented pedagogical ideas would be tried out, such as admitting students who did not have the traditional academic credentials. Evidently another radical idea at Livingston was that writing teachers could benefit from reading scholarship on writing and on education in general. From a fellow graduate student who was teaching at Livingston, Bruce Herzberg, I received my first two books on education and writing: Paulo Freire's *Pedagogy of the Oppressed* and Mina Shaughnessy's *Errors and Expectations*.

Shaughnessy's definition of a category called "basic writing" or "basic writers" came to me as a dramatic revelation. I had felt that my students had some kind of serious problem, expressed by the "remedial" or "developmental" name and approach attached to the course I was teaching. But at the same time I had felt that they did not deserve to bear the entire onus of this problem themselves. Now, under the model of basic writing, I could see them as beginners, newcomers to a complex discursive world with whose ways of using language they were relatively unfamiliar. Using this model, I could shape the masses of errors in their writing into patterns that made sense in terms of the newcomers' attempts to approximate what they thought academic writing was. Even their dogmatic arguments and quick-closing clichés could be seen as attempts to claim academic authority. Shaughnessy's analysis seemed to diagnose exactly what I needed by way of a pedagogy: some method of demystifying academic writing, laying bare its habitual patterns and mindsets so that students could imitate them more easily.

At the same time, what I gathered from Freire was an even stronger sense than my student liberalism had provided of the connection between political oppression and academic disadvantage. My students' initial unfamiliarity with academic writing could be understood in terms of group membership, with some groups experiencing disenfranchisements and exclusions that had kept them from encountering much academic writing in the past. My students had been victims for so long of what Freire calls "banking education" that they could hardly break out of the narrow-visioned thinking it enforces. To be sure, I had to start where they were, but I could hope to guide them toward a more critically interactive relationship with their school experience. I could hope to foster what Freire calls "critical consciousness," in which, he suggests, an analytic vision first acquired through literacy schooling can be turned on the inequities in the larger social order.

As I assimilated Shaughnessy and Freire into my thinking, I began to reformulate my pedagogical goals. Now I would not have said that I was teaching Standard English and academic forms of prose in order to enable students to graduate and better themselves in American society while also trying to reform society from within. Now I would have said that I was teaching academic discourse—meaning to imply something that influenced thinking profoundly, even as it embodied stylistic conventions—and that I hoped what would issue from the teaching would be the development of critical consciousness in students so that they would want to work not just for reform, but for radical change in American society. Thus I was able to continue to justify to myself the project of teaching writing in an American college.

After Bruce Herzberg and I got married in the summer of 1977, we went to the University of California at Irvine which was then hosting the School of Criticism and Theory so that Bruce could study with Stanley Fish and Edward Said. I remember being over-whelmed with Said's ideological analyses of orientalism and Fish's versions of reader-response criticism. I was still arguing against it all. I claimed that texts limited the readings that could be produced from them, if not to a single reading at least to a range; I claimed that social conventions constrained individuals but did not determine them completely; and without ever giving up any of these argumentative positions I found that by the end of the summer, I believed that "everything" was constituted by discourse. I saw in Fish's "interpre-tive community" the academic community my students were trying to enter. What I had to do was to interpret its interpretive strategies.

I saw myself as starting on this project in the first essay I published in the area of composition studies, "The Ethos of Academic Dis-course." The direct inspiration for this piece was Mina Shaugh-nessy's last published essay, "Some Needed Research on Writing."[1] Shaughnessy had called for a "taxonomy" of "ways of winning argu-ments in academe." I attempted to provide theoretical support for the importance of such a project. Following what I was beginning to learn from Fish, and from another book I was reading that summer in California, *The New Rhetoric* by Chaim Perelman and Lucie Olbrechts-Tyteca, I suggested that arguments get treated as rational by academic readers when the writer knows how to evoke the com-mon wisdom of the academic discourse community and how to em-ploy its interpretive strategies. I called for writing teachers to under-take to describe the common academic wisdom, to analyze and teach academic discourse conventions. My own work, I supposed, would soon be contributing to this taxonomy.

I learned, however, that the kind of research other composition specialists seemed to feel was needed did not match what I, and I thought Shaughnessy, desired. For instance, Maxine Hairston called for research that was social-science-oriented, rather than literary-critical in method as I took Shaughnessy's interpretations of basic writers' texts to be. This research, it seemed, would focus on individual writers and their mental processes in isolation, rather than on the social and cultural contexts of writing where I thought Fish's interpretive emphasis led, especially the academic context.[2] I was concerned that this empirical, individualistic focus would draw attention away from the political considerations that had always been important for me and that were foregrounded by my reading of Paulo Freire.

I was especially disturbed to hear Thomas Kuhn being used in support of this research agenda, because I thought that he gave more support to my own position. Kuhn's book *The Structure of Scientific Revolutions* formed part of the intellectual horizon for those of us at Rutgers and at Irvine who were interested in theories treating discourse as constitutive of knowledge. Kuhn, as we read him, suggested that "even" in the natural sciences, where the claim to demonstrable empirical truth might seem to be most unassailable, rhetorical processes in actual practice played a decisive role in the acceptance or dismissal of scientific theories. One could not say, then, that a theory prevailed because it was presented in discourse so transparent that the convincing power of the evidence supporting the theory was conveyed in the most unfiltered way. Rather, one would have to say that a theory prevailed because it and its supporting evidence were presented in discourse that argued the way scientists were prepared by their training, by their socialization to their discipline, to hear a position argued. In short, Kuhn, as I read him, provided the most powerful sort of argument against scientism.

Moreover, by calling attention to the power of discourse to constitute knowledge, Kuhn pointed not to the empirical social sciences but to more humanistic and rhetorically based research methods as the best source for defining the emerging field of composition studies. I was still hoping that if we were able to analyze academic discourse conventions in such a way as to demystify them for students, we would be contributing, if not to a political revolution, at least to the groundwork for major social change through preparing previously marginalized students to speak with powerful voices against the mainstream. I tried to speak for this reading of Kuhn, and to argue again for my own preferred agenda for composition studies, in "Thomas Kuhn, Scientism, and English Studies."

Looking back, I now feel that this was one of the most important essays in my career—but not because everyone listened to my call for composition research on discursive practices. On the contrary, the cognitivist agenda seemed to be carrying the day. But the Kuhn essay was important because it got me the attention of Ann Berthoff. At the 1979 Conference on College Composition and Communication, one of the first meetings I attended, I sat in a large lecture hall listening to Ann give a major address and suddenly heard her praise my Kuhn essay, which had appeared only a month before. I experienced a feeling of pure pleasure I thought was only available to little girls being praised by their mothers. Later, at a conference social gathering, Ann asked David Bartholomae to introduce us (David I had known from our graduate student days at Rutgers, where he had been Bruce's close friend).

I can't overemphasize the importance to me of having Ann's encouragement. I was never sure if we meant exactly the same thing when we talked about the mind's meaning-making powers—in spite of years, now, of tutelage, I'm still barely grasping Ann's uses of C. S. Pierce—or when we talked about how we were inspired by Paulo Freire's deep respect for learners. I never found myself citing her work as frequently as that of other thinkers. But I still felt somehow that our ultimate goals were in harmony, and that she had confidence in my ability to further those goals. For someone whose graduate professors had not given her much encouragement to take composition theory and pedagogy seriously, I found Ann's sheer fascination with the classroom experience and its intellectual and emotional rewards for teachers and students tremendously inspiriting.

Perhaps it was especially important for me to meet Ann Berthoff in 1979 because in the previous fall, I had left Rutgers to start my first tenure-track job, at Holy Cross College. It was important not only for the general boost of confidence it gave to a tentative assistant professor, but also for the more specific ratification it gave to my preference for moving to a college rather than a university. My experience at Rutgers had tended to make me see scholarship and teaching in opposition. It seemed that the most published and eminent university professors, even though I saw they were fine teachers of graduate students, were not particularly interested in discussing teaching or engaging in the labor-intensive task of teaching writing. The structure of the department implied that the more brilliant a person was, the more he or she published and the fewer and brighter the students he or she taught. Lesser lights taught undergraduates; mere sparks taught undergraduate composition.

The conclusion I was now able to draw from this, bolstered by my acquaintance with composition scholarship and the nurturing atmosphere of CCCC, was not that composition was not a worthy endeavor. Rather, it was that I ought to go someplace where composition work might be regarded more highly than it seemed to be in the university: specifically, I ought to go to a liberal arts college, where I might expect to find all sorts of pedagogical interests more valued. I did not want to define myself professionally as a scholar who also taught; I wanted the opportunity to be a teacher-scholar. I didn't want to have to take too much time away from my teaching to write a book in order to get tenure.

I also hoped by going to a liberal arts college to get away from the sort of multiple-course requirement-driven writing program with which I had been involved at Rutgers. I knew that such programs could scarcely exist at places without a ready pool of graduate teaching assistants, and Holy Cross had no graduate programs of any kind. Of course, in the mid-1970s when I was looking for a tenure-track job, almost the only kind of job open to people who defined themselves primarily as composition specialists was a position as director or assistant director of just such a large program. But my doctoral training had actually been in American literature, and I hoped to be able to find a college that would hire me as a combination person, to teach American literature and to act as a resident specialist in composition. This role is exactly what Holy Cross wanted me to play.

My reservations about large writing programs did not stem from particular weaknesses I perceived in the Rutgers program. I thought, and think, it was a fine example of its kind. But large writing programs as such seemed to me to embody several contradictions.

My sense of these contradictions began in my growing conviction that writing could not be seen as a skill or set of skills, analogous to the set of skills one must master in order to ride a bicycle. My theoretical understanding of discourse as constitutive of knowledge, as epistemic, entailed the idea that learning to write meant immersing oneself in the discursive practices of a community composed of present social relations, cultural assumptions, textual traditions, political circumstances—the whole complex web more recently indicated by Marilyn Cooper's concept of the "ecology of writing."[3]

Moreover, along with this gradual internalization of the community's discursive practices would proceed internal adjustments and external discursive innovations as this community's practices were juxtaposed with those of other communities to which each writer might be presumed to belong. This model suggests that one is always learning to write, that it is a lifelong process. A person could learn to ride a bike in a summer, and then never forget it. A person could be said never to finish learning to write.

Yet, I thought, to require a first-year composition course is to imply that writing can be learned in a brief time, as a skill, like riding a bike. When this turns out not to be the case, when many students exit the one-semester course still apparently not knowing how to write to their college teachers' satisfaction, then the first-year course becomes a multiple-course sequence. The first-year course becomes a two-semester course; perhaps it is preceded for some students by a basic writing course. And each of these courses must be passed before the next requirement can be completed. At Rutgers, we had students who completed their sophomore year in college without completing their "first-year" composition requirement. As juniors they might be found still trying to pass English 102. I didn't think I could go on treating composition as a skill that most "should" be able to master in a semester, in spite of the many student experiences suggesting otherwise.

Meanwhile, too, these students' other teachers might be found grading them negatively for their poor writing while doing no more to address the problem than to lambast the English department for not solving it in the first year. This situation implies another contradiction in the multiple-course requirement-driven program. To require courses is to imply that something can be gained here that can be gained nowhere else: presumably, the ability to write. University faculties can then forget about teaching writing anywhere else, because the English department is presumed to be taking care of it.

But if writing isn't a skill, if it is instead a more complex discursive process such as I have suggested above, then it follows that writing will be learned better the more opportunities one has to practice it, the more teachers of writing one has, the more guides one acquires to the discursive practices of the community one is trying to enter. In short, it follows that writing should be taught by every college teacher, not just those designated as writing specialists. Indeed, many undergraduates now get their firmest grasp on academic writing through practicing the discourse of their majors, whether or not the major is English. Yet the existence of a separate writing program continues to imply that here is where the writing instruction will be done.

I don't suppose that then I really wanted writing programs to wither away, nor do I wish to be read as priggishly calling for such a development now. It would be a mistake to sacrifice on the altar of theoretical correctness a program that one felt might still be doing some good. But in going to Holy Cross, I hoped to develop a writing program that would be college-wide, diverse, and voluntary. This helps to explain my intense interest in the ideas supporting writing-across-the-curriculum programs and peer tutoring workshops, ideas that now certainly will not seem new.

When I got to Holy Cross, the faculty had recently passed a resolution stating that learning to write formed a central part of liberal arts education and teaching writing a major responsibility for all faculty. I think this resolution reflected the Jesuit tradition of commitment to training in rhetoric as much as the back-to-basics educational atmosphere of the mid-1970s. But the only courses then being offered with an explicit focus on writing instruction were electives in the English Department. Almost all of the tenured and tenure-track faculty in the department (there were no part-timers) regularly took a turn teaching one of these courses, but my colleagues had little desire to expand their writing course offerings and no desire to shoulder the burden of a required course.

I volunteered to teach a writing course every semester, as well as courses in American literature; and I offered workshops from time to time on issues in writing instruction, informed by current scholarship. My colleagues participated in these workshops, and also supported my efforts to convince the dean of the college that Holy Cross needed a writing program based in his office, not in the English department. After consulting, too, with faculty outside the English department, I finally developed a writing program that began in 1982. This program consisted, and consists, of two parts: a writing-across-the-curriculum program and a peer-tutoring workshop. With the assistance of faculty colleagues within and outside the English department and head student tutors, I manage this two-part program and teach one course each semester.

The Writing-across-the-Curriculum Program comprises writing-intensive courses offered outside the English department every semester; a newsletter informing faculty of writing activities on campus and notes from the scholarship; and faculty workshops on writing instruction offered from time to time. While I have urged my colleagues to see themselves as teaching about academic discourse, my approach to developing this program has been collaborative in that I have attempted to use my knowledge of writing instruction to help faculty teach better the courses they want to teach, rather than urging the wholesale importation of any one writing technique. I have encouraged them to teach writing processes, especially by working over drafts, and to offer students a variety of kinds of writing, such as journals and prepared speeches, not all of which need be graded. Also, faculty workshop topics have frequently arisen from concerns expressed to me by colleagues either individually or as departments, rather than from what happened to be current in the field at the time.

The Peer-Tutoring Workshop is staffed by undergraduate students above the first-year level who have taken or are taking the tutor training course, a full-credit English course in composition theory and pedagogy. Once tutors have completed the course, they are paid for their tutoring hours. The workshop, in a small, crowded room down the corridor from my office in the main office building on campus, is open on weekday afternoons and evenings. Neither I nor the colleagues who have helped me manage the workshop stay in the room as tutors. I have tried to encourage everyone to think of the facility as being "by students for students," more a formalization of dorm study groups than an adjunct to the regular curriculum. Here, too, the implicit theory is collaborative learning. I encourage the tutors to share with their peers the secrets they as good students have learned about negotiating academic discursive practices.

Students may drop in for help with any stage of the writing process, or students may be referred to the workshop by teachers, academic advisors, or class deans. Holy Cross has no basic writing course and no English-as-a-second-language course; for the small number of first-year students in each entering class who might need such courses, the workshop provides individualized academic support. Faculty members also sometimes assign an entire class to use the workshop for help with one or all writing assignments, and usually these faculty members will simply request that one or several tutors be designated specifically to work with them and their students. In the typical recent year, 20 to 25 percent of our student body of 2,800 use the workshop.

Except for the situation in which a faculty member assigns a student to visit the workshop, no part of this writing program is ever required of any student. There is no requirement to take a writing-intensive course, or to avail oneself of tutors if one's native language is not English, and so on.

There does now seem to be a writing-rich environment at the college, as evidenced by the large number of student-sponsored journals. But I have not gone on at such length about the Holy Cross program because I wish to offer it as a model; indeed, I suspect that writing programs are not easily transplantable as models because to be good, they must be indigenous. Moreover, I see problems with the program, not the least of which is that probably most of the participants in it see themselves as teaching academic discourse so that students can succeed in college and better themselves in the larger society—that is, there is probably little radical political content to the program. But I want to take responsibility for what I was doing at Holy Cross while I wrote most of the essays collected in this volume.

As noted above, when I came to Holy Cross, the research agenda in composition studies seemed to be heading exclusively toward a cognitivist focus that worried me. While I was still at Rutgers, I had read *The Philosophy of Composition* by E. D. Hirsch, Jr., and found it a particularly clear-cut example of an attempt to use empirical evidence concerning what Hirsch calls "absolutes of human psychology" to establish a theoretical position on literacy, as Hirsch says, "above mere ideology." I wrote a seventy-five-page diatribe against the book upon that first reading, from which Bruce Herzberg carved the essay published as " 'Inherent' Ideology, 'Universal' History, 'Empirical' Evidence, and 'Context-Free' Writing: Some Problems in E. D. Hirsch's *The Philosophy of Composition*." When I look back, it seems as if I first articulated what I would now call my social-constructionist approach to the study of discourse by anatomizing just how Hirsch's argument goes wrong.

As far as I know, this essay had no more influence than the piece on Thomas Kuhn, although Hirsch has now repudiated the argument of *The Philosophy of Composition*. That is, he now agrees with Bruce and me that language is rendered intelligible by shared context rather than by structures inherent in the language independent of context. It is his new conviction of the importance of context that has urged Hirsch to promote a scheme for "cultural literacy." Cultural literacy comprises the contextual knowledge that renders Standard English discourse intelligible in national public fora.

Of course, Hirsch would inculcate cultural literacy in the same manner he once advocated inculcating a Standard English "grapholect"—the form of the argument is the same, and its political motives remain overt. In *The Philosophy of Composition*, Hirsch attempts to justify teaching a privileged dialect to everyone so that everyone can participate in the national life; but in order to make this case he has to ignore the fact that there are privileged people for whom the grapholect is much closer to a native tongue than it is for others, and who hence will have an advantage in mastering this condition for political participation. Social class differences call into question Hirsch's claim, as we put it, that "the grapholect's linguistic conservatism is transformed into political liberalism by universal schooling." Hirsch now almost echoes our words in promoting his specification of cultural literacy: "The inherent conservatism of literacy leads to a subtle but unavoidable paradox: the goals of political liberalism require educational conservatism. We make social and economic progress *only* by teaching myths and facts that are predominantly traditional."[4] For Hirsch, this is a paradox; for me, it is a contradiction that reveals the dangers of educational schemes that claim universality.

Unease about claims to universality prompted me to raise questions in a review-essay concentrating on the early work of Linda Flower and John R. Hayes, "Cognition, Convention, and Certainty: What We Need To Know about Writing." My principal objection to their work in this essay is that they seek a kind of "authoritative certainty" that, I argue, following Kuhn, no scientific research can provide. I did not want to allow them certainty because I feared that any model claiming to be above debate would be imposed Procrustean-fashion on all students, with relatively greater harm being done to students at greater social removes from the culture-bound assumptions about thinking and writing that, in my view, informed the model.

Rather than directing the attack against claims for the authority of empirical evidence, however, here I adopted the tactic of arguing that the view of composing offered by the cognitivist approach is incomplete. In part this tactic was motivated by a desire to be respectful to the many scholars who were eagerly taking up cognitive research as a way to "do" composition studies, a badly needed modus operandi in view of the field's fledgling status. But I also wanted to create a research space for another approach, one that would focus upon the elements of the social context that influence writing, such as the textual conventions of discourse communities, which I suggested might be studied by more humanities-oriented research techniques.

The concept of "discourse community" thus was initially used to define an alternate research site for scholars in composition studies. Indeed, in my review-essay I pretended that research was already going on at that site; as far as I knew, it really wasn't, but I hoped to invoke it with my essay. I don't remember whether the concept of discourse community was "my own idea." I don't really believe that people have their "own" ideas or "own" them. The formulation of the concept in my review-essay was not taken from anywhere else in its present form, but it was certainly profoundly influenced by my reading in Kuhn, Fish, Richard Rorty, and the sociolinguists, and by discussions with Bruce Herzberg. Indeed, given the concept's provenance in a review-essay—which Dominic LaCapra calls the characteristic genre of our intellectual era—I think it would be fair to say that Flower and Hayes also influenced its development. And in turn, it would seem that this essay has influenced the work of the cognitivists who now define their research as "socio-cognitive," seeming to attempt to build in the supplement I called for; and it has influenced the work on discourse conventions done, for example, by scholars in writing across the curriculum.

I began to try to make my own contributions to the demystification of academic discourse conventions in "College Composition: Initiation Into the Academic Discourse Community." This essay was commissioned for *Curriculum Inquiry*, a journal published by the Ontario Institute for Studies in Education, by Henry Giroux. Henry was working at the Boston University School of Education at this time, enabling Bruce and me to come in from Worcester for inspiriting discussions with him, his wife, Jeanne Brady, and other left-oriented educators. We kept struggling with a critique of Marxist-influenced theories of education, which we felt were too rigid in their diagnosis of schools as sites of "reproduction," where oppressive cultural patterns were simply deposited in unresisting student minds by automaton teachers. We all felt that there should be, and our teaching experiences confirmed that there might be, opportunities for resistance and the promotion of egalitarian social and political values even within admittedly oppressive institutional structures. Giroux has codified this thinking in his concept of the "pedagogy of possibility."

In writing the "Initiation" essay, then, I was attempting to serve a utopian educational project by suggesting that initiation into academic discourse could be a good thing from a left-oriented point of view. I based this argument on two premises. One, perforce, is that basic writing students are educable—that is, alleged limitations in their prose should be traced to their social and political circumstances, which can be resisted, rather than to biologically hardwired cognitive deficiencies that would presumably be very difficult to change. I argued for this premise in my discussion of Andrea Lunsford's early work on basic writers.

The other premise is that the circumstances that produce these limitations in student writing can be resisted through mastering academic discourse because academic discourse fosters "critical un-

derstanding" or something like Paulo Freire's "critical consciousness." I did not argue for this premise here, however, and my
failure to do so constitutes a serious argumentative flaw in the
paper. I intended to argue for it in "Academic Discourse and Critical Consciousness," an essay forthcoming in *Social Text*, but that
essay never appeared.

There was perhaps a conscious ambivalence in my choice of the
term "initiation." Entering college could be seen as an initiation
ritual in a positive sense, as a process that provides mechanisms of
inclusion and empowerment, especially for so-called nontraditional
students. Initiation could also be a useful concept simply to suggest
that we understand students' entry into college as a social ritual,
entailing various kinds of subjective exchanges between initiates
and initiators, rather than as some sort of objectively monitored,
digital test of who should be in or out. In other words, initiation
foregrounds the personal feelings and culturally constructed, perhaps unconscious prejudices and assumptions in teachers and students that condition the entry process. But this view slides over
into a more negative or ironic connotation invoked by initiation,
images of physically and emotionally punishing rituals imposed on
newcomers by powerful people abusing their power. Initiation as a
negative concept invites us to see learning academic discourse as
running a gauntlet—hardly the sort of process that might be presumed to conduce to critical consciousness.

My doubts about the position I had been taking on the potential
of academic discourse to foster critical consciousness came to a
head about this time, as I was working on "Academic Discourse
and Critical Consciousness."

The key point in this argument is that learning academic discourse can change the thinking of basic writers in much the same
way that literacy, according to Paulo Freire, changes Brazilian peasants. Freire believes that human beings can "detach themselves
from the world"; that when they "enter into" social reality from this
detached perspective, the "true interrelations" they will "discover"
will embody injustices which the people will then be able to diagnose and correct. At this point they have embarked on the process
Freire calls "critical consciousness." Oppressive social systems will
seek to prevent people from developing critical consciousness, so

as not to be challenged and disrupted. Freire's peasant students have been operated on in this way, so that they are unable to exercise their innate human ability to "penetrate" reality but instead see themselves as seamlessly part of reality or part of nature: "more *part* of the world than transformers of the world."[5] Freire's project is to provide literacy education in which students learn-by-doing that they *can* detach from the world, analyze it, and take hold of it to change it.

In "Academic Discourse and Critical Consciousness," I find this language of detachment, penetration, and objective analysis very congenial to typical methods of academic thinking, and so I argue that academic discourse can be a form of literacy that encourages critical consciousness. The bulk of the essay is then spent in discussing how to teach academic discourse in this way: by emphasizing its culture-bound qualities, as the language of a particular community with a particular history and current socioeconomic and political interests. Thus academic discourse is not allowed to masquerade as the clearest or most rational or most efficient form of language use, to the detriment of the students' home languages, and the students are encouraged to relativize their acquisition of academic discourse, to see it as one more addition to their discursive repertoires, useful for specific purposes, rather than to see it as a means of growing up or learning to think. Nevertheless, like Freire, I assume here that with the critical detachment academic discourse affords when it is acquired in a (supposedly) liberatory manner will more or less automatically come insight into social injustices and the will to correct them.

I never published this essay because I developed serious doubts about the argument while writing it. The doubts did not really focus on whether academic discourse and critical consciousness could be linked. It seemed that they could be, although in thinking back over my teaching experience, I began to feel that my confidence in their causal relationship, in the idea that teaching academic discourse could *cause* critical consciousness in students, was somewhat exaggerated. I was more dissatisfied with critical consciousness itself as a goal for pedagogy. I began to doubt that critical detachment in the Freirean sense could be achieved, that *any* critical method could automatically lead to a left-oriented view of the socio-political world without any ideological arguments having to be made.

I think this doubt began to grow due to my continued contact with postmodern and deconstructive theories of literary interpretation, which implied that one could not get "out of" the cultural text by any critical means. The process was a continuation of what had happened to me at the School of Criticism and Theory: I never "accepted" these postmodern theories, I often argued against them and violated them shamelessly in my teaching of literature by American women writers, and yet increasingly I found that these theories came to feel "right" to me. Hence the rationale to which I had been clinging for some time as a justification of my teaching was seriously undermined.

Eventually I came to realize that the key issue here is embodied in the phrase above, "without any ideological arguments having to be made." My objection to Freire came to be precisely that he pretended his critical literacy methods merely pointed out truths in reality for students to discover—that is, that his methods were strictly objective and value-free. Eventually I would begin to work on the idea that education for critical consciousness could be saved by open recognition of its ideological agenda and the dropping of all pretense to objectivity. This development would lead me to reject Freire—a very difficult move given his earlier importance to my thinking.

I now believe that Freire does not so much pretend to absolute objectivity as he takes his ideological allegiances for granted, assuming that his Brazilian audience is well aware of them. I have the impression that within Brazilian Roman Catholic society, Freire is readily recognized as a kind of "liberation-theology" Catholic, pursuing left-oriented political goals out of an ultimate concern for the souls of his students. He can perhaps rely on his primary audience's identification of him in this way to underly the seemingly detached language he uses to characterize his students' gains. But if I'm right in this reading of the ideology in Freire's arguments, then it means that his work cannot be naively imported into American discussions of the politics of education without adding acknowledgement of his Christianity.[6]

Around 1982, however, when I abandoned the essay "Academic

Discourse and Critical Consciousness," I was not immediately ready to address the issue of how to open the ideological agenda of one's teaching. I had of course been trained, like all good American academics, to regard discussion of values in one's intellectual life as taboo. So I entered what now looks like something of a period of temporizing. With respect to my teaching, the abortive effort embodied in the "Academic Discourse and Critical Consciousness" essay left me in a much bleaker moral universe. I would go on teaching academic discourse and urging others to do so with much less confidence that I was doing good and doing no harm. Meanwhile, without having worked out of this theoretical impasse, I wrote three essays, two on the work of William Perry and one on modern research into composing processes.

The essays "William Perry and Liberal Education" and "What Happens When Basic Writers Come to College?" were written together in 1983, in an attempt to continue my researches into academic discourse in spite of theoretical doubts. In the Perry essay, I worked to prevent what I regarded as scientistic uses of Perry for the classification of students according to his developmental scheme, a process almost always detrimental to basic writers (who, with sadly typical stigmatization, are usually found to be "dualists," or thinkers in the very beginning stages of development). I argued that Perry's scheme is culture bound, or one might even say Harvard bound, but that if we understand this, his scheme becomes uniquely valuable as a taxonomy, if not exactly of the textual conventions of academic discourse, then of the philosophical assumptions or world view that informs academic discourse and that it creates. In other words, his scheme can be read as providing some of that needed research on writing for which Mina Shaughnessy called in her late work.

With Perry's picture of the academic world view in mind, then, in the "What Happens?" essay I wished to dignify the struggles of basic writers by characterizing these struggles as confrontations not just with a new language or new genres but with a whole new world view. At the same time, I attempted to preserve the project of teaching academic discourse to basic writers by arguing that there are grounds for hoping they can learn to work comfortably within the academic world view without abandoning home perspectives or becoming deracinated. Thus I followed out an agenda established in my earlier work, such as the essays on ethos and on initiation.

Although I had begun internally to question this agenda, I also pursued it around this time through a session proposed in 1984 for the 1985 CCCC, a session in which Bruce and I debated Lil Brannon and Cy Knoblauch concerning the political advisability of teaching academic discourse. The four of us agreed that all writing is socially embedded—that is, there is no writing outside discourse communities, no individually isolated creator. We agreed that students entering college should learn academic discourse, and indeed, would do so eventually. We all endorsed a workshop method of teaching writing, in which students would be encouraged to move from "expressive" or personal to "transactional" or academic forms of writing (Brannon took the terminology from James Britton), while modifying academic discursive practices in light of the styles and modes of thought preferred in the other discourse communities to which students belonged.

We disagreed about how academic discourse might be taught directly. Brannon and Knoblauch seemed to see a separation between form and content. They deplored the teaching of academic stylistic conventions or what they called "formal shells," and argued instead that allowing students to frame personally relevant meanings through writing would eventually lead students to academic habits of thought. Bruce and I agreed that the ultimate object was to familiarize students with academic habits of thought, but we doubted whether this project could be separated from consideration of what *kind* of papers students wrote as they moved toward this thinking; while not wanting at this point to teach some putative taxonomy of a generic academic discourse, we thought that students could be taught to argue, support assertions, and evaluate evidence in ways that would lead more directly to academic thinking than would writing in which they simply presented personal experience the authenticity of which few could question, which would require little "support."

Knoblauch suggested that even if we were correct in our hope that academic ways of thinking were cognate with critical consciousness, we were taking up a sort of "white man's burden" approach to teaching academic writing to marginalized students. We responded that social domination was a reality we could not wish away, but that we hoped to use our privileged position as middle-class teachers to create circumstances in which the whole structure of privilege could be challenged by those most oppressed by it. Once again, the whole force of our argument seemed to depend upon the power of academic discourse to generate critical consciousness, or something more politically effective than the overly detached and rational critical consciousness.

Still without coming to grips with whether this power would be forthcoming, I also followed out an old agenda in "Composing Processes: An Overview." The old agenda is that of the "Cognitive, Convention, and Certainty" essay, namely the attempt to create research space for a socially, textually, or as I would now say, rhetorically oriented approach to composition studies. Hence, in this essay I treated composing as involving plural processes, and research on composing processes as a very large category which can include work on authentic voice (or personal style, as it is called here), classical invention, writing across the curriculum, and collaborative learning, as well as cognitivist research. Thus I aimed both to diminish the authority of cognitive research on composing, by suggesting that it is not the only legitimate kind of research in this area, and to encourage reading other kinds of work in composition studies as bearing on composing, so as to emphasize the social and political effects on composing. Research on composing has now diversified to the point that these suggestions will not seem novel.

During the time I was writing these essays, I was undergoing some kind of complex mental gestation, which would result, among other things, in the last four essays in this book. These essays represent a definite break with the thinking expressed in my earlier work. I now see my crisis of confidence and theoretical revisionism as related somehow to Bruce's and my adoption of two little girls in 1984. I took a leave of absence from Holy Cross from the summer of 1984, when six-month-old Rachel and two-year-old Anna arrived from Korea, until the spring of 1986. Pulled away from my job, with no time to follow so closely the scholarly debates in which I had been involved,—I lost two sources of pleasure and self-worth; and at the same time I found it very hard to learn to be a mother and I was beset with feelings of inadequacy which I now know are not uncommon, but which I then thought were simply accurate self-assessments. All these factors tended to diminish my confidence to think through and articulate a position, feeding the doubts that had begun to develop several years earlier.

At the same time, being forcibly removed and distracted from my professional and scholarly business-as-usual aided me in imagining a constructive revision of what I wanted to do. Having my momentum interrupted made it easier to imagine alternative pursuits, new directions in which to start up again. One path I decided to follow was to rebuild my confidence on firmer scholarly ground, by undertaking projects that would give me a wider grasp of contemporary and premodern rhetoric and composition work. Bruce and I accepted offers to produce new editions of an annotated bibliography of current scholarship and an anthology of selections from premodern texts accompanied by historically oriented introductions. We signed the contract for the anthology in the spring of 1985, a little less than a year after the children came.

I was now inhabiting a world that was not organized. I could not plan my time or my reading. I was "reading around" both in the sense that I was reading in desultory fashion, trying things out, reading a little here and a lot there, as I looked for materials for the bibliographies and the anthology; and also in the sense that I was always reading around the children's nap times and the other exigencies of domestic life. I could now write this period into my tale as one of unexpected (and at the time unrecognized) freedom, which might have made me more open to a new theoretical angle when I happened upon one.

The angle I was looking for would help me address the lack I had felt in Freire's work, that is, the lack of a way to make articulate one's ideological agenda. What started me off on this new and, it seemed, more satisfying direction was Stanley Fish's work in the then-current controversy over the consequences of literary theory.

"Foundationalism and Anti-Foundationalism in Composition Studies" seemed then and seems now to be a first step in a new direction for me. The direct theoretical inspiration for this essay was Fish's essay "Consequences."[7] Fish's concept of "anti-foundationalist theory hope" sorted out a lot of difficulties for me, and it dominates my essay. I already understood the contemporary philosophical term "foundationalism" to refer to projects claiming to base knowledge on absolute grounds of truth; because such knowledge schemes could be and so often were used oppressively, foundationalism became the name of a philosophical orientation I opposed. At the same time I thought I embraced "anti-foundationalism," a philosophical position which holds that there are no absolute grounds of truth, or if there are, we cannot know them—that all "truth" is contingent, provisional, subject to establishment and change by rhetorical means.

But I had been getting into difficulties by clinging to the hope that the anti-foundationalist position could allow one to see what was "really" there in the social world, to see through the ideological mystifications of the dominant foundationalisms. In other words, I had hoped that the method of anti-foundationalist critique could itself provide the kind of authoritative certainty I condemned in foundationalism. When I began to reject the Freirean concept of critical consciousness as being too close to the rationalism of the academic point of view, I had hoped to turn instead to the power of the anti-foundationalist critique to confer the kind of authority for which I seemed to be looking, the authority that would justify continuing to teach academic discourse. Reading Fish, I found my difficulty named and anatomized precisely as "anti-foundationalist theory hope": the hope of the anti-foundationalist that her theory can function effectively as if it were absolute grounds for truth.

Hence with Fish's help I began to reject the notion that any critical method could confer detachment from the world and objective analysis of the world. In the first part of my essay, I attack this belief as it is found in the claims made for literacy by Thomas J. Farrell. I now see the attack on Farrell as a kind of acceptable displacement of my questions about theoretically similar claims made for literacy by Paulo Freire. I reject the idea that any form of literacy in and of itself can provide critical distance on the world or, one may as well say, critical consciousness. Then in the second part of the essay, I attack applications of Freire's theory of critical consciousness to academic discourse work, my own and others' work on writing across the curriculum, although again without mentioning Freire.

The problem facing me then becomes how to argue in an anti-foundationalist universe of discourse for left-oriented or egalitarian social values. The critical method does not confer the authority to make this argument. The argument can only be made ideologically, with interests acknowledged (hence my concluding this essay with a strong plea for forthrightness concerning our political allegiances and responsibilities). I am still trying to figure out how to make this kind of argument.

While I was working on "Foundationalism and Anti-Foundationalism in Composition Studies," I became aware from conversations at conferences that others shared my doubts about my own earlier advocacy of teaching academic discourse as a means to critical consciousness. I was alarmed to hear that I was now regarded in some quarters as advocating the imposition of academic discourse on all students at all costs with total disregard for whatever knowledge they might bring to school from other discourse communities.

These attacks have subsequently taken the form of treating the concept of "discourse community" as if it were meant to name a totally unified entity with impermeable boundaries.[8] I did not feel that I had explicitly used the concept in this way in my earlier work; indeed, I thought I had emphasized the multiplicity of personal, social, cultural, and political factors that conditioned discourse in a community. But I did see how I could be read as advocating the inculcation of academic discourse; I did in fact advocate teaching academic discourse, while trying to find ways of doing it that were not quite so dominating as the notion of "inculcation" might imply.

Included here is an essay entitled "What Is a 'Discourse Community'?" which I began to work on in preparation for the 1987 CCCC, as I framed a respondent's comments on essays by Carol Berkenkotter, Thomas Huckin, and John Swales, to be presented in a session Carol had organized. I initially thought of this project as an attempt to elaborate a definition of the concept of discourse community that would emphasize the dynamic, not the static, in discursive relations. I was assembling this new definition from materials that happened to be at hand, namely the CCCC papers, and anti-foundationalist stuff I happened to be reading, namely Jane Tompkins, with a certain amount of freedom and lack of concern for linearity characteristic of my "reading around" mode of thought, or what I allude to in the paper as David Bartholomae's concept of "combinatory rhetoric."

The first complete version of this paper was presented at the 1987 Conference on Rhetoric at Pennsylvania State University, where I was spending the summer with Bruce, Anna, and Rachel, teaching a graduate course on contemporary uses of classical rhetoric and mining Penn State's fabulous, Borgesian library to research our anthology, *The Rhetorical Tradition.* This first version was entitled "Some Uses of the Concept of Discourse Community," indicating both my eclecticism ("some") and my attempt to emphasize the dynamic ("uses"). After the conference, I produced the version printed here for the first time, the new title indicating an attempt to tighten up the eclecticism somewhat in the interests of clarifying the definition. I feel that this version still does not adequately emphasize the most important point I wanted to make, namely that discourse communities, particularly the academic discourse community, are not monolithic and impervious to influence by new voices joining the conversation. But the next version I produced, "How Do Discourse Communities Change?", fell into pieces under pressure from various readers to make it more linear. So let one version stand here to record my struggle to represent the dynamism in discourse communities.

In the process of working over these versions, I think I have begun to feel that I do not want to fight for the concept of discourse community, either in the sense of fighting for my own conception of this speculative instrument, or in the sense of fighting to keep the term current in debate in the field. I have felt that I have little more to offer to my long tussle with the issues revolving for me around the concept of discourse community, issues which I have been addressing here also as related to whether academic discourse can be, or should be, used to promote critical consciousness. I have felt that the agenda should be passed to other scholars and that I do not have to defend myself if they take it in other new directions. I may be foolish to sound so valedictory here. But this essay can be seen as one of my last attempts to grapple with the putative linkage of academic discourse and critical consciousness, a struggle which I have suggested forms the theme of this book.

The last two essays, "Arguing About Literacy" and "Beyond Anti-

Foundationalism to Rhetorical Authority," present attempts to develop responses to the problem of how to avow one's ideological agenda or, I may as well say, moral values, in a postmodern philosophical climate that will not allow such values to be grounded, or justified, transcendently. I embark on another struggle, not only against the cultural literacy work of E. D. Hirsch but also against many of those who have attacked him. Looking at these essays in the context of this book, I am struck by the way I have often been moved to argue against E. D. Hirsch. Whereas I may once have seen his position as the antithesis of my own, as for example in the essay on *The Philosophy of Composition*, I think I would now characterize his role in my imagination as more that of dark double. Especially in his cultural literacy work, Hirsch provokes me because, while rejecting his conclusions, I find myself drawn to much of what he says. For example, in specifying a content for academic discourse in "Academic Discourse and Critical Consciousness," I came perilously close to doing just what I condemn Hirsch for doing in his specification of a national cultural literacy: I set myself up as an expert who could in fact undertake such a task unilaterally.

The conclusion of "Arguing About Literacy" attempts to characterize ways of constructing beliefs and bases for action that would be "rhetorical," that is, frankly culture bound and collaborative. Thus I attempt to find some way to achieve direction without playing the expert. Both of these efforts are important, I feel—to not play the expert, yes, but also to meet what I increasingly regard as a professional responsibility to try to give my students' education some direction. It is the crying need for some direction that motivates me to question what appears to be quietism in the positions of some who have attacked Hirsch, as I argue in "Beyond Anti-Foundationalism." Of course, when I call for direction, I don't mean to imply that any old direction is okay. Rather I find that I am still seeking for ways to foster social justice, defined in some left-liberal way, in my teaching. Indeed, I think that many who attack Hirsch share that goal with me. If they do, that makes me all the more eager to enlist them in a more utopian critical process, imagining where we could go from here as well as what's wrong with now.

In working for these values, however, I no longer see myself as the privileged advocate for marginalized basic writers. No doubt my life is safer and more comfortable than the lives of many Americans; this is a "privilege" it would be fatuous to deny. But I increasingly see my situation as analogous to that of the basic writers—what I had thought of as specifically their experience I now see as paradigmatic for all American experience. Another way to put this would be to say that I now see all teachers as more like students, and all students as more like basic writers, than I once did.

I would link this re-vision with my current teaching situation at Holy Cross, in which most of my students come from the upper social classes. My task is to interest them in a social justice project for which they may not presently see any compelling reason. They know their lives are safer and more comfortable than most. They are tired of hearing that they are complicit in an unjust social order, at least in part because they know no strategies for changing it. I have to figure out how to persuade them to identify with social justice as the common good. I have to figure out how we can all use rhetorical power to effect democratic political change.

NOTES

1. Mina Shaughnessy, "Some Needed Research on Writing," *College Composition and Communication* 28 (December 1977): 318–21.

2. See Maxine Hairston, "Winds of Change: Thomas Kuhn and the Revolution in the Teaching of Writing," *College Composition and Communication* 33 (February 1982): 76–88.

3. Marilyn Cooper, "The Ecology of Writing," in Marilyn Cooper and Michael Holzman, *Writing as Social Action* (Portsmouth, N.H.: Heinemann-Boynton/Cook, 1989).

4. E. D. Hirsch, Jr., Joseph Kett, and James Trefil, *Cultural Literacy: What Every American Needs to Know*, 2d ed., revised and enlarged (New York: Vintage-Random House, 1988), xii. Hirsch's emphasis.

5. Paulo Freire, "Extension or Communication," trans. Louise Bigwood and Margaret Marshall, in *Education for Critical Consciousness* (1969; rpt. New York: Seabury Press, 1973), 105. Freire's emphasis.

6. For further development of these ideas, see my essay "Marxist Ideas in Composition Studies," in *Contending with Words*, ed. Patricia Harkin and John Schilb (New York: MLA, 1991).

7. Stanley Fish, "Consequences," *Critical Inquiry* 11 (1985): 433–58.

8. See Joseph Harris, "The Idea of Community in the Study of Writing," *College Composition and Communication* 40 (February 1989): 11–22.

The Ethos of Academic Discourse

I recall reading a survey of viewers of the televised Ford-Carter debates, which presented the perhaps unsurprising findings that those who had favored Carter before the debates felt that he won, while those who had favored Ford were convinced that their man came out ahead. In other words, few people's minds were changed by what purported to be a reasonable, persuasive exposition of the candidates' views. More recently, a televised "debate" between candidates for governor of New Jersey gave the viewers even less chance to be persuaded; the number of candidates (a dozen or so) attempting to present their views in a very short time (one hour) precluded any exposition at all. Most of the candidates didn't attempt it but instead chose to rely on a variety of rhetorical gestures. For example, one candidate decided he could best convey his views by sitting in frowning silence, with folded arms, throughout the "debate," while another chose to initiate a shouting match with the moderator early in the program and then to storm out of the studio, shaking his fist.

Feeble as the reasoning in political debates may seem to the teacher of rhetoric, such debates provide just about the only examples on television of any attempt at extended rational presentation of ideas. "Ideas" appear more often on television in the talk-show format. A celebrity's views on abortion or censorship are solicited, not to begin a consideration of the reasonable or defensible positions that may be taken on such debatable issues but to establish what classical rhetoric terms the speaker's "ethos." The audience's interest in a talk-show guest is determined, it seems to me, mainly

Reprinted with permission from *College Composition and Communication* 29 (Dec. 1978). Copyright 1978 by the National Council of Teachers of English.

by a series of aphorisms that contribute, along with his or her physical appearance, dress, and gestures, to make up the guest's "media image." This concept is probably much more familiar to television viewers than the classical notion of ethos, which it replaces in the rhetorical situation of the talk show. An analysis of parodic talk shows, such as "Fernwood 2-Night," would probably yield a clearer idea of the function of this "media image." And its operation can also be seen in the introductory questioning of the contestants on game shows, another popular item of television fare.

I would like to suggest that the dearth of extended rational presentation of ideas on television and the medium's dependence instead on the ethos of the speaker may help create freshman students of composition who have trouble with "the skills of elucidation and validation and sequencing in expository writing," as Mina Shaughnessy defined the problem.[1] For my proposition to have merit, I do have to assume that our students are socialized in language use much more through watching television than through reading and writing in academic discourse, but the findings of a panel appointed by the College Board to study declining verbal S.A.T. scores give some support to this assumption.[2] I would like to examine in what way television may be detrimental to the acquisition of the skills Shaughnessy mentions, by examining some functions of a speaker's ethos.

Edward P. J. Corbett cogently summarizes Aristotle's concept of ethos or ethical proof:

> Sometimes an author or a speaker comes to us with an antecedent reputation that disposes us to react to him either favorably or unfavorably. But while recognizing this fact, Aristotle insisted in his *Rhetoric* that the ethical appeal depends ultimately and crucially on what is said and how it is said in the discourse itself. Aristotle maintains that a speaker or writer will establish his credibility with us—that is, his persuasiveness—if he projects an image of himself as being a man of good sense, good moral character, and goodwill.[3]

Corbett emphasizes the importance of the ethical appeal even more strongly when he draws on its analysis by another classical master of rhetoric, Quintilian:

The ethical appeal is especially important in rhetorical discourse, because here we deal with matters about which absolute certainty is impossible and opinions are divided. Quintilian felt that of the three kinds of rhetorical discourse, deliberative oratory had the most need for the ethical appeal (he called it *auctoritas*). (93)

Although Corbett himself doesn't make this connection, I would like to suggest that his discussion of enthymemes, in a chapter subsection entitled "The Appeal to Reason," sheds some light on how a speaker goes about convincing his audience of his "good sense, good moral character, and goodwill." Corbett explains:

Aristotle was shrewd enough to see that we base persuasive arguments not only on what usually or generally happens but also on what people believe to be true. . . . Every civilization has a body of accepted opinions that influence the conduct of its affairs—a body of "truths" which have never really been demonstrated but in which the people have faith, almost to the point of accepting them as self-evident. (74)

Corbett argues that the speaker should familiarize himself with these "truths" and use them as the basis for the enthymemes or truncated syllogisms with which the speaker hopes to persuade an audience. Surely one uttering "self-evident opinions" will impress his or her audience as a judicious reasoner. Indeed, if the speaker is also a member of the "civilization" that holds these beliefs, he or she probably believes them with at least some of the sincerity that the audience does and can thus impress the audience as a "good" person.

Frank D'Angelo, in an article on proverbs, seems to be arguing that proverbs also fall into this category of accepted opinions. After watching a televised interview with a Boston protestor against busing, he concludes "that proverbs are not just outworn sentiments from an earlier age but that they are still being used by people every day to win arguments. Because proverbs are so familiar, they often win uncritical acceptance from the audience."[4] He concludes his argument by stating that proverbs "still have a vital relevance for modern man in the presentation and preservation of ethical values" (36). D'Angelo, however, apparently does not see the meaning of "ethical" to which I am pointing as he devotes his article to an extremely interesting discussion of proverbs as heuristics for invention, without considering their underlying function in developing the ethos, or moral appeal, of the one who uses them. But I have a more serious quarrel with D'Angelo's approach: he remains squarely within the "civilization" for which the proverbs express "accepted opinions," to use Corbett's terms. He seems to regard the problem of finding arguments as a problem in uncovering logical appeals that are therefore universal almost by definition; and Corbett's discussion of enthymemes seems prone to a similar misemphasis.

For our students, the problem of capitalizing on the preeminent power of the ethical appeal is more of a problem in figuring out the conventions of academic discourse, as Mina Shaughnessy clearly recognizes. In discussing the more complex writing problems of her students, she finds that "beginning adult writers. . . do not know the rituals and ways of winning arguments in academia. Indeed, so open and vulnerable do they appear in their writing that teachers often turn sentimental in their response to it, urging them into the lion's den of academic disputation with no more than an honest face for protection" (319). Shaughnessy senses that the ethos of the "honest face" is not adequate for academic discourse, as she complains that "the emphasis in writing instruction over the past years has not encouraged a close look at academic discourse nor favored such images as the contest or the dispute as acceptable metaphors for writing" (319–20).

Students' reliance on the "honest face" ethos leads them into many of the rhetorical postures that writing teachers complainingly identify as weaknesses in argumentation. I'm thinking of such familiar practices as the bald assertion of an opinion about some controversial issue, without supporting arguments or extensive evidence, as if the assertion itself constituted "proof"; and the defensive tactic, when the instructor attacks such assertions by asking the students how they would meet various opposing arguments, of exclaiming indignantly that "everyone is entitled to their [sic] own opinion." I contend that students rely on this expression of the "honest face" ethos not only because their teachers have waxed "sentimental" over it but also because the students are unfamiliar with the "rituals" of academic discourse. I contend that they most often see "ideas" presented in the mass media in just this aphoristic, "self-evident" way: a way that assumes that rational debate cannot resolve controversial problems, so that all that remains of importance is to identify what side one is on, to solidify the personal image or ethos one has found to be most acceptable to the peer audience with which one is most concerned.

My point, however, is not to launch fruitless accusations that students are guilty of murdering the tradition of rational argument due to subliminal intoxication with television talk shows. I do suggest that we turn our energies away from the project of attempting to delineate usable heuristics for inventing arguments of universal appeal. This project, it seems to me, dead-ends right now in psychology and related fields, which cannot yet provide us with a paradigm of basic human cognitive modes. While we wait for, or contribute to, research in this area, I think we can work on ways of making the ethos of academic discourse more accessible to our students. To do so will probably require students to think about what kind of person the intellectual work of college seems to be asking them to be. Perhaps we can help them begin their deliberations by a sort of revamping of our theories of teaching writing through consideration of the audience, already explored so brilliantly by James Kinneavy and James Moffett. I'm thinking of the kind of analysis that already goes on in some technical writing courses, where students may be asked to analyze the format of a professional journal in their major field and then tailor an essay for publication in it. Once again, I think Mina Shaughnessy has pointed our way in her insightful characterization of academic discourse, in which

> the writer, often with great cunning, strives to present his or her intent in a way that will be seductive to an academic audience, which, while it aspires among other things to high standards of verification and sound reason, is nonetheless subject to other kinds of persuasion as well—to the deft manipulation of audience expectations and biases, to shrewd assessments of what constitutes "adequate proof" or enough examples in specific situations, to the stances of fairness, objectivity, and formal courtesy that smooth the surface of academic disputation. (319)

Lest we feel that a full pursuit of Shaughnessy's analysis would lead us into an unmanageable exercise of cultural anthropology, performed upon ourselves, she has indicated a particular area in which we can begin our researches—what she calls "vocabulary": "We have done even less to describe the common stock of words teachers assume students know—proper names, words that have transcended their disciplines, words that initiate academic activities, (*document, define,* etc.), words that articulate logical relationships, etc" (320). I suggest that this "common stock of words" constitutes for academic discourse the "accepted opinions" upon which, Corbett explains, enthymemes are based; and I have tried to argue that it is through the judicious manipulation of such a "common stock" of opinions, or ways of thinking about things, that a speaker convinces his or her audience that he or she is a worthy, intelligent person. I don't think that we risk creating bullshit artists by making the ethos of academic discourse available to beginning adult writers. Rather, I think we may begin to save ourselves, and our students, from the frustration of feeling that their learning to write is blocked by kinds of ignorance not usually attacked directly in writing classes. For example, I was convinced that one failing student was really very bright, even though her malapropisms made the other teacher in my office laugh. And I know that after struggling to compose an essay on the relation of the Declaration of Independence to the fight for black civil rights, one student was enraged to find his failing grade attributed to his assumption that Abraham Lincoln influenced the Declaration's framers. By calling for a "taxonomy" of academic discourse, Shaughnessy has suggested how we might begin to make the academic ethos available to these students.

What might be the elements in this taxonomy? It seems to me they might cover a wide range. One element, indicated by Shaughnessy's "proper names" and "words that have transcended their disciplines," might be something like a compendium of knowledge that anyone should possess who has grown up in this culture. I'm thinking, for example, of a rudimentary knowledge of the Bible, of the chronology of Western history, of modern developments in physics and economics, and even of the "current events" of popular culture in the last ten years. I realize that any attempt to outline such a compendium lies open to charges of cultural bias— but in a way, that's just the point. Whatever his or her background, the student who is attempting to master academic discourse is attempting to pass for a member of a particular cultural group who shares this "common stock" of knowledge. I know that failure to share it is one of the most salient ways a student destroys his or her ethos in the world of college intellectual life.

In *Errors and Expectations*, Shaughnessy has noted what may be another element in the taxonomy of academic discourse, when she characterizes the advanced student-writer as making his or her "greatest gain" "in the use of relational words. . . . Not only do we find most of the idioms of connection, both logical and rhetorical, that produce the web of discourse in analytical writing but we find the syntactical structures that underlie many of these idioms."[5] This increased mastery of logical connections leads to a related gain, the reduction of pronoun-reference errors. Perhaps the very forms of sentences using relational words can be used as an heuristic to initiate students into the kind of reasoning acceptable in academic discourse.

Here Shaughnessy also notes advanced writers' use of "nouns that name attitudes, ideas, tendencies" (*Errors*, 207), Latinate words (often imprecisely used) (208), and "predictable phrases" (209) of the sort that George Orwell deplores in that perennial freshman reading assignment, "Politics and the English Language." The point here may be that Orwell's advice is not appropriate for most freshman today, who have not yet mastered academic discourse. As Cleo McNelly has argued, "Of course, the major problem is that Orwell presumes his readers have already been taught to write—badly."[6] Perhaps they should be encouraged to experiment with making their prose sound formal, if such experimentation is coupled with instruction in the necessary forms of academic argument. Probably all of us composition teachers have early productions of our own whose pomposity now embarrasses us but which we see as stages in our progress to a more manageable yet respectable style.

My suggestions here are tentative. I suspect that before we can arrive at a taxonomy of academic discourse, we will have to consult our colleagues in other college departments. Does the ethos of historians, music theorists, chemists, present any common features? Further, I do not want to suggest that we can arrive at a taxonomy only by cataloguing the stylistic features of our professional prose. It is for this reason that I have emphasized the function of ethos. As Shaughnessy has suggested, academic discourse seems to require not only certain apparently analyzable features of vocabulary and syntax but also such ethical qualities as "formal courtesy" and "shrewd assessments of what constitutes 'adequate proof.' " We must be willing to be self-conscious about the value we place on the ethos of academic discourse. We must also be willing to confront the social ramifications of this ethos, if we are to persuade our students that it is in their best interests to pursue their intellectual work beyond the television image.

NOTES

1. Mina Shaughnessy, "Some Needed Research on Writing," *College Composition and Communication* 28 (December 1977), 318. All further references to this work appear in the text.

2. Willard Wirtz, chairman, et al., *On Further Examination: Report of the Advisory Panel on the Scholastic Aptitude Test Score Decline* (New York: College Entrance Examination Board, 1977), 35–37.

3. Edward P. J. Corbett, *Classical Rhetoric for the Modern Student,* 2d ed. (New York: Oxford University Press, 1971), 19. All further references to this work appear in the text.

4. Frank D'Angelo, "Some Uses of Proverbs," *College Composition and Communication* 28 (December 1977), 365. All further references to this work appear in the text.

5. Mina Shaughnessy, *Errors and Expectations* (New York: Oxford University Press, 1977), 206. All further references to this work appear in the text.

6. Cleo McNelly, "On Not Teaching Orwell," *College English* 38 (February 1977), 555.

Thomas Kuhn, Scientism, and
English Studies

In *The Structure of Scientific Revolutions*,[1] Thomas Kuhn elaborates the concept of the "paradigm," a comprehensive theoretical model that governs both the view of reality accepted by an intellectual community and the practice of that community's discipline. This concept has increasing interest for English studies because new demands on our composition courses, along with new developments in literary theory, have contributed to a hot debate over the premises of our discipline. Maxine Hairston, for one, has explained in an address to the 1978 convention of the Conference on College Composition and Communication that we should understand this debate as the sort of profound revolution in accepted thinking that accompanies a new paradigm, rather than as an unrelated group of local disagreements over critical tastes and pedagogical methods. Professor Hairston wants to dignify our debate as a paradigm debate because she fears, with good reason, that its beginnings in literary theory and composition pedagogy have allowed too many practitioners in English studies to regard it as tangential to their main business. Therefore, Hairston emphasizes the comprehensive nature of the "paradigm," as Kuhn explains it.

Having characterized our situation as a paradigm debate, however, Hairston goes on to support her own candidate for our new paradigm by an appeal to empirical evidence. But it is Kuhn's most striking point that a paradigm determines the identification and interpretation of "empirical evidence" in a given discipline. "Empirical evidence" makes sense only when considered in light of a paradigm; therefore, empirical evidence cannot be imported to establish a paradigm above debate. Hairston and others (Janet Emig and E. D. Hirsch, for example) have sought, however, to establish a paradigm based on such evidence, under the misapprehension that only a paradigm so established can raise English studies to the status of a truly rigorous discipline. On the contrary, Kuhn argues that a paradigm is established, even in the natural sciences, not because of compelling empirical evidence, but because of a rhetorical process that delimits the shared language of the intellectual community governed by the paradigm. Indeed, he suggests that he has derived his concept of "paradigm" for the sciences from a study of the theoretical models that govern the humanistic disciplines. In following Kuhn, we should not be misled into a scientistic faith in empirical evidence as compelling. Instead, the special province of our new paradigm may be indicated in his analysis of the ways in which any paradigm is constituted by language.

Early in *The Structure of Scientific Revolutions,* Kuhn does create the misleading impression that English studies might be more aptly described as being in a "pre-paradigm state," in which practice has not yet become sufficiently rigorous to allow the establishment of one theoretical model as the discipline's paradigm. In describing the discourse of physical optics before the ascendance of Newton's unifying paradigm, Kuhn explains:

> Being able to take no common body of belief for granted, each writer in physical optics felt forced to build his field anew from its foundations. In doing so, his choice of supporting observation and experiment was relatively free, for there was no standard set of methods or of phenomena that every optical writer felt forced to employ and explain. Under these circumstances, the dialogue of the resulting books was often directed as much to the members of other schools as it was to nature. That pattern is not unfamiliar in a number of creative fields today, nor is it incompatible with significant discovery and invention. It is not, however, the pattern of development that physical optics acquired after Newton and that other natural sciences make familiar today. (13)

I take it that the phrase "creative fields" includes English studies; Kuhn's phrase "discovery and invention" suggests the rhetorical nature of the development of knowledge in any discipline. Yet Kuhn seems to be suggesting that the welter of competing "schools" can be united under a paradigm only when research can be directed "to nature" rather than "to the members of other schools." In other words, he seems to be downgrading theoretical work in favor of work that finds empirical evidence in "nature" to support a paradigm. The current uncertainty about premises in English studies has led many of us, I believe, to feel surfeited with the claims of competing theoretical schools. We may feel that we recognize in English studies the pre-paradigm characteristics Kuhn notes: "no common body of belief," "no standard set of methods," and so on. Thus, if we read no more deeply in Kuhn, we may decide that the way out of our difficulties lies in the discovery of empirical evidence to establish one theoretical model as an absolutely true picture of reality in our field of study.

It is true that in the passage I have quoted, Kuhn seems to be contrasting the internal debates within "creative fields," to which he condescends, with the presumed disposition of natural sciences to examine nature directly and discover its truth. On closer examination, however, the main thrust of Kuhn's entire argument counters this view. His historiography of science has been controversial in his own field precisely because he questions its traditional view of science as a discipline that progresses ever closer to accurate description and prediction of the phenomena of reality. As I understand him, Kuhn concludes that there are no "scientific discoveries," if by that we mean isolable events performed by geniuses. Instead, the change in perspective traditionally labeled a discovery by historians of science typically comes about over a long period of time, as a result of community effort. Furthermore, there is no "progress" in science, if by that we mean an ever-closer approach to the truth about the phenomena of reality, because science does not deal in "truth," but rather in the cataloguing of sense perceptions and generalizations about them. Kuhn is at pains to argue, especially in the lengthy "Postscript" to the second edition of his book (1970), that we cannot know whether science tells us "what's really there." Finally, Kuhn argues that science is not ahistorical, although it attempts to depict itself that way:

Scientists are more affected by the temptation to rewrite history, partly because the results of scientific research show no obvious dependence upon the historical context of the inquiry, and partly because, except during crisis and revolution [in the scientific community], the scientist's contemporary position seems so secure. . . . The depreciation of historical fact is deeply, and probably functionally, ingrained in the ideology of the scientific profession . . ; the sciences, like other professional enterprises, do need their heroes and do preserve their names, . . . [but] scientists have been able to forget or revise their works. The result is a persistent tendency to make the history of science look linear or cumulative, a tendency that even affects scientists looking back at their own research. (138–39)

Not for nothing does Kuhn begin his chapter on "The Nature and Necessity of Scientific Revolutions" with a comparison of scientific revolutions with political revolutions that is more than mere analogy (92–94). He argues that a paradigm enforces a particular ideology, or way of seeing the world. Therefore, Kuhn is acutely alive to the limitations imposed by a paradigm, limitations that may not only restrict free inquiry, but vitiate the social usefulness of the discipline:

We have already seen, however, that one of the things a scientific community acquires with a paradigm is a criterion for choosing problems that, while the paradigm is taken for granted, can be assumed to have solutions. To a great extent these are the only problems that the community will admit as scientific or encourage its members to undertake. Other problems, including many that had previously been standard, are rejected as metaphysical, as the concern of another discipline, or sometimes as just too problematic to be worth the time. . . . One of the reasons why normal science seems to progress so rapidly is that its practitioners concentrate on problems that only their own lack of ingenuity should keep them from solving. (37)

To gain a critical perspective on the paradigms that govern the sciences, Kuhn explains in the "Postscript" to the second edition that he has adapted the historiographic methods of *The Structure of Scientific Revolutions* from the very humanistic disciplines that are attempting to dignify themselves as paradigm-governed communities under his aegis. Therefore, their anxiety to achieve paradigm-governed status puzzles him:

A number of those who have taken pleasure from [my book] have done so less because it illuminates science than because they read its main theses as applicable to many other fields as well. I see what they mean and would not like to discourage their attempts to extend the position, but their reaction has nevertheless puzzled me. To the extent that the book portrays scientific development as a succession of tradition-bound periods punctuated by non-cumulative breaks, its theses are undoubtedly of wide applicability. But they should be, for they are borrowed from other fields. Historians of literature, of music, of the arts, of political development, and of many other human activities have long described their subjects in the same way. Periodization in terms of revolutionary breaks in style, taste, and institutional structure have been among their standard tools. If I have been original with respect to concepts like these, it has mainly been by applying them to the sciences, fields which had been widely thought to develop in a different way. (208)

In other words, historians of and within English studies and other humanistic disciplines are already guided by a paradigm which Kuhn finds superior to the dominant one in the history of science. The anxiety that leads us into scientism may arise not from working in a pre-paradigm discipline, but in a discipline undergoing a paradigm shift, one of those breaks from a tradition-bound period Kuhn sees when he looks at the histories of many intellectual activities. In becoming constructively self-conscious about our paradigms, and working to hasten the emergence of a new one to meet our current problems more effectively, perhaps we should take a hint from the direction Kuhn wants to pursue in his own work: "Having opened this postscript by emphasizing the need to study the community structure of science, I shall close by underscoring the need for similar and, above all, comparative study of the corresponding communities in other fields" (209).

The concept of "community," toward which Kuhn points in his attempt to answer his critics, may ultimately be more useful to English studies than his concept of "paradigm." Kuhn emphasizes in his "Postscript" that any paradigm, or way of seeing and acting on reality, must be understood as the joint product of a community, whether it be a community bound together for study or for survival. We must understand that a paradigm has the following social characteristics: "it has been transmitted through education; it has, by trial, been found more effective than its historical competitors in a group's current environment; and, finally, it is subject to change both through further education and through discovery of misfits with the environment" (196). The paradigm is so deeply implanted in the members of the community that it achieves the status of tacit knowledge, invisible so long as its effectiveness is not challenged. But in considering what happens when a paradigm is challenged, Kuhn's argument takes a very interesting turn, for he uncovers the crucial operation of "shared language" in binding the community together under the paradigm.

We can see that if a paradigm is "transmitted" through education, then language must at the very least be an important transmitting device. But Kuhn's analysis is much deeper; he sees that the language of the paradigm is the substance of the paradigm, so that the sudden failure of familiar language to unite the community often initiates a paradigm shift. Kuhn explains that in the process of abandoning an old paradigm for a new one,

> a particular set of shared values interacts with the particular experiences shared by a community of specialists to ensure that most members of the group will ultimately find one set of arguments rather than another decisive. That process is persuasion, but it presents a deeper problem. Two men who perceive the same situation differently but nevertheless employ the same vocabulary in its discussion must be using words differently. . . . Such problems, though they first become evident in communication, are not merely linguistic, and they cannot be resolved simply by stipulating the definitions of troublesome terms. . . . Briefly put, what the participants in a communications break-down can do is recognize each other as members of different language communities and then become translators. . . . [but] To translate a theory or worldview into one's own language is not to make it one's own. For that one must go native, discover that one is thinking and working in, not simply translating out of, a language that was previously foreign. (200–204)

If we accept Kuhn's account of the relationship between a community and its paradigm, we can make two applications to English studies. First, we can understand our current unsettled condition as a state of paradigm shift. Following Kuhn's analysis, we should be alert to the means used by the proponents of the current competitors for paradigm status. Specifically, we should be aware that the traditions of the community of English studies, the needs of the larger community that includes our students, and the politics and culture of the even larger historical community in which we all live will be as important—if not more important—in shaping the outcome of our debate, as any empirical evidence adduced and interpreted by the competing schools of thought. In feeling the power of these various means by which a paradigm eventually establishes itself, the situation of the English studies community is exactly analogous to the situation of modern physics as it accommodates to Einstein's theories, or of China as it develops a Marxist ideology appropriate to its own culture, or of a family as the desires and responsibilities of its members shift under the pressure of feminism. In short, Kuhn's analysis provides a powerful insight into the ways ideas shape our lives as our lives shape our ideas.

Second, Kuhn's analysis of the importance of language to the relationship between a community and its paradigm may suggest the area of intellectual work that will be the special province of English studies when our current paradigm shift is completed. It is extremely difficult to characterize a paradigm until long after it has passed out of favor. It is true that self-consciousness about language has always been the special province of English studies. But it seems to me that under our current paradigm the conventions that shape this self-consciousness have been taken for granted. Thus, we treat language as providing its own context, in effect, and this premise allows stylisticians, for example, to assert confidently that so many instances of a certain grammatical structure in a prose passage prove that the writer is communicating a certain meaning. The current paradigm has allowed psycholinguists to go even further and assert that certain grammatical structures mimic or represent basic structures of the human brain. The current paradigm also allows composition teachers to define their students' main problem as the choice of the best or most correct words to convey their thoughts. In short, the current dominant paradigm seems founded in a conception of language as a system of references to a knowable reality external to it.

The current paradigm is under attack, however, because more and more students are not simply unpracticed in academic discourse, but unaware of the entire constellation of premises by which under its current paradigm the English studies community understands the operations of language. Faced with the new problem of explaining what had been tacit knowledge, many in English studies are now attempting to understand how we ourselves gained this knowledge. Many of those working on the new paradigm are turning to the study of language as the product of a community, reflecting the community's shared values, its historical situation, its cultural traditions, and so on. In other words, we are turning in the direction Kuhn indicates, toward the study of language as social product and embodiment of ideology. As we uncover the ways we learned to be self-conscious about language, we will be better able to pass this knowledge along to our uninitiated students. But more important, we may develop a new paradigm to place the study of this process of self-consciousness in the center of our discipline; and we will begin studying the process v hereby all paradigms exercise their influence through language.

A powerful theoretical analysis of the function of language in determining standards of reasonableness, which may help to advance our new paradigm, may be found in *The New Rhetoric*.[2] Here, Chaim Perelman and Lucie Olbrechts-Tyteca discuss language in terms reminiscent of those Kuhn uses to describe the protocols binding together a paradigm-governed scientific community:

> All language is the language of a community, be this a community bound by biological ties, or by the practice of a common discipline or technique. The terms used, their meaning, their definition, can only be understood in the context of the habits, ways of thought, methods, external circumstances, and traditions known to the users of the terms. . . . Adherence to particular linguistic usages normally expresses the explicit or implicit adoption of certain positions which are neither the reflection of an objective reality nor the manifestations of individual arbitrariness. Language . . . only undergoes revolutionary modifications where there is a radical failure to adapt to a new situation . . . [language] is linked to a social and historical situation which fundamentally conditions any distinction that one might wish to draw between judgements of reality and value judgements. (513)

Perelman and Olbrechts-Tyteca argue that one cannot draw a distinction "between judgements of reality and value judgements"— that is, between empirical evidence and ideology, or between what a poem "really says" and what the student thinks it means. One must attempt to uncover the "social and historical situation" of a community to understand its language, for that language expresses "certain definite positions"—an ideology or paradigm—and cannot be taken simply as "the reflection of an objective reality."

At the same time, however, the language of a community, precisely because it is shared by that community, cannot be taken as "manifestations of individual arbitrariness" with no useful reference to the reality in which the community finds itself. Perelman and Olbrechts-Tyteca argue that "the transcendence of these social and historical conditions," falsely claimed, for example, by science self-styled as ahistorical, "is only possible through the adoption of a philosophical position," or paradigm, "which, if it is rational, is only conceivable as the consequence of a preceding argumentation" (513–514). Thus, as Kuhn argues, a paradigm gains ascendancy not because it is proved true, but because "preceding argumentation" within the community has persuaded most of its members that it is a reasonable choice. But, as Kuhn also argues, a paradigm established by reasonable debate is no less useful to the community for being, in a sense, provisional. Here Perelman and Olbrechts-Tyteca extend Kuhn's argument persuasively, redeeming his account of the transition to a new paradigm from the charge that community members can only submit to it passively:

> The theory and practice of argumentation are, in our view, correlative with a critical rationalism that transcends the duality 'judgements of reality-value judgements." . . . Only the existence of an argumentation that is neither compelling nor arbitrary can give meaning to human freedom, a state in which a reasonable choice can be exercised. If freedom was no more than necessary adherence to a previously given natural order, it would exclude all possibility of choice; and if the exercise of freedom were not based on reasons, every choice would be irrational and would be reduced to an arbitrary decision operating in an intellectual void. . . . The theory of argumentation will help to develop . . . the justification of the possibility of a human community in the sphere of action when this justification cannot be based on a reality or objective truth. (514)

Under the new paradigm, the domain of English studies can be the study of the ways in which a language community's methods of argumentation establish standards for thinking and acting together that are "neither compelling nor arbitrary," but reasonable—in other words, the domain of rhetoric. An example of the kind of study for which Perelman and Olbrechts-Tyteca provide a theoretical base can be seen in Mina Shaughnessy's "Some Needed Research on Writing."[3] She calls for "a precise taxonomy of the academic vocabulary" (320) which could assist students in mastering "the skills of elucidation and validation and sequencing for expository writing," which she sees as their most pressing need (318). At first glance, such a taxonomy might appear to require a purely scientistic approach, cataloguing "what's really there" in the stylistic features of academic texts. But Professor Shaughnessy makes clear that she is urging a more profound inquiry, an inquiry into the ways that the language of the academic community binds this particular community together:

> The [experienced academic] writer, often with great cunning, strives to present his or her intent in a way that will be seductive to an academic audience, which, while it aspires among other things to high standards of verification and sound reason, is nonetheless subject to other kinds of persuasion as well—to the deft manipulation of audience expectations and biases, to shrewd assessments of what constitutes "adequate proof" or enough examples in specific situations, to the stances of fairness, objectivity, and formal courtesy that smooth the surface of academic disputation. One has but to re-read such brilliant performances as Freud's introductory lectures on psychoanalysis to observe this craftiness at work. Now, beginning adult writers . . . do not know the rituals and ways of winning arguments in academia. Indeed, so open and vulnerable do they appear in their writing that teachers often turn sentimental in their response to it, urging them into the lion's den of academic disputation with no more than an honest face for protection. (319)

Note that Shaughnessy says the academic community "aspires among other things to high standards of verification and sound reason." That is, the academic communities of the sciences and the humanities may place a high value on objective truth. But no community possesses it, and, furthermore, each is largely influenced in its judgment of "truth" by the rhetorical strategies of academic discourse, as her example from Freud illustrates. Therefore, it is important to understand that a student's paper may sound poorly reasoned not because he or she is irrational, but because he or she is unaware of "what constitutes 'adequate proof' or enough examples" in the eyes of an academic audience. Further, Shaughnessy suggests that the study of these rhetorical strategies should be the special province of English studies—to make accessible in our composition classes what I have called the ethos of academic discourse. If we can uncover the rhetorical conventions that help us, in our own professional work, to establish this ethos and make our arguments respectable, we can cease to make the insulting claim that a badly argued essay contravenes universal standards of rationality verified by simple inspection of the natural order.

But, by the same token, we can prevent students from claiming that in the absence of universal standards, everyone is entitled to his or her own, unsupported opinion. Having exposed some of the "craftiness" of academic discourse, Shaughnessy still feels justified in urging that we teach this craft. Perelman and Olbrechts-Tyteca provide persuasive support for her confidence. No doubt at present the language of the academic community is at variance with the language of the larger community from which most of our students come. But if we believe that the language of our smaller community offers better opportunities for rational criticism of the here and now that we share with the larger community, we in the community of English studies need not continue to recommend it merely with exhortations to "Be clear!" "Be concise!" "Be coherent!" Instead, we should recover the ethos of academic discourse that presumably enticed us to join the English studies community in the first place. We need to elucidate our assumption that our rhetorical methods can develop "the justification of the possibility of a human community in the sphere of action," to "give meaning to human freedom, a state in which a reasonable choice can be exercised," as Perelman and Olbrechts-Tyteca argue.

I have argued that English studies is undergoing a shift toward a paradigm in which the theoretical bases will generate research into our processes of self-consciousness about language. I hope that our interest in Kuhn can facilitate this shift, both by helping us to understand the kind of debate we are experiencing, and by indicating a productive field of research for our particular community, under a new paradigm. In any community undergoing such a shift defenders of the old paradigm often feel, as Kuhn's examples show, that traditional and timeless values will slip into oblivion. But in the current situation in English studies, those who hope to buttress their established position with empirical evidence are really undermining their own professed allegiance to the individual as a reasonable being interacting critically with reality. I believe that this old allegiance is really better served by new methods that make academic techniques of argumentation accessible to more and more students from our diverse society. Thomas Kuhn is of value to English studies only if he does not lead us into scientism. Rather, we should work toward a new paradigm that allows us to examine the ways in which language sharpens and directs critical analysis of the historical situation in which we and our students and our society find ourselves.

NOTES

1. Thomas Kuhn, *The Structure of Scientific Revolutions*, 2d ed. (Chicago: University of Chicago Press, 1970). All further references to this work appear in the text.

2. Chaim Perelman and Lucie Olbrechts-Tyteca, *The New Rhetoric* (1958; trans. John Wilkinson and Purcell Weaver, South Bend, Ind.: University of Notre Dame Press, 1969). All further references to this work appear in the text.

3. *College Composition and Communication* 28 (December 1977), 317–20. All further references appear in the text.

"Inherent" Ideology, "Universal" History, "Empirical" Evidence, and "Context-Free" Writing: Some Problems in E. D. Hirsch's *The Philosophy of Composition*

In *The Philosophy of Composition*, E. D. Hirsch translates his theories of literary criticism into principles of composition teaching.[1] In his critical books, *Validity in Interpretation* (1967) and *The Aims of Interpretation* (1976), Hirsch champions an anti-relativistic critical position. He opposes the purportedly objective explication of literary texts by formal methods, from the New Criticism to Derridean deconstruction. When the text is detached from the conditions of its creation, he argues, it becomes subject to readings that depend more upon the interpreter than the work itself, readings that do not bring us any closer to the meaning of the text. Hirsch's own phenomenological approach is an attempt to find the *principles* of interpretation that should orient critical perspectives. The task that Hirsch set for himself in literary criticism—to determine the premises of validity—is amplified in his search for the philosophy of composition. The problem now is to locate the Archimedean Point of *literacy:* "An authentic ideology of literacy inheres in the subject itself, and should guide our teaching of it. This

Bruce Herzberg co-authored this essay. Reprinted with permission from *MLN* 95 (Spring 1980): 1181–1202.

51

privileged ideology is the common ground on which we can all stand in our common enterprise" (xiii).

If an ideology is *inherent* in literacy, its *authenticity* is assured; we are then well justified in granting it the *privilege* of guiding our work. Thus, the privilege that Hirsch will grant to the ideology that he presents in his book must be grounded in certain kinds of *absolutes*. He promises to deduce the inherent ideology of literacy from "absolutes of human psychology" (58) and from "principles which transcend historical and cultural contingencies" (52). These absolutes and transcendental principles will be supported, he claims, by empirical evidence as well as common sense. Hirsch's appeal to empirical evidence is extremely problematic. The necessary implication of such an appeal is that "empirical" means "true," and Hirsch does not shrink from the further implication that "true" means "beyond ideology": "the empirical evidence which I have adduced and interpreted has raised my argument above mere ideology" (4).

Any philosopher's claim to speak from a perspective that is above ideology should be regarded with suspicion. Hirsch attempts to quiet that suspicion by asserting that "answers to our questions about goals can be determined from the nature and history of writing, rather than from ideology and personal taste—two potent sources of our conflict over goals" (3). Hirsch's tactic here is to equate the "inherent" ideology of literacy with "empirical" facts about writing itself. By implying that ideology is merely uninformed prejudice, he suggests that any empirical evidence is therefore above ideology.

Hirsch's introductory appeals to positivistic arguments, long before he presents the evidence itself, announce that his argument will be a reasoned polemic. This is the strategy that he employs in *Validity and Aims*, though in a somewhat different way. In the critical books, Hirsch stresses the need for the critical community to agree on principles of interpretation in order to combat interpretive anarchy and "cognitive atheism."[2] Although it is clear that Hirsch himself believes in "the stable determinacy of meaning,"[3] upon which he bases his position, he argues for its reasonableness as a standard that we should maintain even if we are not wholly converted to his belief. Now, in *The Philosophy of Composition*, the call for a standard of arbitration is gone—or buried, at least, in assertions to the effect that if Hirsch is not correct, composition teachers might as well "close up shop" (87). *The Philosophy of Composition* is a committed polemic on the inherent and indisputable basis of literacy itself. One correlative of his stronger position is Hirsch's defense of the authority of the teacher as a social engineer, a specifically political figure operating in the classroom. The teacher's authority, if it is not to be politically suspect, must be grounded in the *inherent* ideology of the subject itself.

Anyone who has experienced the frustrations of teaching composition or recognized the politically sensitive situation of the teacher of "basic" or "remedial" writing may well be susceptible to arguments for a privileged ideology that is based on something more than privilege. In general, a privileged ideology is a set of assumptions about goals and methods that governs theory and practice in a society, in a culture or sub-culture, or in a discipline. The effective privileged ideology guides the work of practitioners without their being conscious of its governing power. Hirsch suggests that our present state of confusion about goals and intentions could be cleared away by a stable set of premises. A privileged ideology would act as a filter, focusing energy on soluble problems. Moreover, an *inherent* ideology raises privilege to necessity. In effect, such an ideology is transparent; it ceases to have the appearance of an ideology at all; it makes "other" ideologies appear to be matters of prejudice or personal taste; it puts on the cloak of Empirical Truth, and rises "above mere ideology." It is the purpose of a polemical argument to justify and promote ideological transparency—the sense that one's position is natural, and not an ideology at all.

Although Hirsch presents his position as the only philosophy of composition that is consistent with the "nature and history of writing," he is, in effect, presenting a candidate for "privileged ideology." Therefore, as we examine his candidate, we must remember that the argument is polemical and that self-effacement is part of its ideological strategy. We must decide whether Hirsch's arguments support his position on its own terms—that is, whether the "empirical evidence" is evidence of inherent and transcendental qualities of writing. We should try to determine the implications of acting on the principles that Hirsch proposes. And we should consider what we will sacrifice, along with our self-consciousness, if we assent to this or any other "privileged ideology."

Hirsch's presentation is complex and his points are strongly inter-related, but there are four points, central to his position, which are particularly worth examining: (1) the problem of context (Hirsch argues that "the functional peculiarity of written speech is its need to furnish its own context"[7]); (2) the "grapholect" and the histori-cal development of a "classless" language; (3) the status of empirical research in psycholinguistics; (4) the possibility of an inherent ideol-ogy of literacy.

Hirsch actually begins his argument in the introduction, where he summarizes the argument of each chapter. This strategy is note-worthy: each sub-position is derived deductively, so generalizations precede their supporting analyses and are later recuperated as conclusions. Hirsch's initial distinction, between "oral speech" and "written speech," shows the effect of this strategy. Hirsch asserts that "oral speech normally takes place in a concrete situation that supplies external, extra-verbal clues to meaning, while written speech, lacking this dimension, is able to communicate effectively only if it supplies much of its context within the verbal medium alone" (7). It is evident that the presence of the interlocutors in oral communication is a distinctive sort of context. "Extra-verbal clues to meaning" might include gestures and facial expressions, events and objects at hand, the time, place, and circumstances of the verbal exchange. But to those of us who teach writing as a rhetori-cal act that takes place between the writer and an audience, that has intentional effects, an intentional persona, and a conventional organization, the assertion that "students should be taught how to make their writing self-contextual" (8) may sound like a contradic-tion in terms. The form of a piece of writing, the conventions employed in it, the vocabulary, the mode of argument, and the subject itself are all context-*markers* that identify the rhetorical mode of "written speech." Yet surely, context-markers aren't con-text; surely written communication still takes place in time and circumstances. How can writing lack the "dimension" of extra-verbal conditioning? How can writing "furnish its own context" (7)?

In chapter 1, Hirsch will severely limit the meaning of "context" in order to answer these questions; but because of his rhetorical strategy, he will nonetheless return to the initial, unqualified statement of his position on the context-independence of written speech and treat it as proved in its generalized form—"the important distinctive feature of written discourse . . . is its isolation from any particular situational context" (21). Hirsch's insistence on this point recalls his defense, in *The Aims of Interpretation*, of "the stable determinacy of meaning." In Hirsch's usage, the phrase is not redundant: it indicates that the determinants of meaning are fixed, in his view. This is the basis of the earlier argument for *validity* in interpretation. Hirsch's position is that interpretation is a valid activity only if there is a determinant meaning to be gleaned from the object of interpretation. In short, the text must contain its meaning. If the meaning of the text is dependent on *con*textual information—on its situation—then we cannot establish *the* meaning. Even the author's intention must be contained in the text itself, according to Hirsch's formulation. If context is outside the text, then meaning will be relative to the context that is adduced or assumed by the individual interpreter.[4] But if writing can determinately constrain the conditions of its interpretation—that is, contain its own context—then the meaning of the text can be recovered.

Much of Hirsch's argument in *The Philosophy of Composition* rests on this proposition and on the mode of argument that supports it. The first part of the argument demonstrates very pointedly that *oral* communication is often difficult to understand when it is taken out of context. Hirsch uses the example of the tapes and transcripts of Nixon's White House conversations to show that timing and intonation, and even more significantly, the historical circumstances of the conversations, are essential to an understanding of the recorded exchanges. But then Hirsch implies that in contrast to this sort of "oral speech," which is difficult to comprehend because it is context-tied, "written speech" which is comprehensible must therefore be context-free. He then formalizes this implied dichotomy by invoking Basil Bernstein's theory of "elaborated" and "restricted" codes.

Hirsch's use of Bernstein is crucial and deserves careful analysis. By "elaborated code" Bernstein designates a use of language that is relatively less context-bound and more explicit than the use of language in a "restricted code." Bernstein does indeed mean kinds of language use, not the poles of a continuum of explicitness, and as Hirsch points out, this is analogous to his own distinction between written and oral speech.[5] Bernstein is always careful, however, to speak of the *circumstances* in which an elaborated or restricted code is *chosen* by the speaker. All of Bernstein's work shows that certain sub-cultural groups (children, adolescents, criminals, soldiers, and most notably, members of the working class) habitually use a restricted code and have *limited access* to an elaborated code. Most speakers ordinarily use a restricted code, regardless of their group or class (Nixon and his friends, for example). Thus, the *choice* of a restricted or elaborated code on a given occasion depends upon the speaker's ability to use an *elaborated* code, and further depends upon the speaker's ability to decide upon the circumstances in which an elaborated code is appropriate.

Bernstein's research into the social determinants of language use has shown, as we might expect, that an elaborated code is more commonly used by the middle class than the working class. An elaborated code is necessary for working in a world that is "finely and extensively controlled . . . with reference to a distant future," for example.[6] The elaborated code provides the logical complexity that is appropriate for future-oriented processes. The restricted code, on the other hand, "tends to emphasize *things* rather than *processes.*"[7] Bernstein—who began this research as a result of his experiences as a teacher—notes that "the school is an institution where every item in the present is finely linked to a distant future, consequently there is not a serious clash of expectations between the school and the middle-class child."[8]

Hirsch quotes, at length, one of Bernstein's demonstrations of the differences between uses of the two codes. Several children are shown a series of drawings and asked to describe them. One of the middle-class children explains: "Three boys are playing football and one boy kicks the ball and it goes through the window the ball breaks the window and the boys are looking at it and a man comes out and shouts at them. . ." A working-class child gives this description: "They're playing football and he kicks it and it goes through there it breaks the window and they're looking at it and he comes out and shouts at them. . ."[9] The first description is given in an elaborated, the second in a restricted code. Bernstein comments:

"what we have here are differences in the use of language arising out of a specific context." The context that Bernstein refers to is *not* the story of the boys playing football, but the *request to verbalize* the story: "for the first child the task was seen as a context in which meanings were required to be made explicit, whereas the task for the second child was not seen as a task which required such explication of meaning."[10]

In contrast, Hirsch retains the sense of "context" as referring to the *story:* the first is comprehensible without the pictures, so it is context-free; the second makes sense only in the presence of the pictures, so it is context-tied. It becomes clear that this is what Hirsch means by "context" when he goes on to comment on the social associations of the codes:

> The analogy is striking between Bernstein's analysis of the two codes and my functional distinction between speech and writing. Especially telling is the contrast between speech that is "context-tied" and speech that is "context-free," the typical contrast that I have drawn between oral and written speech. That this contrast should have a correlation with economic class is not surprising, since middle-class children will normally be more intensively educated in writing and reading than working-class children and will tend to use a literate form of speech in completing a schoolroom sort of task. But surely it is their education in literacy, and their experience with a variety of speech partners that has made the difference, not money or family relationships per se. (26)

The last sentence is rather surprising. Bernstein's conclusion—which Hirsch, too, seems to be leading up to here—is that middle-class children, who are socially oriented toward use of the elaborated code, and who therefore sort well with the aims and methods of schooling, will learn to write more easily than working-class children. The very fact that the middle-class child interprets a request by an adult to verbalize a story as a "school-room sort of task," that is, as a request to use the elaborated code, seems to compel this conclusion. Yet Hirsch says the very opposite. Where does he suppose that the "education in literacy" and the "variety of speech partners" have come from? What does he suppose that "class" means? What is "the difference" that he mentions if not family relationships, economic circumstances, education in literacy, and a variety of speech partners?

Hirsch is committed to the idea that "universal schooling" is a democratizing agent. He is plainly willing to assert, against the evidence of an authority that he has just quoted, that "education in literacy" supersedes all other socializing forces. Yet Hirsch's odd conclusion here is more than the effect of his egalitarian impulses. His project requires him to attribute to *language itself* the qualities that Bernstein attributes to the social situation of language *users*. If these qualities are in the language, then teaching "literacy" transmits the qualities. The requirements of Hirsch's premise—that language can determinately constrain the conditions of its interpretation—have produced his paradoxical conclusion, not an examination of Bernstein at all.

Two points must be made here. First, Bernstein has much to teach us. His explanations of the codes are recognizable as the basis of many difficulties in the college composition class. Students frequently seem unaware that academic writing calls for the use of an elaborated code. The particular form and qualities of the assigned essays present problems which are thus at an even further remove from their usual modes of language use.

Second, it appears that Hirsch is willing to treat Bernstein reductively for a number of good reasons. For one thing, the definition of context that Hirsch urges has been the foundation of his long-standing and popular critical theory. He has chosen to test his theory in the sensitive socio-political arena marked out by Bernstein, and it is certainly to Hirsch's credit that he should wish to have Bernstein as his ally. For another, it appears that Hirsch is searching for a theoretical solution to the problem posed by Bernstein and others: how can we justify teaching *our* form of language-use to those who see no value in it because of prior circumstances? And its corollary: is it *possible* to teach standard English under these conditions? These hard questions haunt Hirsch's argument from the beginning.

The next stage of Hirsch's argument (on the "grapholect") reveals how his reading of Bernstein contributes to his answers to the hard questions. But as he concludes his discussion of "context," Hirsch makes a concession to Bernstein's sense of context. He notes that "writing always leaves a great deal unsaid" (27) and that explicitness is often bought at the price of complexity, refinement of expression, and rhetorical effect. Writing and elaborated codes work through conventions, through assumptions about what is "understood," through an implied author and a projected audience. Hirsch spends several pages on this discussion, presenting Wayne Booth's and Chaim Perelman's formulations of the rhetorical sense of context, and apparently modifying his own original assertion that written speech is context-free. But in another startling reversal of his apparent line of argument, Hirsch takes it all back and returns to his initial position:

> In oral speech, a mistaken idea of a speaker's intention or of an auditor's response is constantly open to correction. But in writing, where these feedback signals are absent, the character of the implied author and of the implied reader must be more firmly and securely established *within the verbal medium itself.* Hence, just as *an elaborated code is required for the "context-free" utterances of writing,* in order to replace a situational context through verbal means, so, in writing, an inherent uncertainty about the implied author and implied audience must be compensated for by special conventions [emphasis added]. (29)

Since the implied author and implied reader *are* the conventions that refer to a presumptive situational context, Hirsch must mean that the "special" conventions are conventions-for-conventions. Once again, Hirsch is trying to suggest that all the conventions can be contained "within the verbal medium itself," that where writing is concerned there is no outside.

Hirsch's reassertion of his polemical position on the inherent constraints of writing serves as a preface to the introduction of another source of certainty and a renewed promise that inherent principles will be deduced. "Effective prose," Hirsch says, "was not born full-grown within the history of any language of which we possess records" (31). Effectiveness, that is, develops through the progressive refinement of syntax and style. "Hidden within this historical process, traceable in all modern written languages, may be discovered the underlying principles of composition" (31–32).

There are two parts to this stage of the argument. The first is the assertion that written standard English is a "grapholect," by which Hirsch means that it is standardized, stable, and "normative." Once established, the grapholectic form of a language is highly conservative, resistant to the kinds of changes that alter most oral dialects. While the grapholect *becomes* the grapholect by virtue of the political dominance of the group that used it when it was just a dialect, Hirsch asserts that universal schooling in that dialect fixes its form and makes it transdialectal. The English grapholect, he notes, is derived from "upper-class London English fixed as the unique standard in the sixteenth, seventeenth, and eighteenth centuries" (42). Hirsch explains that every dialect "is correct in its own terms" (41), by which he means that any dialect might have become dominant and acceded to the position of the grapholect. But the grapholect, wherever it came from and however it got to be the grapholect, is now the only transdialectal language we have, our only standard of correctness. This assessment seems to be correct by definition, but in order to set up the terms of the definition, Hirsch has to ignore several logical and political contradictions that he has raised himself.

Hirsch claims that the grapholect's linguistic conservatism is transformed to political liberalism by universal schooling: "The normative character of a national written language lies in its very isolation from class and region. It is transdialectal in character, an artificial construct that belongs to no group or place in particular, though of course it has greatest currency among those who have been most intensively trained in its use" (44). The final subordinate clause here (like the comment on the middle-class child in Bernstein's experiment) is a reminder that Hirsch is speaking of a form of language that is *already* privileged. The grapholect is indeed isolated from *some* classes and regions, but it *is* the language of some other classes and regions. It is transdialectal only if those to whom it is not native are able to gain access to it. If there were no other extant dialects to allow linguistic discrimination, if there were no groups that were more and less trained in its use, if no associations remained between the grapholect and its class origins, then it *might* be fair to claim that the grapholect is not a tool of class division and discrimination.

But there is a deeper and more important issue here. Hirsch has implicitly equated *dialects* with *restricted codes*, while explicitly equating the *grapholect* with an *elaborated code*. Thus, by representing the grapholect as a dialect that has been raised, rather incidentally, to transdialectal status, he suggests that the same relationship subsists between restricted and elaborated codes. This conflation of terms is the result of Hirsch's reductive definition of "context." To define context as greater or less explicitness in an utterance is perfectly reasonable and without prejudice to Bernstein's definition. The difficulty arises over Hirsch's insistence that the conditions of language-use and code-choice are embedded in the codes themselves: one conflation leads to another, to the implicit equation of codes and dialects. Dialects are languages that share the same base, though they differ somewhat in pronunciation and idiom. But learning to write is not a matter of learning a particular dialect. Hirsch himself has just argued that learning to write means learning to use an elaborated code. If the elaborated code represents a different order of perception and expression for those who are socially habituated to restricted-code use, then learning an elaborated code is very little like learning another dialect.

Yet Hirsch advances his argument by combining the language of *class* with a politically innocuous derivation of the dominant *dialect:* "the normative character of a national written language lies in its very isolation from class and region." This is clearly supposed to be the statement of a liberal position; but "class" must refer to differences in socialization and language use, while "region" simply means differences in usage and pronunciation. "Isolation" for the latter implies democracy; but for the former it implies the preservation of privilege. This confusion is fostered partly by Hirsch's assumption about the egalitarianism of "universal" schooling. Here again, he assumes that schooling (and ultimately, the grapholect itself) can overcome socialization, provide everyone with the same order of language use, regardless of social situation. But as Bernstein (if not our own daily experience) shows, schooling participates in socialization. Certain classes of students find themselves in conflict with the very nature of the school—or at least with the parts of it that depend upon the use of an elaborated code. Such conflicts are not to be overcome by the language itself.

As an extension of his position on universal schooling, Hirsch discusses the inevitable linguistic assimilation that is taking place, especially in the United States, as a result of increased interregional mobility. In this discussion—in which linguistic assimilation itself is treated as an historical *fait accompli*—Hirsch clearly means that dialects are being flattened out, yet he again implies that this includes *codes*. He laments the loss of a variety that linguistic assimilation will bring about: "it is useless to pretend that all is for the best in this inexorable process of normalization" (48). Regional and class speech (Hirsch's conflation) is an important part of "a group solidarity which probably fills important psychological needs that cannot be met in normalized grapholectic speech" (49). We must be resigned, he says, because this normalization is "a fact of life, not merely of language" (49). Moreover, Hirsch finds, on balance, "that the benefits are greater than the costs" (49), since we will have increased communication between people. Can Hirsch mean that the flattening of regional accents is of the same order of assimilation as providing everyone with a middle-class mode of language use? And even if we accept both forms of assimilation as proceeding inexorably, will we gain anything, practically or theoretically, by assenting to Hirsch's conflation?

The assertion that the benefits of assimilation outweigh the costs is to be Hirsch's final answer to the hard questions that he has raised. The rest of his book presents the historical and psycholinguistic evidence that supports this answer. The dilemma that Hirsch has thus attempted to pacify has been stated, in another context, by James Sledd: languages are "at once the instruments of power, the vehicles of cultural traditions, and the media of literatures." Standard English, in particular,

> is the language of one of the world's great literatures, and the most accessible storehouse of the world's knowledge, especially the knowledge of science and technology. In its edited and written form it is much the same wherever it is used; as spoken by the educated, it is intelligible with little difficulty everywhere; it is securely established in the full range of functions which a language can serve, from lovemaking to divine worship, from flying airplanes to seeking cures for cancer. Yet standard English is also, as it always has been, an instrument of domination.[11]

It is clearly the responsibility of the English teacher, especially perhaps of the teacher of composition, to teach standard English to the students.

But Hirsch's account of *why* we must teach standard English turns out to be a rationalization of the mechanism that preserves the language's privileged status. Once again, the form of the argument rests on the assumption that the language contains the conditions of its use. The significance of Hirsch's initial formulation of his project is evident here: if the privilege is inherent in literacy, and if, as he now argues, linguistic assimilation is inevitable, then teachers must be satisfied to maximize the positive qualities of the situation:

> Merely to be a teacher of literacy is already to be committed to linguistic social engineering, and, while such intervention can be harmful, its potential for good includes the benefit of instruction in a classless, transdialectal instrument for communication between social and regional groups. To this may be added the benefit of communicating with the dead and yet unborn. When a child of ten can read, with at least verbal comprehension, *Gulliver's Travels,* a book over two hundred years old, the conservative and normative power of the grapholect transcends class, time, and place. (45)

The first and last assertions, that the grapholect is classless, are supported only by *other* assertions that it is classless. The danger of Hirsch's defense of such propositions—which, indeed, are familiar enough without the claims of inherence and inevitability to back them up—is that they support similar assertions, such as Hirsch's own, that a child of ten can read *Gulliver's Travels.* Whose child of ten?

No matter how disturbing the dilemma of privilege may be, it does not justify a theory which amounts to no more than rationalization of that privilege. It is the English teacher's job to teach the middle-class ideolect/code that constitutes what Hirsch calls the grapholect. It is a discursive mode that allows for the expression of causal connection through time; it has a large lexicon and an affinity for logic, complexity, and a variety of rhetorical effects. It is undoubtedly the mode of academic discourse, hence students must master it to succeed academically. When we bury all this in assertions of its classlessness (!), or its historical inevitability, we make it *more* difficult to teach it to students who don't share its basic perceptual and conceptual modes as a result of socialization. The problem is *access* to the grapholect, and access is determined by nonlinguistic conditions. Thus, the problem engendered by continued assertions of classlessness and inevitability is the effacement of the marks of the ideolect's differential position and quality. Every college student has at least partially acceded to the status of the dominant ideolect (i.e., by being in college), but the socialization process that will give the student access to the grapholect may be just beginning.

Thus, even if we assume that the teaching process brings about assimilation (and it is by no means a necessary assumption), Hirsch's analysis does not provide a differential or dialectical means of initiating the socialization process. Linking the ideolect to the natural, the human, the physiological, the inevitable, has indeed a negative effect, for it reinforces the ideolect's highly privileged standard of exclusion. Arguments to the effect that the grapholect is classless, that it is merely a dialect, are part of the process of erasure, and must make us less sensitive to the complex situation that already distresses the composition teacher so much.

After his discussion of linguistic assimilation, Hirsch does not mention the socio-political situation of language or teaching again. Everything that follows is represented as either common-sense demonstration or empirical evidence of his original assertions about the characteristics of written speech. This evidence, drawn from "certain absolutes of human psychology," will establish "in absolute terms, as transcending cultural and historical bias" (58), that the characteristics which Hirsch has identified are inherent not only in language, but in human physiology. Many of Hirsch's arguments are susceptible to the same objections that can be raised against his interpretation of Bernstein and his determination to recover his initial assertions. [12] All of his arguments about the absolute validity of empirical evidence, however, are subject to an epistemological critique of the nature of empirical evidence, and in particular to a critique of the nature of the psycholinguistic evidence that is his major resource.

Thomas Kuhn has examined the character of empirical research in *The Structure of Scientific Revolutions*. [13] In brief, Kuhn's thesis is that the practitioners in any mature intellectual discipline operate under its "paradigm," or shared set of assumptions and methods. The paradigm determines what experiments the workers in a scientific community will perform, and how they will interpret the evidence produced by these experiments. Kuhn argues that scientists do not examine "reality" directly; instead, they interpret their perceptions according to the assumptions and methods of the paradigm under which they are educated. What a scientist "sees" when he or she examines "empirical evidence" is really an interpretation enforced by education in the way of seeing determined by the paradigm.

One of Kuhn's most striking illustrations concerns the discovery of the planet Uranus. In the early eighteenth century, the paradigm governing astronomy precluded the existence of undiscovered planets. Therefore, although many professional observers saw an object "in positions that we now suppose must have been occupied by Uranus," they all identified it as a "star" and failed to note "the motion that could have suggested another identification," even though their apparatus could record such motion.[14] Late in the century, Sir William Herschel observed the object with an improved telescope that revealed "an apparent disk-size that was at least unusual for stars."[15] Herschel did not yet question that this object was a star, but at least it had now become "unusual" for him. Later, he recorded its motion, but still unwilling to overturn the dominant assumption precluding new planets, he identified the object as a comet: "Only several months later, after fruitless attempts to fit the observed motion to a cometary orbit, did Lexell suggest that the orbit was probably planetary. When that suggestion was accepted, there were several fewer stars and one more planet in the world of the professional astronomer."[16] Historians of science traditionally do not award the honor of "discovering" Uranus to the astronomer who first observed it while identifying it as a star; but neither do they award the honor to Lexell, who first identified the disputed object as a planet. Sir William Herschel is given the honor, in part because of his eminence in the field, but also because he opened the debate on this particular problematic bit of empirical evidence. As Kuhn points out, the conceptual interpretation of empirical evidence is crucial to its value.

Kuhn opposes the popular notion that science "progresses" ever closer to an empirically true description of reality. The belief that it does is called "scientism," a faith in empirical evidence as compelling and above debate. Kuhn explains that scientists do observe reality, but only as filtered through the protocols established by each discipline's paradigm. Changes in the paradigm and in the way it is transmitted through education come about through a process which Kuhn likens to a political revolution because it involves not only the scientific community, but the larger movement of the society in which it works.[17] Thus, even if we attained complete knowledge of the physiology of the human *brain*, that knowledge would not be sufficient to explain how the *mind* learns to interpret through a paradigm:

> We try . . . to interpret sensations already at hand, to analyze what is for us the given. However we do that, the processes involved must ultimately be neural, and they are therefore governed by the same *physico-chemical* laws that govern perception on the one hand and the beating of our hearts on the other. But the fact that the system obeys the same laws in all three cases provides no reason to suppose that our neural apparatus is programmed to operate the same way in interpretation as in perception. . . . What is built into the neural process that transforms stimuli to sensations has the following characteristics: it has been transmitted through education; it has, by trial, been found more effective than its historical competitors in the group's current environment; and, finally, it is subject to change both through further education and through the discovery of misfits with the environment.[18]

Kuhn is far from arguing that what science discovers is worthless. Rather, he wants to make us aware that the "truth" about "reality" provided by science is a provisional truth.

In seeking empirical support for his theory and by characterizing it as inherent and universal, Hirsch overlooks the historical process whereby "empirical evidence" gains its authority. For example, in support of his proposition that two texts can mean the same thing, Hirsch asserts: "It has been proved experimentally that what [the reader or listener] mainly remembers is stored as meaning, not as linguistic form" (86). He draws this conclusion from experiments in which the test subject, asked to recall a sentence or passage, makes frequent errors in the exact syntactic or lexical elements of the text, but recalls its "gist" or "meaning" very well. Test subjects may recall active voice sentences in the passive voice, for instance, or substitute synonyms for the original words (122–123). When he discusses these experiments, Hirsch repeats his conclusion that "discourse *meaning*" is "recorded in memory in an abstract, nonverbal form" (122). This conclusion is not based upon the evidence; it is based upon the "paradigmatic" premise of synonymy that Hirsch argues for in *The Aims of Interpretation*. Even an authority that Hirsch cites as the source of this evidence, P. N. Johnson-Laird, is more equivocal about its interpretation than Hirsch. "No one knows how meaning is represented within memory," according to Johnson-Laird, "but there is no evidence to show that any form of *syntactic* structure is directly involved" (123, emphasis added). Even if *syntactic* structures are not involved, this observation by no means warrants Hirsch's conclusion that no *verbal* structures of any kind are involved. Indeed, Hirsch contradicts this position himself:

> The writer will assist the reader by continually repeating a rather small number of thematic tags which *represent* [the] meaning. If the thematic tags are too numerous, they cannot be held at once in working memory (123–124).

What prevents the "thematic tags" from being *words?* Hirsch attempts to finesse the connection between verbal thematic tags and meaning by his stress on "*represent*," but the gesture does not constitute an argument against the possibility that we remember discourse in an abbreviated or paraphrased but still linguistic form.

In addition, Hirsch passes over Johnson-Laird's warning that "how meaning is represented within memory" is still very much an open question. This warning is repeated more forcefully by Judith Greene in her survey of research in *Psycholinguistics*.[19] Greene's analysis of psycholinguistic experimental practice confirms Kuhn's theoretical conclusion that empirical evidence is problematic:

> When trying to sum up the contribution of transformational grammar to psychology, one point that must be stressed is that the psycholinguistic approach has opened up totally new ways of conceptualizing language. The experiments described in this book [many of which are also cited by Hirsch], which it is fair to say would never have been carried out except under the stimulus of transformational grammar, are a far cry from *simpliste* pre-Chomskyan attempts to look at verbal associations and so on. By directing attention to subjects' behavior when using sentences, the search for an exact one-to-one relationship between

grammatical rules and subjects' performance has by its very failure brought to light the influence of many unexpected factors.

Faced with this sort of experimental evidence about subjects' language use, it is, of course, perfectly logical for Chomsky to fall back on the position that it is a misunderstanding of generative grammar to treat it as a model for the production and perception of sentences. It is a fair point, too, that for purposes of grammatical analysis it is necessary to concentrate on standard usage, ignoring moment to moment fluctuations in individual utterances. But when Chomsky makes the stronger claim that he is describing the structure of cognitive processes, can he ignore the extreme complexity of the relation between speakers' linguistic knowledge and how it is put to use in the real world? It would be a pity if the previous blindness of psychologists were to be matched by an equal reluctance on the part of transformational linguists to face up to facts about language that do not square with their account of the organization of linguistic rules.[20]

By accepting psycholinguistic "empirical" evidence as compelling, Hirsch reproduces many of the same methodological errors that plague that field. As Greene points out, in spite of their *failure* to produce evidence that the biochemical processes of the brain are synonymous with the thought processes of the mind, psycholinguists persist in the claim that grammatical rules describe "the structure of cognitive processes." They too readily ignore "the extreme complexity of the relation between speaker's linguistic knowledge and how it is put to use in the real world"—in other words, the problem of context. The tests that Hirsch and Greene cite explicitly omit the rhetorical context in which language use ordinarily occurs. The experimenter is not trying to communicate with the test subjects by saying words at them, and does not regard their responses as attempts at communication. But "in the real world," one processes a verbal communication for a purpose that is determined by the rhetorical situation and conditioned by the larger social and historical context. Typically, the purpose and conditioning factors determine what one notices in a verbal communication, what one decides is worth storing in the memory, and so on.

After introducing some of his psycholinguistic evidence, Hirsch tries once again to account for the problem of context by subsuming it under the information-theory concept of "constraint." Once again he asserts that our questions about composition can be answered "only by referring them to root psychological principles" (93). Hirsch brings in information theory because it is "a powerful tool of psychological research . . . its concepts approximate certain actual functions of the mind, particularly certain functions of language processing" (99–100). Since information theory is designed to deal with the function of electrical circuits, its application to the neural circuits of the brain is at best a problematic analogy; moreover, as Kuhn and Greene explain, brain function cannot be taken as synonymous with mind function. Nonetheless, Hirsch calls upon information theory in the form of the "cloze" test. In this test, a prose passage is presented to the subject with words left out, and the "readability" of the passage is judged by the subject's ability to fill in the blanks "correctly." The subject's guesses are presumably limited by the very structure of the passage, and that limitation is known in information theory as "constraint." Hirsch takes this concept one step farther: "*Constraint* is a precise, functional term for *context*" (102).

This application of information theory is problematic even on its own terms. The cloze test is based on the information-theory principle that the information content of a "bit" of information in a circuit can be calculated by the formula for thermodynamic entropy. By analogy, the *less* predictable a "bit" of information is, the *more* information it conveys. The cloze test calculates the probability that a reader will fill in the blanks in a text "correctly." But high probability means high predictability which in turn means low information content. Therefore, a text edited by cloze test standards to ensure high "readability" will convey *less* information per sentence than a more "unpredictable" text. The cloze test gives us no means to reconcile the conflict between making a text "readable," and making a text "convey" the most information in the shortest possible reading time.

Hirsch's appeal to information theory as a source of empirical information about language and language "processing" presupposes that language is an "instrument for communication" (45) in the mechanical sense: a tool for transmitting messages. By this definition, writing is not like a radio announcer's message, but like the electronic device that transmits it. The cloze test works only within the limits of this definition, and so never raises the problem of "matching" between transmitted code and received message. But the "matching," not the transmission itself, determines comprehension. If language is equated to electronic signals—or any other mechanical encoding and relaying system—then the question of the *conditions* of meaning is left out. Any such mechanistic analogy gives us no clue to what is missing when, for example, a child of ten reads *Gulliver's Travels* with "verbal comprehension" only.

Finally, the cloze test itself reveals the weakness of its own premise. The test works on the notion that language itself provides "constraint," as if the structure of language were the same for all language users. If the structure of a given language were universal, then native speakers would produce similar scores on a given test. But Hirsch notes a "large variation in cloze-test scores for different classes of readers" (104), and consequently modifies the notion of "constraint" that he has just established:

> But, obviously, the larger-scale context of prose is still more important than small-scale constraints in reducing uncertainty and enhancing readability. . . . [The larger-scale context] embraces large domains of tacitly shared knowledge, and it includes tacit suppositions about the theme and tendency of the text as a whole. . . . This suggests that . . . the writer's correct assessment of the relevant knowledge already possessed by his principal audience . . . may be the most important decision the writer makes. (104–05)

Though he has returned here to the previously discarded idea of "understood" meaning and implied authors and audiences, Hirsch is working up to the next part of his presentation—the derivation of "maxims" for writers which will embody the "root psychological principles" that he has demonstrated. But "the larger-scale context" cannot be subsumed under these principles or contained in maxims. This will not deter him, however, because "a neglect of these large-scale convert constraints is rarely the chief cause of unreadable writing" (105).

Hirsch's maxims set forth the precepts of the inherent ideology of literacy, the "paradigm" for composition research and teaching. Unfortunately, he has adduced no evidence for any transcendental principles that account for "large-scale covert constraints"—except, of course, for the principles that account for them by exclusion. All of his research focuses on acontextual language, while, by his own account, the problems of teaching writing have a great deal to do with context and convention.

Mina Shaughnessy has addressed the problems of "academic discourse" that Hirsch has attempted to circumvent:

> The [academic] writer, often with great cunning, strives to present his or her intent in a way that will be seductive to an academic audience, which, while it aspires among other things to high standards of verification and sound reason, is nonetheless subject to other kinds of persuasion as well—to the deft manipulation of audience expectations and biases, to shrewd assessment of what constitutes "adequate proof" or enough examples in specific situations, to the stances of fairness, objectivity, and formal courtesy that smooth the surface of academic disputation.[21]

The persuasiveness of academic discourse does not rely on absolute truth or perfect logic. Rather, academic discourse is persuasive when it employs conventions and rituals that are "seductive to an academic audience." Beginning writers cannot succeed in academic disputation merely by being "clear" and "logical." Shaughnessy urges teachers to help students gain the power to initiate themselves into the discursive practices of academia. The conventions governing academic discourse are bound to the social context that constitutes the rhetorical situation of academic discourse. If these conventions can be specified, they can be transmitted through education. If they are "genre rules," presumably they are established by practice and can be expounded in the composition class.

But Hirsch wants to identify the governing conventions with certain logical forms of thought that can be taken as "understood" because all normal humans are assumed to have the ability to understand them. Thus, he rules out just the sort of critical analysis that a "priviliged ideology" of composition requires if it is to be made pedagogically useful: an analysis of the social sources of its power and the ways writers are initiated into the use of its conventions.

The "privileged ideology" that Hirsch presents in *The Philosophy of Composition* is, after all, the ideology of literacy that reigned *before* Shaugnessy's proposals needed to be enunciated—an ideology for which the qualities and uses of conventions and the context of academic literacy were, indeed, *understood.* It may therefore be disappointing, though not surprising, to find that the maxims that Hirsch finally proposes are contained in Strunk and White's *Elements of Style.* Hirsch announces in his Preface that "the book argues for certain privileged goals in the teaching of literacy" (xiii). Clearly, though, the book provides no new theoretical synthesis but an apologia for certain goals which are already privileged, and whose failure has been the source of the controversy over curriculum goals that prompted Hirsch to write.

Hirsch regards the Strunk-and-White approach as "timeless." Indeed, it is only fair to acknowledge the value of their maxims and also the value of Hirsch's pedagogical advice in his chapter on "Inproving Teaching Methods," although this advice, too, is familiar.[22] Hirsch has assumed that students learn to write through the conscious application of maxims, and now asserts that "practical experience in the classroom coincides pretty well with the psychological principles of readability" (154). If these assumptions were correct, we would expect all of our problems in teaching composition to be solved, as Hirsch's familiar maxims (e.g., "omit needless words") and advice have been available long enough to have been given a thorough trial.

Hirsch's challenge to the teaching community, particularly to those engaged in research in composition, is not in his advice or his conclusions, but in his premises and mode of argument. It is, undoubtedly, much more difficult to analyze our own unconscious assumptions about the conventions of academic discourse, as Shaughnessy suggests, or to become sensitive to the social circumstances that shape our students' language use, as Bernstein suggests, than it is to appeal to features of language that *must* be common to all of us. But the difficulty, or the impossibility, or even the inutility of developing a taxonomy of the conventions of academic discourse or of surveying our classes the way that Paulo Freire, for example, surveys his groups of Brazilian peasants does not make a *theory* of inherent linguistic ideology an appropriate goal. Hirsch would have us believe that "authoritative knowledge" of the physiology of the human brain will resolve our problems of language teaching. His purpose is "to encourage a conviction that we *can* gain that authoritative knowledge within a decade" (6). To predict that we can attain such knowledge for such a purpose is to predict that we will be able to judge whether people respond to the "real" world in an "unfiltered" way, with minimal "interference" between biochemical processes and human action. Education would then, without doubt, have an absolute standard and an absolute goal, but it would be a process of closing off human possibilities in accordance with the standards of a privileged ideology even more impervious to debate than our present one.

NOTES

1. E. D. Hirsch, *The Philosophy of Composition* (Chicago, 1977). Hereafter page numbers of citations are included in the body of the text.

2. Hirsch, *The Aims of Interpretation* (Chicago, 1976), p. 4 *et passim.*

3. Hirsch, *Aims,* p. 1 *et passim.*

4. This conclusion does not necessarily follow from the conditions set up in Hirsch's anti-relativism argument. It is quite possible to discuss circumstantial determinants of meaning without declaring them to be either absolutely stable or completely relative. For relevant examples, see Stanley Fish, "What is Stylistics and Why Are They Saying Such Terrible Things About It?" in *Approaches to Poetics,* ed. Seymour Chapman (New York, 1973), pp. 109–152; Terry Eagleton, *Criticism and Ideology* (London, 1976); William E. Cain, "Authority, 'Cognitive Atheism,' and the Aims of Interpretation: The Literary Theory of E. D. Hirsch," *College English* 39 (November 1977), pp. 333–345.

5. Bernstein refers only to oral utterances.

6. Basil Bernstein, *Class, Codes, and Control* (New York, 1971), p. 29.

7. Bernstein, *Class,* p. 44.

8. Bernstein, *Class,* p. 29.

9. Quoted by Hirsch in *Philosophy,* p. 25; Bernstein, *Class,* p. 178.

10. Quoted by Hirsch in *Philosophy,* p. 26; Bernstein, *Class,* p. 179.

11. James Sledd, "Language Differences and Literary Values: Divagations From a Theme," *College English* 38, (November 1976), p. 235.

12. Cf. Cain, *op. cit.;* Wallace W. Douglas, review of *The Philosophy of Composition* in *College English* 40, (September 1978), pp. 90–99; Donald C. Freeman, "Toward 'Relative Readability': A Criterion for Good Writing," *The Chronicle of Higher Education,* April 7, 1978, p. 18.

13. Thomas Kuhn, *The Structure of Scientific Revolutions,* 2d ed. (Chicago, 1970).

14. Kuhn, *Structure,* p. 115.

15. Kuhn, *Structure,* p. 115.

16. Kuhn, *Structure*, p. 115.

17. Kuhn, *Structure*, pp. 92–94.

18. Kuhn, *Structure*, pp. 195–196.

19. Judith Greene, *Psycholinguistics* (Harmondsworth, 1972).

20. Greene, *Psycholinguistics*, p. 196.

21. Mina Shaughnessy, "Some Needed Research on Writing," *College Composition and Communication* 28 (December 1977), pp. 319–320.

22. Cf. Kenneth E. Eble, "Part Three: Grubby Stuff and Dirty Work," *The Craft of Teaching* (San Francisco, 1976), pp. 83–134.

Cognition, Convention, and Certainty: What We Need to Know About Writing

What do we need to know about writing? Only recently have we needed to ask this question, and the asking has created composition studies. We have needed to ask it because of changing circumstances in the classroom, and our answers will be put to the test there with a speed uncommon in other academic disciplines. The current theoretical debate over how to go about finding these answers, therefore, is not merely an empty exercise. Students' lives will be affected in profound ways.

This profound effect on students is the more to be expected because of the terms in which the "writing problem" has appeared to us—terms that suggest that students' thinking needs remediation as much as their writing. Seeing the problem this way makes it very clear that our teaching task is not only to convey information but also to transform students' whole world view. But if this indeed is our project, we must be aware that it has such scope. Otherwise, we risk burying ethical and political questions under supposedly neutral pedagogical technique. Some of our answers to the question of what we need to know about writing are riskier in this regard than others.

We now see the "writing problem" as a thinking problem primarily because we used to take our students' thinking for granted. We used to assume that students came to us with ideas and we helped them put those ideas into words. We taught style, explaining the formal properties of model essays and evaluating students' prod-

Reprinted with permission from *Pre/Text* 3, no. 3 (1982): 213–43.

ucts in the light of these models. Some students came to us with better ideas than others, but these were simply the brighter or more mature students. All we could do for the duller, more imma- ture students was to hope that exposure to good models might push them along the developmental path.[1]

Over the last twenty years, however, we have encountered in our classrooms more and more students whose ideas seem so ill- considered, by academic standards, that we can no longer see the problem as primarily one of expression. Rather, we feel, "Now I have to teach them to think, too!" And at the same time, students have so much trouble writing Standard English that we are driven away from stylistic considerations back to the basics of grammar and mechanics. Teaching style from model essays has not prepared us to explain or repair these students' deficiencies. The new de- mands on us as teachers can only be met, it seems, by reconsidera- tion of the relationship between thought and language. We are pretty much agreed, in other words, that what we need to know about writing has to do with the thinking processes involved in it.

Composition specialists generally agree about some fundamental elements in the development of language and thought. We agree that the normal human individual possesses innate mental capaci- ties to learn a language and to assemble complex conceptual struc- tures. As the individual develops, these capacities are realized in her learning a native tongue and forming thought patterns that organize and interpret experience. The mature exercise of these thought and language capacities takes place in society, in interac- tion with other individuals, and this interaction modifies the indi- vidual's reasoning, speaking, and writing within society. Groups of society members can become accustomed to modifying each other's reasoning and language use in certain ways. Eventually, these famil- iar ways may achieve the status of conventions binding the group in a discourse community, at work together on some project of interac- tion with the material world. An individual can belong to more than one discourse community, but her access to the various communi- ties will be unequally conditioned by her social situation.

If composition specialists generally agree about this description, however, we disagree about what part of it is relevant to composition studies. One theoretical camp sees writing as primarily inner-directed, and so is more interested in the structure of language-learning and thinking processes in their earliest state, prior to social influence. The other main theoretical camp sees writing as primarily outer-directed, and so is more interested in the social processes whereby language-learning and thinking capacities are shaped and used in particular communities. In the current debate, each camp seeks to define what we *most* need to know about writing.

Inner-directed theorists seek to discover writing processes that are so fundamental as to be universal. Later elaborations of thinking and language-using should be understood as out-growths of individual capacities (see figure 1). Hence, inner-directed theorists are most interested in individual capacities and their earliest interactions with experience (locations 1 and 2, figure 1). The inner-directed theorists tend to see the kinds of reasoning occurring at all four locations as isomorphic—all the same basic logical structures.[2] They also tend to see differences in language use at different locations as superficial matters of lexical choice; the basic structure of the language cannot change from location to location because this structure is isomorphic with the innate mental structures that enabled one to learn a language, and hence presumably universal and independent of lexical choice. Nevertheless, looking for an argument to justify teaching one form of a language, some inner-directed theorists treat one set of lexical choices as better able than others to make language embody the innate structures. Insofar as these better choices fall into the patterns of, for example, a "standard" form of a native tongue, they make the standard intellectually superior to other forms.[3]

Inner-directed theorists further claim, in a similar paradox, that the universal, fundamental structures of thought and language can be taught. If our students are unable to have ideas, we should look around locations 1 and 2 for structural models of the mental processes that are not happening in these students' minds. Once we find these models, we can guide students through the processes until the students' own thought-forming mechanisms "kick on" and they can make concepts on their own. A heuristic procedure is often presented as such a process model.[4] Similarly, if our students are unable to write English, we should look in the same locations for patterns of correct syntax, which we can then ask the students to

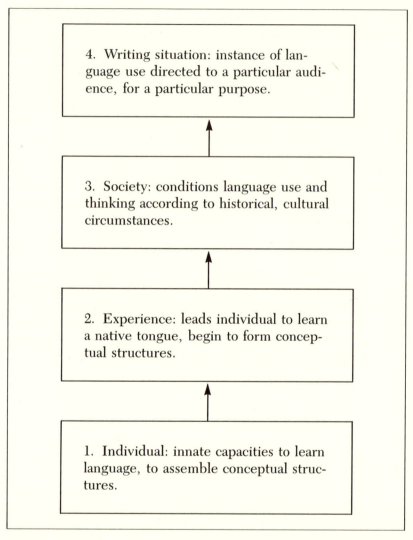

Figure 1. An inner-directed model of the development of language and thought in writing. Arrows indicate direction of individual's development, beginning with innate capacities and issuing finally in particular instances of use.

practice until they internalize the patterns. Sentence-combining exercises offer such pattern practice.[5]

Once students are capable of cognitively sophisticated thinking and writing, they are ready to tackle the problems of a particular writing situation. These problems are usually treated by inner-directed theory as problems of audience analysis. Audience analysis seeks to identify the personal idiosyncracies of readers so that the writer can communicate her message to them in the most persuasive form. The changes made to accommodate an audience, however, are not seen as substantially altering the meaning of the piece of writing because that is based in the underlying structure of thought and language.[6]

In contrast, outer-directed theorists believe that universal, fundamental structures can't be taught; thinking and language use can never occur free of a social context that conditions them (see figure 2). The outer-directed theorists believe that teaching style from model essays failed not because we were doing the wrong thing but because we weren't aware of what we were doing. Teaching style from model essays, in this view, is teaching discourse conventions of a particular community—in this case, a community of intellectuals including, but not limited to, academics. But because we were unaware that we were in a discourse community, we taught the conventions as formal structures, as if they were universal patterns of thought and language. What we should do is to teach students that there are such things as discourse conventions.

The outer-directed theorists are sceptical about how we can obtain knowledge of what thinking and language-learning processes are innate. Moreover, they would argue that the individual is already inside a discourse community when she learns a native tongue, since the infant does not learn some generalized form of language but rather the habits of language use in the neighborhood, or the discourse community into which she is born.[7] Since this discourse community already possesses traditional, shared ways of understanding experience, the infant doesn't learn to conceptualize in a social vacuum, either, but is constantly being advised by more mature community members whether her inferences are correct, whether her groupings of experiential data into evidence are significant, and so on.[8] Some outer-directed theorists

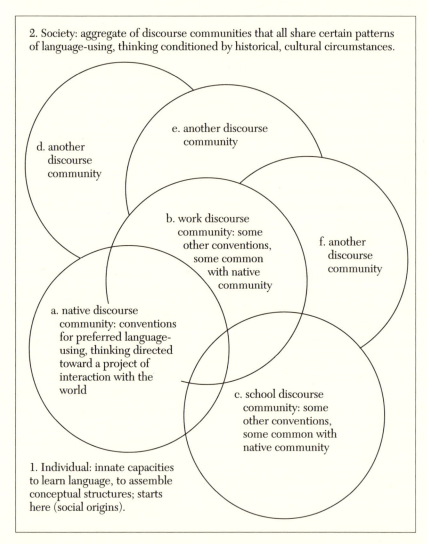

2. Society: aggregate of discourse communities that all share certain patterns of language-using, thinking conditioned by historical, cultural circumstances.

e. another discourse community

d. another discourse community

b. work discourse community: some other conventions, some common with native community

f. another discourse community

a. native discourse community: conventions for preferred language-using, thinking directed toward a project of interaction with the world

c. school discourse community: some other conventions, some common with native community

1. Individual: innate capacities to learn language, to assemble conceptual structures; starts here (social origins).

Figure 2. An outer-directed model of the development of language and thought. Note that innate capacities have no expression outside discourse communities and that society is made up entirely of discourse communities. Individual has unequal access to different communities. Direction of development is outward from native community.

would go so far as to say that the lines of development of thought and language merge when the native tongue is learned, since one learns to think only by learning a language and one can't have an idea one doesn't have a word for.[9]

Outer-directed theorists would argue that we have no reason to believe, and no convincing way to determine, that our students can't think or use language in complex ways. It's just that they can't think or use language in the ways we want them to. To help them, then, we should be looking for ways to explain discourse conventions. We might find patterns of language use and reasoning that are common to all members of a society, patterns that are part of the set of conventions of every discourse community within the society. Conventions that are common in the society could be used as bridges between different discourse communities—for example, to ease the transition into the academic discourse community for students who come from discourse communities far removed from it.[10]

The staple activity of outer-directed writing instruction will be analysis of the conventions of particular discourse communities (see figure 2). For example, a major focus of writing-across-the-curriculum programs is to demystify the conventions of the academic discourse community.[11] Discourse analysis goes beyond audience analysis because what is most significant about members of a discourse community is not their personal preferences, prejudices, and so on, but rather the expectations they share by virtue of belonging to that particular community. These expectations are embodied in the discourse conventions, which are in turn conditioned by the community's work. Audience analysis aims to persuade readers that you're right; it is to dress your argument in flattering apparel. Discourse analysis aims to enable you to make that argument, to do intellectual work of significance to the community, and hence, to persuade readers that you are a worthy coworker.[12]

Answers to what we need to know about writing will have to come from both the inner-directed and the outer-directed theoretical schools if we wish to have a complete picture of the composing process. We need to explain the cognitive and the social factors in writing development, and even more important, the relationship between them. Therefore, we should think of the current debate between the two schools as the kind of fruitful exchange that enlarges knowledge, not as a process that will lead to its own termination, to a theory that silences debate. I would like to show here how one inner-directed theoretical model of writing can be enlarged by an outer-directed critique.

The inner-directed school has been distinguished by its fostering of research on writing that follows scientific methodology, and two of the most important researchers are Linda Flower, a professor of English at Carnegie-Mellon University, and John R. Hayes, a professor of psychology at the same school. They have been conducting research for about six years on what people do when they compose. The goal of this research is to formulate "A Cognitive Process Theory of Writing," according to the title of their recent *College Composition and Communication* essay.[13] Their work's roots in cognitive psychology can be seen in *Cognitive Processes in Writing,* the proceedings of a 1978 symposium at Carnegie-Mellon.[14] Flower and Hayes see composing as a kind of problem-solving activity; what interests them are the "invariant" thought processes called into play whenever one is confronted with a writing task. In other words, they assume that although each writing task will have its own environment of purposes and constraints, the mental activity involved in juggling these constraints while moving to accomplish one's purposes does not change from task to task. This problem-solving thought process is the "cognitive process of writing."

In figure 1, location 2 is approximately where Flower and Hayes would place what they are studying. The cognitive process is triggered by what goes on at location 4 (imposition of a particular writing task); the process may also be shaped by attitudes absorbed at location 3 and modified in the light of success or failure in problem-solving at location 4. Not everyone uses the same cognitive process in writing, some processes are more successful than others, and one's process can be consciously or unconsciously modified. Flower and Hayes seek to describe a model of the most complete and successful composing process they can find through their research.

Protocol analysis is their principle research tool. First, the researcher asks a person (the test subject) to say aloud whatever she is thinking while solving a problem posed by the researcher. For example, Flower and Hayes have asked English teachers to describe what goes through their minds while composing an article describing their jobs for the readers of *Seventeen* magazine. The transcription of what the subject says is the protocol. Next, the researcher scans the protocol looking in the subject's self-description for features predicted by the theory of cognitive activity guiding the research. Flower and Hayes have looked for descriptions of behavior common to current accounts of the writing process, such as "organizing" and "revising." In analyzing the protocol, the researcher must bridge gaps in the protocol caused by the subject's forgetting to mention some of her problem-solving steps. The theory is tested by its ability to bridge these gaps as well as by the appearance in the protocol of features it predicts (Flower and Hayes explained their procedure in "Identifying the Organization of Writing Processes," *Cognitive Processes*, 3–30).

Through their research, Flower and Hayes have been gradually refining a process model of composing (see "Process Theory," 370). Its most current version divides the writing situation into three main parts: one, the "task environment," subdivided into "rhetorical problem" and "text produced so far"; two, the "writing process," subdivided into "reviewing" (further subdivided into "revising" and "evaluating"), "translating," and "planning" (further subdivided into "generating," "goal-setting," and "organizing"); and three, the "writer's long-term memory." The task environment is outside the writer, the writing process is inside the writer, and long-term memory can be both inside and outside—that is, in the writer's mind or in books. Task environment and memory are seen as information sources upon which the writer draws while performing the composing activities grouped under "writing process."

This model is hierarchical and recursive rather than sequential in structure; that is, Flower and Hayes do not see the writing process as an invariant order of steps. What is invariant, in their view, is the structural relation of the steps. A writer can "access" memory or task environment, and switch from one composing subprocess to another, at any time while the writing task is being completed; an entity in the model called "monitor" executes these switches. This model does not tell us how to proceed through the composing process, but only that in proceeding, there are certain sub-processes we must include if we want to compose successfully.

Flower and Hayes see this model as resolving current theoretical disagreements about what guides composing. Beginning their "Process Theory" essay with summaries of different but compatible views on composing, Flower and Hayes seem to suggest that while other theorists are like blind men describing an elephant, in the Flower-Hayes model we see the whole beast—or at least we can infer its shape when the porpoise occasionally breaks water, to switch to the animal metaphor Flower and Hayes use (*Cognitive Processes*, 9–10). It is the hierarchical and recursive structure of this model, in Flower and Hayes's view, that makes it superior to other theorists' work and able to control and reconcile other theorists' work.

The Flower-Hayes model may, however, strike many readers as a surprising mix of daunting complexity and disappointing familiarity. When we finally get the new terminology straight in our minds, we find in the model's elaborate cognitive processes just the same writing activities we have been debating about. Consider, for example, the Flower-Hayes model's "monitor," the entity that executes switches between composing subprocesses. On the one hand, the term, borrowed from computer programming, is rather intimidating, especially if we imagine that it names something we didn't know was there before. On the other hand, we find out eventually that "monitor" means simply "the writer's mind making decisions." Borrowing a term from programming masks the question of *why* the writer makes certain decisions. The Flower-Hayes model consistently presents a description of *how* the writing process goes on as if it were capable of answering questions about *why* the writer makes certain choices in certain situations. While it is useful for us to have an overview of the "how," such as the Flower-Hayes model offers, we should not suppose that this will enable us to advise students on difficult questions of practice. To put it another way, if we are going to see students as problem-solvers, we must also see them as problem-solvers situated in discourse communities that guide problem definition and the range of alternative solutions. Outer-directed theory can thus shore up the Flower-Hayes model in two critical areas, planning and translating.

"Translating," according to Flower and Hayes, is "the process of putting ideas into visible language" ("Process Theory," 373). They treat written English as a set of containers into which we pour meaning, regardless of how meaning exists before the pouring. The containers may not seem to be in convenient sizes at first—we have to struggle with their "constraints" or "special demands"—but once we internalize these, written language as a factor in the composing process essentially disappears. Writing does not so much contribute to thinking as provide an occasion for thinking—or, more precisely, a substrate upon which thinking can grow. Beyond minor matters of spelling, diction, and so on, we do not have to worry about how students are going to find out about the features of written language because these are already innate.

"Translating," then, remains the emptiest box in the Flower-Hayes model, while "planning" becomes the fullest. During planning, the writer generates and organizes ideas before struggling to put them into words. Language itself is not seen as having a generative force in the planning process, except insofar as it stands as a record of the current progress of the writer's thinking in "text produced so far." Planning processes, therefore, have to be elaborated because they are all the writer has to guide her toward a solution to the particular writing problem. What's missing here is the connection to social context afforded by recognition of the dialectical relationship between thought and language. We can have thoughts for which we have no words, I think, but learning language, though it doesn't exactly teach us to think, teaches us what thoughts matter. To put it another way, we can *know* nothing but what we have words for, if knowledge is what language makes of experience.

Vygotsky has characterized this dialectical relationship of thought and language as the development of "verbal thought." At first, language use and thinking develop separately in the child. But eventually the child comes to understand that language not only names ideas but develops and evaluates them, and then, *"the nature of the* [child's] *development itself changes,* from biological to historical."[15] The child's linguistic and cognitive development culminates in "verbal thought," which "is not a natural, innate form of behavior but is determined by a historical-cultural process and has specific properties and laws that cannot be found in the natural forms of thought and speech" (Vygotsky, 51). To illustrate the mature relationship between thought and language, Vygotsky uses situations that are strongly context-bound, such as conversations between lovers or among actors in a play.

Vygotsky's analysis suggests that a model that separates planning and translating will not be fruitful for describing adult language-using because these activities are never separate in adult-language-using. There is, to be sure, a basis in the human organism for language-using behavior; Vygotsky calls it "biological," Flower and Hayes call it "cognitive." But while this basis is a legitimate object of study in its own right, even the most complete anatomy of it will not explain adult language-using because, as Vygotsky emphasizes, with the advent of verbal thought the very nature of language-using processes changes. The writing process can only take place after this change has occurred. Vygotsky's analysis would suggest, then, not only that we should not separate planning and translating but also that we should understand them as conditioned by social context.

If we accept Vygotsky's analysis as indicating the need to fill in Flower and Hayes's empty "translating" box, then to look for knowledge to fill it, we can turn to sociolinguistics. This discipline seeks to analyze the ways thinking and language-using are conditioned by social context. In studying writing, sociolinguists look for the verbal ties with context. They argue that certain genres, implying certain relations between people, are typical of certain situations. Furthermore, readers do not perceive a text as hanging together logically unless its connections with the social context are as clear as the markers of internal coherence.[16] Therefore, for example, students who struggle to write Standard English need knowledge beyond the rules of grammar, spelling, and so on. They need to know: the habitual attitudes of Standard English users toward this preferred form; the linguistic features that most strongly mark group identity; the conventions that can sometimes be ignored; and so on. Students who do know the rules of Standard English may still seem to academics to be writing "incorrectly" if the students are insensitive to all these other features of language use in the community—then the students are using academic language in unacademic ways.[17]

Composition specialists can learn from sociolinguists to avoid what

George Dillon has called the "bottom-to-top" fallacy: the notion that a writer first finds meaning, then puts it into words, then organizes the words into sentences, sentences into paragraphs, etc.[18] Dillon argues, rather, that it is the sense of her whole project that most stimulates a writer's thinking and guides her language use. The discourse gives meaning to the words and not vice versa. For example, such phrases as "it seems to me" and "these results suggest . . ." do not themselves tell us how to interpret such a pattern of qualifying statements. When we encounter these words in a student paper, we are likely to chide the writer for covering up poor research or for being unduly humble. When we encounter the very same words in a scholarly paper, we simply take them to mean that the writer is establishing a properly inquiring persona (see Dillon, 91).

Even something as cognitively fundamental as sentence structure takes on meaning from the discourse in which it is deployed. For this reason, for example, revising rules are notoriously unhelpful: they always require further knowledge in order to be applied. We can't "omit needless words" unless we have some additional criteria for "needlessness." We can't even "avoid passive voice" all the time. Passive voice might be preferred by a writer who wants to head her sentence with words that tie it closely to the previous sentence, especially if the kind of discourse she is producing places a high value on markers of internal coherence.[19]

"Putting meaning into words," then, cannot be seen as a mechanical process of finding the right size containers. Instead, with a form of discourse we take on a whole range of possibilities for making meaning. Language-using in social contexts is connected not only to the immediate situation but to the larger society, too, in the form of conventions for construing reality. This relationship between language and world view has prompted M.A.K. Halliday to argue that "the problem of educational failure is not a linguistic problem, if by linguistic we mean a problem of different urban dialects"; at bottom, "it is a semiotic problem, concerned with the different ways in which we have constructed our social reality, and the styles of meaning we have learned to associate with the various aspects of it."[20] In short, educational problems associated with language use should be understood as difficulties with joining an unfamiliar discourse community.

To look at writing as situated in a discourse community is to blur over the lines between translating and planning in the Flower-Hayes model. Finding words is not a separate process from setting goals. It *is* setting goals, because finding words is always a matter of aligning oneself with a particular discourse community. The community's conventions will include instructions on a preferred form of the native tongue, a specialized vocabulary, a polite technique for establishing persona, and so on. To some extent, the community's conventions can be inferred from analyzing the community's texts. But because the conventions also shape world view, the texts can never be an adequate index of community practice.

Therefore, we should not think of what I am calling a discourse community simply as a group who have decided to abide by certain language-using rules. Rather, we should see the group as an "interpretive community," to use Stanley Fish's term, whose language-using habits are part of a larger pattern of regular interaction with the material world.[21] Because this interaction is always a historical process, changing over time, the community's conventions also change over time. This is not to say that the community's interpretive conventions are arbitrary or that they totally determine individual behavior. They are not arbitrary because they are always conditioned by the ongoing work in the community and sanctioned by consensus. At any given time, community members should have no trouble specifying that some kinds of thinking and language-using are obviously appropriate to the community and some are not. Changes in conventions can only define themselves in terms of what is already acceptable (even if such definition means negation of the currently acceptable).

At the same time, some kinds of thinking and language-using are not obviously either appropriate or inappropriate; they are open to debate. An individual who abides by the community's conventions, therefore, can still find areas for initiative—adherence is slavish adherence only for the least productive community members. These "open" areas may be the unsolved problems of the community, experiences that remain anomalous in the community's interpretive scheme, or they may be areas the community has never even considered dealing with. An individual may, however, bring one of these open areas into the range of the community's discourse if her argument for an interpretation of it is sufficiently persuasive in terms the community already understands. As an example of this activity, Mina Shaugnessy has cited Freud's introductory lectures on psychoanalysis.[22]

Producing text within a discourse community, then, cannot take place unless the writer can define her goals in terms of the community's interpretive conventions. Writing is always already writing for some purpose that can only be understood in its community context. Fish has argued not only that the community of literary critics proceeds in this way but furthermore, that the main business of English studies should be to investigate the nature of discourse communities (see Fish, 338–55). It is exactly this sort of analysis that the Flower-Hayes model lacks when trying to explain planning. For Flower and Hayes, "generating" (a subdivision of planning) means finding ideas by using heuristics, not by responding with individual initiative to the community's needs. "Organizing" (another subdivision) means fitting ideas into the range of logical structures available from human thought processes, not finding out what's reasonable in terms of a community's interpretive conventions. In other words, all that's needed for generating and organizing is access to the invariant, universal structures of human cognition (for a critique of this assumption, see Dillon, 50–82).

The weakness of this approach is most apparent in Flower and Hayes's treatment of "goal-setting." They correctly identify goal-setting as the motor of the composing process, its most important element, but in their model they close it off in the most subordinate position (a subdivision of a subdivision of the writing process). In the "Process Theory" essay, Flower and Hayes elaborate their description into "process goals" (directions for the writing process) and "content goals" (directions for affecting the audience), and they also classify goals in terms of levels of abstraction (see "Process Theory," 377). Their model's structure cannot order this multifarious account.

Flower and Hayes end the "Process Theory" essay with analysis of a "good" writer's protocol, aimed to explicate the process of goal-setting. The writer is having trouble deciding how to tell *Seventeen* readers about his job as a college English teacher until he decides that many girls think of English as a "tidy" and "prim" subject and that "By God I can change that notion for them." He goes on to frame an introduction that recounts a "crazy skit" his 101 class liked on the first day of school ("Process Theory," 383, 385). Of his "By God" moment of decision, Flower and Hayes say that "he has regenerated and elaborated his top-level goals," and "this consolidation leaves the writer with a new, relatively complex, rhetorically sophisticated working goal, one which encompasses plans for a topic, a persona, and an audience" (383).

Notice the verbs in this explanation: "regenerating" and "elaborating" goals "leave" the writer with regenerated ("new") and elaborated ("complex") goals—which "encompass" what he needs to know to go on writing. The action described here has no force as an explanation not only because it is circular (regeneration causes regeneration), but also because we still don't know where the new goals come from. Flower and Hayes suggest that going through a process simply "leaves" one with the goals, as if the process itself brought them into being. Upon arrival, the goals are found to contain ("encompass") the necessary knowledge—but we still don't know how that knowledge got there.

The *Seventeen* article writer's process of goal-setting, I think, can be better understood if we see it in terms of writing for a discourse community. His initial problem (which seems to be typical of most subjects confronted with this writing task) is to find a way to include these readers in a discourse community for which he is comfortable writing. He places them in the academic discourse community by imagining the girls as students ("they will all have had English," 383). Once he has included them in a familiar discourse community, he can find a way to address them that is common in the community: he will argue with them, putting a new interpretation on information they possess in order to correct misconceptions (his "By God" decision). In arguing, he can draw on all the familiar habits of persuasion he has built up in his experience as a teacher (his "crazy skit" decision). He could not have found a way to write this article if he did not have knowledge of a discourse community to draw on.

The Flower-Hayes model does, of course, include a "long-term memory" where such knowledge could be stored, and Flower and Hayes even acknowledge its importance: "Sometimes a single cue in an assignment, such as 'write a persuasive . . . ,' can let a writer tap a stored representation of a problem and bring a whole raft of writing plans into play" (371).

A "stored representation of a problem" must be a set of directions for producing a certain kind of text—what I have been calling discourse conventions. I would argue that the writer doesn't just tap this representation sometimes but every time a writing task is successfully accomplished. Flower and Hayes give this crucial determinant of text production very offhand treatment, however. They seem to see writing in response to discourse conventions as response to "semi-automatic plans and goals" that contrast with "goals writers create for a particular paper" (381). Evidently they are seeing discourse conventions simply as rules to be internalized, similar to their treatment of the "constraints" of written English. This reduction of conventions to sets of rules is also suggested by their choice of the limerick as a good example of a "genre" (379).

Hence, although Flower and Hayes acknowledge the existence of discourse conventions, they fail to see conventions' generative power, which is to say that their notion of conventions does not include the interpretive function for which I have been arguing. This neglect of the role of knowledge in composing makes the Flower-Hayes theory particularly insensitive to the problems of poor writers.

> Poor writers will frequently depend on very abstract, undeveloped top-level goals, such as "appeal to a broad range of intellect," even though such goals are much harder to work with than a more operational goal such as "give a brief history of my job." Sondra Perl has seen this phenomenon in the basic writers who kept returning to reread the assignment, searching, it would seem, for ready-made goals, instead of forming their own. Alternatively, poor writers will depend on only very low-level goals, such as finishing a sentence or correctly spelling a word. They will be, as Nancy Sommers's student revisers were, locked in by the myopia in their own goals and criteria. (379)

The implication here seems to be that cognitive deficiency keeps poor writers from forming their own goals, keeps them locked in the myopia of goals appropriate to a much earlier stage of cognitive development. The physical image of poor eyesight is revealing of Flower and Hayes's assumptions about the innate sources of writing problems.

I think these students' difficulties with goal-setting are better understood in terms of their unfamiliarity with the academic discourse community, combined, perhaps, with such limited experience outside their native discourse communities that they are unaware that there is such a thing as a discourse community with conventions to be mastered. What is underdeveloped is their knowledge of the ways experience is constituted and interpreted in the academic discourse community and of the fact that all discourse communities constitute and interpret experience. Basil Bernstein has shown that British working-class students are not cognitively deficient but that, first, their native discourse community's conventions are very different from school conventions, and, second, their lack of a variety of speech partners makes it hard for them to see their problems in school as problems of learning to relate to new speech partners (or an unfamiliar discourse community).[23]

Such students may be unable to set a more operational goal because they do not know the conventions of language-using that define such goals as, for example, a "history." Without such knowledge, they may fall back on goals that worked in the past—perhaps in grammar school where close attention to spelling and grammar was rewarded. Or they may sensibly try to enlarge their knowledge by re-reading the assignment, seeking clues to the conventions of this new discourse community or those "ready-made goals" without which no writing gets accomplished. Of course, their search of the assignment may be fruitless if the teacher has not been sufficiently explicit about her expectations. Academics are, perhaps, too ready to assume that such operations as "describe" or "analyze" are self-evident, when in fact they have meanings specific to the academic discourse community and specific to disciplines within that community.

To help poor writers, then, we need to explain that their writing takes place within a community, and to explain what the community's conventions are. Another way of putting this would be to borrow Thomas Kuhn's terminology and explain that "puzzle-solving" writing can go on only under the direction of an established "paradigm" for community activity.[24] As Charles Bazerman's work has shown, the writer within the academic community knows how to relate her text to "the object under study, the literature of the field, the anticipated audience, and the author's own self" via discipline-specific conventions governing "lexicon," "explicit citation and implicit knowledge," "knowledge and attitudes the text assumes that the readers will have," and the "features" of a "public face" (Bazerman, 362–63).

The Flower-Hayes model of writing, then, cannot alone give us a complete picture of the process. We might say that if this model describes the *form* of the composing process, the process cannot go on without the *content* which is knowledge of the conventions of discourse communities. In practice, however, form and content cannot be separated in this way, since discourse conventions shape the goals that drive the writing process. To let the model stand alone as an account of composing is to mask the necessity for the socially situated knowledge without which no writing project gets under way. The problems of letting this model stand alone can be seen in the pedagogy emerging from Flower and Hayes's work. They are inclined to treat the model itself as a heuristic: "Our model is a model of competent writers. Some writers, though, perhaps to their disadvantage, may fail to use some of the processes" (*Cognitive Processes*, 29). Flower has recently published a textbook that aims to guide students through a complete repertoire of composing strategies.[25]

The difficulty with the textbook's view of writing as problem-solving is that it treats problem-solving as an unfiltered encounter with the underlying structure of reality—"the act of discovering key issues in a problem that often lie hidden under the noisy details of the situation" (21). Having defined a problem, one should: first, "fit it into a category of similar problems"; next, decide on a possible course of action against the problem ("make the problem definition more operational"); "tree" the problem or analyze its parts into a hierarchical structure; "generate alternative solutions"; present a conclusion, which weighs alternatives and acknowledges assumptions and implications of the conclusion (see 21–26). But *first,* how does one define a problem? Although Flower says that "problems are only problems for someone," she doesn't talk about this necessary link between problem definition and interpretive communities (21). Rather, it seems that we will *find* (not make) the problem if we strip away the "noisy details of the situation." I would argue, in contrast, that only the noisy details of the situation can define a problem. To "define" a problem is to interact with the material world according to the conventions of a particular discourse community; these conventions are the only source for categories of similar problems, operational definitions, and alternative solutions, and a conclusion can only be evaluated as "well supported" in terms of a particular community's standards.

I certainly do not mean to suggest that students should not be encouraged to look at reality when they compose—far from it, since I have emphasized the function of writing in doing (intellectual) work in the world. But I do mean to point out that we cannot look at reality in an unfiltered way—"reality" only makes sense when organized by the interpretive conventions of a discourse community. Students often complain that they have nothing to say, whereas "real-world" writers almost never do, precisely because real-world writers are writing for discourse communities in which they know their work can matter, whereas students can see little purpose for their own attempts ("essais") other than to get a grade. For example, Erwin Steinberg has suggested that the superior organization of an electrical engineer's report, as compared to a freshman composition, stems from the engineer's superior knowledge of and experience in a field; what looks like a cognitive difference turns out to have a large social component (see "A Garden of Opportunities and a Thicket of Dangers," *Cognitive Processes*, 163–165). Hence, although Steinberg is sympathetic to the project of finding writing models and heuristics, he cautions, "We must always be careful not to think in terms of a single model, because if we do we'll find one and force everyone to use it—the way English teachers used to require students to make formal outlines before they wrote" (163).

The cognitive psychology approach cuts off writing-as-problem-solving from the context of a discourse community precisely because *one* model is sought (Steinberg's caveat notwithstanding). Discourse communities are tied to historical and cultural circumstances, and hence can only be seen as unenlightening instances of the general theory the cognitive approach seeks: the one model is the universal one. All of the theoretical essays in *Cognitive Processes in Writing* seek to find this model. Carl Bereiter offers an account of the stages of development in children's writing processes. Like the Flower-Hayes model, his is recursive—that is, he suggests that children's development includes a certain set of stages but that the order of these stages can be changed. There is, however, a "preferred or 'natural' order of writing development," an order in which the constraints on composing imposed by the necessity of putting thoughts into words are gradually reduced by being "automatized." Bereiter suggests that this order should be adopted in the schools (see "Development in Writing," 89).

Collins and Gentner seek to go even further in schematizing their theory as a rule-governed model because they hope to end with a program enabling a computer to compose (see "A Framework for a Cognitive Theory of Writing," 51–52). This would permit the creation of "Writing Land," where computers would guide students through the patterns of the writing process and enhance the students' cognitive activities (see "Framework," 67–70). Computer-assisted composition will help students reduce the constraints imposed by the struggle to put thoughts into words by separating "idea production" and "text production" ("Framework," 53). Once the ideas are under control, "the next stage is to impose text structure on the ideas" ("Framework," 59).

During text production, Collins and Gentner confidently state, the writer can call on "structural devices, stylistic devices, and content devices"—the term "devices" suggesting rule-governed mechanisms. Yet "unfortunately for the writer, there is no one-to-one correspondence between means and end here"—in other words, no consistency in situation that would permit reliance on rule-governed mechanisms ("Framework," 60). Collins and Gentner's analysis frequently bumps up against language's opacity, the contribution to thinking of densely situation-bound meanings embodied in habits of language-using. Because they cannot account for this situational aspect of writing, Collins and Gentner can only define "good writing" as writing that conforms to a set of rules set by some authority (see "Framework," 52–53). This approach leaves them no way to justify the authority's decisions as other than arbitrary, and hence their "rules" turn out to be situation-bound: "Delete extraneous material," "Shorten long paragraphs," and so on

("Framework," 65). Such advice is unhelpful to students without other knowledge that enables them to identify the extraneous and over-lengthy, as I noted earlier in my discussion of revising rules.

The fundamental problem with this approach is that it assumes that the rules we can formulate to describe behavior are the same rules that produce the behavior. As attempts to program language-using computers have shown, such structures reveal their lack of explanatory power when applied to an actual situation in which discourse conventions come into play. Programming a computer to use language comes up against a problem of infinite regress of context—or, how do we tell the computer how to tell what's important when things are important only in terms of purposive activity? How can we define, for example, what is "extraneous material," when the quality of being extraneous resides not in the material itself but in its relation to discourse? Or, to use a simpler example, how can we tell the computer when a paragraph is too long except by specifying a range of lines that constitute acceptable lengths? Is there any form of discourse in which 20-line paragraphs are acceptable and 21-line paragraphs are not? As the competence/performance debate in linguistics has suggested, it may be that we cannot have a completely descriptive theory of behavior in widely varying specific situations—that is, we cannot formulate universal rules for context-bound activities. If language-using isn't rule-governed in this sense, however, it still may be regular—that is, we may be able to group situations as likely to share a number of language-using features. But to do this is to describe the conventions of discourse communities.[26]

As I have been arguing, then, both the inner-directed and the outer-directed theoretical schools will have to contribute to a synthesis capable of providing a comprehensive new agenda for composition studies. My critique of Flower and Hayes's work is intended to contribute to such a synthesis, not to delegitimate what they are doing. I do want to raise a serious question, however, about another feature of the inner-directed school, a feature that works against fruitful discussion and synthesis: the quest for certainty. In seeking one universal model of the composing process, inner-directed theorists seek a new set of principles for our discipline that will raise their arguments, as one has put it, "above mere ideology" (Hirsch, 4). They seek a kind of certainty they believe is accessible only to science, and their talk of paradigm-shifting invokes Kuhn to announce that our discipline will soon have a scientific basis.[27]

This kind of certainty is presumably analogous to the commonplace elevation of fact over opinion, since it is supposed to end all debate. The inner-directed school therefore has redefined composition research to mean a search for the facts in the real world that prove a theory beyond debate. The Flower-Hayes model claims much prestige from being derived from such supposedly unimpeachable evidence. But its reliance on empirical evidence can be questioned on several grounds. For one thing, protocol analysis is a controversial method even within cognitive psychology because it tends to affect what is being observed (see Gould's remarks, *Cognitive Processes*, 125). Flower and Hayes's work is particularly vulnerable because most of their adult subjects have been English teachers who are familiar with the specialized vocabulary of the theory that Flower and Hayes have used to analyze the protocols. Under any circumstances, protocol analysis can lead to "self-fulfilling" prophecy because its assumption that the subject's words mirror her thinking allows the researcher to claim that certain thought processes have occurred if certain words appear in the protocol. Self-fulfilling prophecy is even more likely when test subjects share expert knowledge of these words with the researchers.

The larger point to be made here, however, is that no scientific research, no matter how rigorously it is conducted, possesses the kind of authoritative certainty inner-directed theorists are seeking.[28] It is always desirable, of course, to know more about composing, but it is also necessary to treat this knowledge as provisional, the way scientists treat their findings, if inquiry is not to end. We may wonder, then, why inner-directed theorists are so ready to invest their results with final authority and rush to pedagogical applications. I think it is that certainty appeals to composition specialists these days for various reasons. For one, until recently composition studies was a low-status enclave it was hard to escape; a powerful theory would help us retaliate against the literary critics who dominate English studies. Moreover, such a theory might help us survive what appears to be the long slide of all humanistic disciplines into a low-status enclave. A scientific-sounding theory promises an "accountability" hedge against hard times.

The strongest appeal of certainty, however, is its offer of a solution to our new students' problems that will enable us to undertake their socialization into the academic discourse community without having to consider the ethical and political dimensions of this act. We are reluctant to take up ethical and political questions about what we do because writing teachers have been under a terrific strain. Pressured with increasing asperity by our colleges to prepare students for their other courses, we have also felt anxious in the classroom both when our teaching worked—because we sensed that we were wiping out the students' own culture—and when it didn't—because we were cheating them of a chance to better their situations. Inner-directed pedagogy meets teachers' emotional needs because it can be defended on grounds that are likely to satisfy complaining faculty and administrators, and because its claim to a basis in universals assures us that when we inculcate it, we aren't touching the students' own culture but merely giving them a way around it and up the ladder of success. The corollary is that students for whom the pedagogy doesn't work need no longer be seen as victims of our incompetence but simply as innately inferior.

Invocation of certainty, then, performs the rhetorical function of invocation of the Deity. It guarantees the transcendent authority of values for which we do not need to argue but which we can now apply with the confidence of a "good cause." I would argue, however, that we must understand such a move as the assigning of superhuman authority to a human construction. All knowledge, that is, is of human origin, even scientific knowledge. Indeed, modern philosophy has centered around a critique of scientific knowledge precisely because such knowledge is most likely now to be treated as certain. As Richard Rorty has recently shown, the history of Western philosophy since the Renaissance can be seen as a series of unsuccessful attempts to fight off the admission that such claims for certainty are no longer tenable.[29] There is no way out of confrontation, except among fellow believers, with the necessity of arguing for one's ethical choices.

This confrontation is especially necessary in a pluralistic society such as the United States, in which a heterogeneous school population ensures that pedagogical choices will affect students unequally. Under such circumstances, as Rorty cautions, claims to certainty often express simply a desire for agreement which masks the question of whose interests are being served (see Rorty, 335). Teachers' individual ethical choices add up to political consequences, responsibility for which we cannot avoid. We are better off, then, with a disciplinary theory that encourages examination of consequences. For example, inner-directed research might come up with a heuristic that is useful in Basic Writing classes. But if we use it there, we should not imagine that the heuristic allows us to forget who the students are in Basic Writing classes, where they come from, what their prospects are—in short, why these particular students are having educational difficulties.

Ultimately, I am calling for the inspection of what some curriculum theorists have called the "hidden curriculum": the project of initiating students into a particular world view that gives rise to the daily classroom tasks without being consciously examined by teacher or students.[30] If we call what we are teaching "universal" structures or processes, we bury the hidden curriculum even deeper by claiming that our choice of material owes nothing to historical circumstances. To do this is to deny the school's function as an agent of cultural hegemony, or the selective valuation and transmission of world views. The result for students who don't share the school's preferred world views is either failure or deracination. I think we must acknowledge cultural differences in the classroom, even though this means increasing our emotional strain as members of one group trying to mediate contacts among various others.

The kind of pedagogy that would foster responsible inspection of the politically loaded hidden curriculum in composition class is discourse analysis. The exercise of cultural hegemony can be seen as the treatment of one community's discourse conventions as if they simply mirrored reality. To point out that discourse conventions exist would be to politicize the classroom—or rather, to make everyone aware that it is already politicized. World views would become more clearly a matter of conscious commitment, instead of unconscious conformity, if the ways in which they are constituted in discourse communities were analyzed.

This is not to say that we can make the school an ideologically neutral place. The whole force of my argument is that there is no way to *escape* all discourse communities, stand outside them and pronounce judgment. Furthermore, I assent to most of the conventions of the academic discourse community and believe that students from other communities can benefit from learning about them, and learning them. But perhaps we can break up the failure/deracination dilemma for students from communities at a distance from academe. Through discourse analysis we might offer them an understanding of their school difficulties as the problems of a traveler to an unfamiliar country—yet a country in which it is possible to learn the language and the manners and even "go native" while still remembering the land from which one has come.

In his discussion of literary criticism and interpretive communities, Stanley Fish has offered us one set of suggestions for how such ethically and politically conscious education might proceed. Richard Rorty offers another in his vision of philosophy becoming not the arbiter of disciplines but the mediator among them. This "edifying" philosophy will have as its task making us realize that agreement that looks like certainty can occur only "because when a practice has continued long enough the conventions which make it possible—and which permit a consensus on how to divide it into parts—are relatively easy to isolate" (321). Rorty's is not a positivist notion of arbitrary conventions; he sees conventions as the product of communities, situation-bound but also subject to change. Rorty generalizes Kuhn's notions of "normal" and "revolutionary" science to argue that the edifying philosopher's task is to keep reminding us that "normal" discourse is evidently clear and above debate only because we agree about its conventions. Education must begin with normal discourse but should not be limited to it, with its unhelpful distinction between facts and values (see 363). For the goal of discovering Truth, Rorty substitutes the goal of continuing conversation, but this will not be a dangerously relativistic goal because always conditioned by and having to answer to a historical framework. Rorty's philosophical community thus resembles Fish's interpretive community.

Finally, then, we should see our answers to the question of what we need to know about writing in the light of a new humanistic synthesis. Philosophy has moved to the position that discourse communities are all we have to rely upon in our quest for certainty. Literary criticism is analyzing how discourse communities function as historically situated interpretive communities. Composition studies should focus upon practice within interpretive communities— exactly how conventions work in the world and how they are transmitted. If the work of these disciplines continues to converge, a new synthesis will emerge that revivifies rhetoric as the central discipline of human intellectual endeavor. In view of such a synthesis, the project to make composition studies merely scientific looks obsolete.

I hope that this rhetorical synthesis, because it turns our attention to questions of value and persuasion, will also reawaken us to the collective nature of the whole educational endeavor. There should be no disgrace in discovering that one's work and the understanding that guides it cannot be achieved autonomously. Then the main casualty of our theoretical debate can be the debilitating individualism that adds so much to classroom strain. In other words, let us emphasize not only discourse but also community. I do not mean that we should seek to eliminate the conflicts that arise from our coming from different historical and cultural situations. We should recognize that being so situated is the most important thing we have in common.[31]

NOTES

1. The attitude I'm describing here has been called current-traditionalism, and it still dominates textbooks in the field; see Donald C. Stewart, "Composition Textbooks and the Assault on Tradition," *College Composition and Communication* 29 (May 1978), pp. 171–76.

2. I am taking this sense of "isomorphic" from Frank D'Angelo, *A Conceptual Theory of Rhetoric* (Cambridge, Mass.: Winthrop, 1975), pp. 16, 26–36.

3. I have in mind here the justification for teaching Standard English advanced in E. D. Hirsch, Jr., *The Philosophy of Composition* (Chicago: University of Chicago Press, 1977).

4. For example, Richard Young has recently characterized his particle-wave-field heuristic as based on "universal invariants that underlie all human experience

as characteristic of rationality itself"; in "Arts, Crafts, Gifts, and Knacks: Some Disharmonies in the New Rhetoric," *Visible Language* 14, no. 4 (1980), p. 347.

5. For an overview of research on sentence-combining and the arguments for teaching it, see Frank O'Hare, *Sentence Combining: Improving Student Writing without Formal Grammar Instruction* (Urbana, Ill.: NCTE, 1973).

6. A new textbook that operates from these principles of audience analysis (and other inner-directed pedagogy) is Janice M. Lauer, Gene Montague, Andrea Lunsford, and Janet Emig, *Four Worlds of Writing* (New York: Harper and Row, 1981).

7. Typically, a discourse community prefers one form of the native tongue, which may be characterized simply by level of formality and specialized vocabulary, or which may be a dialect, or a fully constituted language (in the native tongue's family) with its own grammar rules. The outer-directed theorists thus emphasize "parole" over "langue," to use de Saussure's terms, "performance" over "competence," to use Chomsky's terms. For a good account of such language differences in an American setting, see William Labov, *The Study of Nonstandard English* (1969; revised and enlarged; Urbana, Ill.: NCTE, 1975).

8. See, for example, M.A.K. Halliday, "Language as Social Semiotic," *Language as Social Semiotic* (Baltimore: University Park Press, 1978), pp. 108–26.

9. This attitude has been called the Sapir-Whorf hypothesis, because arguments are advanced for it by linguists Edward Sapir and his pupil, Benjamin Lee Whorf; for a good summary and critique of the Sapir-Whorf hypothesis, see Adam Schaff, *Language and Cognition* (1964; trans. Olgierd Wojtasiewicz, ed. Robert S. Cohen; New York: McGraw-Hill, 1973).

10. This, I think, is the gist of the analysis offered by Mina Shaughnessy, "Beyond the Sentence," *Errors and Expectations* (New York: Oxford University Press, 1977), pp. 226–72.

11. A new textbook that operates from some principles of outer-directed pedagogy is Elaine Maimon, Gerald L. Belcher, Gail W. Hearn, Barbara F. Nodine, and Finbarr W. O'Connor, *Writing in the Arts and Sciences* (Cambridge, Mass.: Winthrop, 1981).

12. For an exemplary analysis of academic discourse conventions and how they lead to the accomplishment of the community's work, see Charles Bazerman, "What Written Knowledge Does: Three Examples of Academic Discourse," *Philosophy of the Social Sciences* 11 (September 1981), pp. 361–87; further references in text.

13. Linda Flower and John R. Hayes, "A Cognitive Process Theory of Writing," *College Composition and Communication* 32 (December 1981), pp. 365–87; further references in text.

14. Lee W. Gregg and Erwin R. Steinberg, eds., *Cognitive Processes in Writing* (Hillsdale, N.J.: Lawrence Erlbaum, 1980); further references in text.

15. Lev Vygotsky, *Thought and Language* (1934; rpt. ed. & trans. Eugenia Hanfmann and Gertrude Vakar; Cambridge, Mass.: MIT Press, 1962), p. 51, author's emphasis; further references in text. Vygotsky's pupil A. R. Luria did

research among Uzbek peasants which suggests that thought and language interpenetrate to such a degree that perception of optical illusions, for example, changes with cultural experience and level of education; see A. R. Luria, *Cognitive Development* (1974; rpt. trans. Martin Lopez-Morillas and Lynn Solotaroff, ed. Michael Cole; Cambridge, Mass.: Harvard University Press, 1976).

16. See M.A.K. Halliday and Ruqaiya Hasan, *Cohesion in English* (London: Longman, 1976), pp. 19–26.

17. My line of argument here is based on Dell Hymes, "Bilingual Education: Linguistic vs. Sociolinguistic Bases," *Foundations in Sociolinguistics* (Philadelphia: University of Pennsylvania Press, 1974), pp. 119–24; in the same volume, Hymes argues that to uncover the extralinguistic attitudes lending significance to language use, linguists need more contributions from folklorists.

18. George L. Dillon, *Constructing Texts* (Bloomington, Ind.: Indiana University Press, 1981), pp. 1–20; further references in text.

19. A critique of the notion of simplicity-as-clarity has been offered by Richard Lanham, *Style: An Anti-Textbook* (New Haven, Conn.: Yale University Press, 1974). Lanham's later work in composition pedagogy suggests, however, that he is cynical about the position taken in *Style* and not really ready to defend "ornate" language choices outside of special literary circumstances; see Richard Lanham, *Revising Prose* (New York: Scribner, 1979). Dillon, pp. 21–49, is more helpful on understanding the problems with revising rules.

20. Halliday, "Language in Urban Society," p. 163; Halliday suggests that our current difficulties in the composition class may be at least in part a function of the increasing number of students who come from urban areas.

21. See Stanley Fish, *Is There a Text in this Class?* (Cambridge, Mass.: Harvard University Press, 1980), further references in text; the following argument is heavily indebted to Fish's work.

22. Mina Shaughnessy, "Some Needed Research on Writing," *College Composition and Communication* 27 (December 1977), p. 319.

23. See Basil Bernstein, *Class, Codes, and Control* (1971; rpt. New York: Schocken, 1975); and to correct the vulgar error that Bernstein is diagnosing a cognitive deficiency in working-class language, see "The Significance of Bernstein's Work for Sociolinguistic Theory" in Halliday, pp. 101–107. Many dangerous misinterpretations of Bernstein could perhaps have been avoided if he had not chosen to call working-class language-using habits a "restricted code" and middle-class (school-oriented) habits an "elaborated code."

24. The seminal text here is Thomas Kuhn, *The Structure of Scientific Revolutions*, 2d. edition, enlarged (Chicago: University of Chicago Press, 1970). Kuhn is now going so far as to say that "proponents of different theories (or different paradigms, in the broader sense of the term) speak different languages—languages expressing different cognitive commitments, suitable for different worlds"; he announces the study of language's function in theory-making as his current project. See Thomas Kuhn, *The Essential Tension* (Chicago: University of Chicago Press, 1977), pp. 22–23.

25. Linda Flower, *Problem-Solving Strategies for Writing* (New York: Harcourt Brace Jovanovich, 1981); further references in text.

26. In my discussion of Collins and Gentner, I am following the line of argument offered by Hubert L. Dreyfus, *What Computers Can't Do* (New York: Harper and Row, 1972; rpt. 2d. edition, San Francisco: Freeman, 1979). Flower and Hayes's sympathy with the Collins-Gentner approach is suggested not only by the large amount of agreement between the two accounts of composing, but also by the numerous borrowings in the Flower-Hayes model from computer terminology and by Flower and Hayes's suggestion that their model will contribute toward "building a Writer" ("Process Theory," p. 368).

27. For an example of this use of Kuhn, see Maxine Hairston, "The Winds of Change: Thomas Kuhn and the Revolution in the Teaching of Writing," *College Composition and Communication* 33 (February 1982), pp. 76–88.

28. This argument follows the account of rhetoric's function in the scientific discourse community given by Kuhn in *Structure* and (in a more radical version) by Paul Feyerabend, *Against Method* (1975; rpt. London: Verso, 1978).

29. Richard Rorty, *Philosophy and the Mirror of Nature* (Princeton, N.J.: Princeton University Press, 1979); further references in text.

30. On the hidden curriculum and its reproduction of oppressive social power relations, see Michael Apple, *Ideology and Curriculum* (London: Routledge and Kegan Paul, 1979).

31. I would like to thank Bruce Herzberg for the many ideas and the editorial guidance that he has, as usual, contributed to my work.

College Composition: Initiation Into
the Academic Discourse Community

Composition studies has become established as an academic discipline. Over the past decade, college writing programs have expanded tremendously, and scholarly attention to writing theory and pedagogy has also grown. Although composition studies are not yet organized under a disciplinary paradigm, some dominant trends are embodied in two recent textbooks, *Four Worlds of Writing* and *Writing in the Arts and Sciences*. The authors of *Four Worlds*, Janice M. Lauer, Gene Montague, Andrea Lunsford, and Janet Emig, are all eminent practitioners in the field, well qualified to produce a text that is based on "premises derived from rhetorical theory of the last decade," as their preface announces (xv). Elaine Maimon, principal author of *Writing in the Arts and Sciences*, directs one of the most successful writing-across-the-curriculum programs in the United States, and her collaborators are colleagues from the departments of History, Biology, Psychology, and Philosophy at Beaver College in Pennsylvania. The sophistication of the new textbooks shows how far composition studies have come.

Yet, the composition specialist who reads these books may wonder just how much progress has been made. Both books aim to teach students how to write for their other college courses; in other words, to initiate students into the academic discourse community. Teachers who are not composition specialists may find this aim quite unsurprising, especially because the recent expansion of college writing programs has been justified largely in terms of their "service" to the whole academic community, in preparing students to do college written work. But to the specialist, the new books present a paradox. On the one hand, their theoretical premises and pedagogical techniques clearly are the products of the recent decade of growth. In this decade, however, college writing teachers frequently have found themselves at odds with the institutional goal of initiation into academic discourse, and much of our work has been directed to redefining the nature of "good" writing. Now these innovative textbooks seem to be reaffirming the traditional academic discourse values. The specialist may be perplexed by this apparent regression.

One great advance represented in these new textbooks is, at least, the acknowledgement that what the community requires is academic discourse. Fifteen years ago, college writing teachers were usually not so aware of their own assumptions. Harvey Wiener, professor of English at LaGuardia Community College in New York, and president of the N. C. T. E.-affiliated Council of Writing Program Administrators, recalls that at that time: "University and college level writing programs were little more than required courses in freshman English. Instructors hoped that the study of *Walden* and *Sons and Lovers* would open the floodgates of correct, intelligent, stylish prose. The Freshman English Director . . . kept out of the way of senior faculty members who rarely taught a course in composition" (1981, 1). My memories of my first years of teaching match Wiener's recollections. Freshman English students were supposed to be brushing up their ability to produce a certain kind of written product; they were not so much taught about this product as reminded of its characteristics by those marginal English department members not needed for rigorous scholarly tasks. Because the nature of the required product—"correct, intelligent, stylish"—was taken to be virtually self-evident, there seemed to be little necessity for an organized teaching approach, and none for a theory to inform our teaching. Writing instruction was dominated by the sort of product-oriented textual analysis that controlled literary criticism.

This kind of writing instruction treated all differences between students simply as a matter of innate and individual abilities. The students' thought processes and their various social circumstances were ignored. Yet, the composition class rewarded writing that tallied with standards of correctness and stylishness already established in the academic discourse community. "Intelligent" writing was defined by its meeting this audience's expectations. As shown by Basil Bernstein (1975), and by Pierre Bourdieu and Jean-Claude Passeron (1977), students from different social classes come to school with different abilities to deal with academic discourse: middle-class students are better suited by their socialization in language use to deal with academic discourse's relative formality and abstraction than working-class students are. This unequal removal from academic language is, of course, exacerbated for students whose home language does not resemble the so-called Standard English, as Mina Shaughnessy has shown (1977a, 1977b). Under the guise of polishing students' written products, then, the freshman English course often "served" the college mainly by culling those students who had not already begun their initiation into the discourse community. At large state schools obligated to set somewhat inclusive admissions standards, the freshman English course regularly "flunked out" a certain percentage of each entering class.

Over the past decade, however, more and more students have come to college while at a very elementary stage of their initiation into the academic discourse community; that is, more and more students have come who cannot easily produce written Standard English, who cannot sustain an argument in an essay, who cannot adopt the relatively objective persona academics prefer, and so on. When such students began to be the majority in most college writing classrooms, what could be treated as self-evident quickly became problematic. Instead of trying to cull so many students, writing programs began to expand to allow more time for initiation. For some undergraduates, one, two, or even three semesters of "remedial" composition preceded the "regular" freshman requirement, hence, of course, calling into question the meaning of "remedial" in this context. The notion of who should be "served" and why began to change.

At the same time that the classroom population has been changing in these ways, college writing teachers have found their situation in the academy changing, too. We used to assume that although our position was "marginal," it was also temporary; when we got our

Ph.D.s, or when a tenure-track line opened, we would move out of the composition ghetto and take on the more challenging—and professionally rewarding—literary work. Early in the 1970s, however, we began to find the upward ladder blocked by funding problems in higher education, and by an attendant, pervasive loss of morale. Our most prestigious professional organization, the Modern Language Association, could not respond to our plight, other than to give cold comfort to jobseekers and to warn undergraduates away from doctoral study. We began to feel that we had little stake in the institutional goals of the English department, including the composition course's questionable "service." But we also saw that if we were to find any security for ourselves in the academy, we were going to have to find ways to make professionally rewarding the field in which we were remaining.

Composition studies began to organize into an academic specialization, then, at a time when changes in our students and ourselves prompted a rejection of received wisdom on what "good" writing was and what a composition course ought to do. We realized that if we were to go on teaching academic discourse, two things would have to change: our understanding of the students' writing processes; and the relationship between the academic discourse community and the students' discourse communities. Thus we turned to those aspects of our students' lives that had been ignored in the old composition course: their thought processes and their social circumstances.

We have not been entirely successful in reforming freshman English, however, because we have not given equal attention to the two neglected areas. We have spent much scholarly energy on exploring students' writing processes. But we have not sufficiently considered the nature of academic discourse as a form of language use that unites a particular community, and we have not examined the relationship between the academic discourse community and the communities from which are students come: communities with forms of language use shaped by their own social circumstances. We have not demystified academic discourse.

The first wave of innovative composition pedagogy simply rejected the academic community's discourse expectations. Instead, the goal became the liberation from academic trammels of each student's "authentic" writing voice; Peter Elbow's influential book here is revealingly entitled *Writing Without Teachers* (1973). But this strategy of rejection has not succeeded because its focus is too individualistic. "Authentic voice" adherents cannot adequately critique academic expectations because they do not realize the extent to which their own pedagogy depends on their students' having had teachers at one time or another. The "authentic voice" cannot be created in a cultural void. Ken Macrorie predicted in a 1968 essay that unless we reform our writing classes, they will be destroyed along with other corrupt "American establishments" because "now we are living in a great series of revolutions, testing whether the present forms of school, church, state, family, and relationships between blacks and whites will endure." Macrorie fails to notice that only readers with a conventional academic discourse education will be well equipped to appreciate his device of alluding to President Lincoln's Gettysburg Address.

A related and perhaps more serious criticism of the "authentic voice" pedagogy is that, since it makes certain assumptions about students' previous education, it leaves unexamined whatever education they do bring to college. "Remedial" or basic writing students may therefore find the "authentic voice" classroom initially a very welcoming place for two reasons. First, the cultural capital that informs their writing will be treated simply as "interesting material." Middle-class students have an advantage over working-class students in cultural capital as well as in formal language structures, as suggested in my analysis of the Macrorie quote above, but their unequal removal from the world of college will not be noticed in the "authentic voice" classroom. Second, the working-class students may even have an advantage here. In many cases, their life experience has been more varied than that of their sheltered classmates, and they are also more likely to be emotionally in touch with this experience. Their papers, then, may strike the instructor as more interesting and "authentic" than those of middle-class students.

Initial success in the "authentic voice" writing class can be ultimately all the more damaging, however. In a critique of Macrorie's *Uptaught,* James Vopat has observed: "I was disturbed to find that students who had recently written well and excitedly about their personal experience were at a loss when asked to write about ideas, when asked to question values" (1978, 42). Vopat is focusing here on students' failures in other college courses, and I know his point is not an unimportant one because I, too, have heard the complaints of former students who do not understand why I was pleased with their writing when no one else in the academy seems to be. Whether or not everyone else in the academy is unjust, composition teachers who have shared my experience have felt compelled to ask themselves whether or not their students were learning what they really needed to learn to grow intellectually. I decided, finally, while teaching Basic Writing students at Rutgers, that the "authentic voice" writing class was too easy for them precisely because it postponed their confrontation, and mine, with the great inequalities in their preparation for the world of college.

In general, however, the movement of composition studies away from "authentic voice" pedagogy has not brought any political analysis to bear on it, but has retained its individualistic bias in the current emphasis on writing as a cognitive process. Wanting to get even closer to the individual student writing, composition specialists have enlisted the aid of cognitive psychologists and psycholinguists to get inside the writing student's head. The emphasis on writing as a process does contrast neatly with the old composition course's stultifying concentration on written product. Also, insofar as the writing process admits of scientific analysis, the intellectual credentials of composition specialists are enhanced with their demoralized humanist colleagues, a gratifying development to those who once were "marginal." Furthermore, this new cognitive focus on process promises the elaboration of a universal set of writing "skills," which, once elaborated, can be taught with selective intensity to bring today's students of varied backgrounds up to the level of academic discourse. But in the focus upon writing process, neglect of students' social circumstances and the normative function of discourse communities continues.

For example, the sort of cultural capital that once simply earned the "authentic" essay a rapt classroom audience is now subjected to psychological testing so that it can be changed. Andrea Lunsford has recently compared basic writers with more skilled student essayists, and has arrived at this conclusion: "The basic writers I have been quoting, then, seem to represent the egocentric stage of cognitive development and the conventional stage of moral development, to conceptualize and generalize with great difficulty, and, most of all, to lack confidence" (Lunsford 1980, 284). When these students employ the first person and rely on evidence drawn from personal experience, techniques that would have been encouraged in the "authentic voice" class, Lunsford diagnoses their writing as evidence of egocentricity. Their personal focus also seems to be responsible for her perception of them as unable to conceptualize and generalize. In place of abstractions carefully derived from well-selected evidence, these students refer their value judgments to maxims received uncritically from authority, prompting Lunsford to place them at an early stage of moral development. Their lack of self-confidence is revealed in their frequent, anxious portrayals of themselves as victims of social forces.

Lunsford nods toward rejection of academic discourse expectations when she asserts (1980, 287) that "the basic writers' prose is more vital, more engaging and more true to their own experience than the impersonal, strangely disengaged prose often produced by our more skilled students"; nevertheless, she believes that we should be "helping our students become more proficient at abstracting and conceptualizing and hence at producing acceptable academic discourse, without losing the directness many of them now possess." This goal may well be attractive to former "authentic voice" pedagogues who, like Vopat, want their students to be better able to write about such abstract matters as ideas and values. The problem is that by retaining an individualistic focus, though in the now-more-fashionable scientific guise rather than the old-fashioned soft-hearted liberal one, Lunsford, like Macrorie, finesses the essential conflict between academic discourse and the cultural capital expressed in the prose she analyzes.

It seems to me that all of Lunsford's symptoms would be better explained in social and political terms. The personal focus of her students' writing and their uncritical references to moral authority are quite typical of the working-class language usage that Basil Bernstein (1974) has called a "restricted code." As Bernstein has repeatedly insisted, however, he sees restricted code use as a function of social context rather than cognitive development. The point is that all of us use restricted codes in some situations. The middle-class students' real advantage is that they are already familiar not only with a range of codes (including the one most appropriate to school usage, which Bernstein calls "elaborated"), but also with the range of social cues that indicate where and when a code is appropriate. In its focus on cognitive writing skills, process-oriented composition studies prejudge those unequally prepared for school as unequal in mental development.

Even more pernicious is treating as neurotic the students' views of themselves as victims. Neither the "authentic voice" pedagogues nor the process-oriented ones have built anything into their theoretical systems that would allow them to take account of the possible truth of these views as affecting student writing. Indeed, it seems to me that basic writing students clearly are victims—of institutionalized social injustice. What they need from their education is not therapy but the critical training to trace their victimization to social forces rather than to "fate," and hence to work toward control of their own destinies.

It is to attain this sort of critical understanding that politically oppressed students need to master academic discourse. They need composition instruction that exposes and demystifies the institutional structure of knowledge, rather than that which covertly reintroduces discriminatory practices while cloaking the force of convention in concessions to the "personal." The cognitive focus of process-oriented composition studies cannot provide the necessary analysis.

In addition to process analysis, however, discourse analysis has increased its influence in composition studies over the past decade. If process analysis tends to strip away social circumstances in favor of cognitive universals, discourse analysis keeps awareness of the social situation of writing alive. If process analysis can "forget" how its anatomy of skills may be used to serve oppressive institutional goals, discourse analysis keeps us aware of the social functions of the writing activity. But until very recently, discourse analysis has focused mainly on the relationship of social function to rhetorical structure, as in James Kinneavy's A Theory of Discourse (1971). Writer, audience, "medium of communication," and "referent" or matter to be communicated are all treated as more or less discrete entities. Discourse can then be classified in terms of the element given preeminence: a scholarly essay focuses on the matter to be communicated, a work of literary art on the medium of communication itself, and so on. This formal approach to discourse analysis, while not claiming to transcend social circumstances as process analysis aims to do, still does not encourage the critical evaluation of writing situations. Hence, formalist discourse analysis cannot demystify academic discourse in use in a community.

Four Worlds of Writing and *Writing in the Arts and Sciences* reflect the latest developments in process theory and, more importantly, in discourse theory. They are also based upon the now reinstated assumption that initiation into academic discourse is the college writing course's goal. The question we have to ask of these books, I think, is not why they are teaching academic discourse. The simple rejection of academic discourse expectations has failed. More important, we do not want simply to reject these expectations, because initiation into the academic discourse community may be just what oppressed students need to gain the critical distance on their experience provided by an elaborated code. I agree with Bourdieu and Passeron (1977) that the academy cannot be separated from its language; indeed, taking a cue from Michel Foucault (1970), I would argue that academic discourse *constitutes* the academic community. Unlike Bourdieu and Passeron, however, I do not think that the connection between the academy and its language absolutely bars access to academic knowledge for some students. What we must do is to inquire whether these new textbooks initiate students into academic discourse in such a way as to foster a productive critical distance on the social processes whereby knowledge is generated and controlled. The books' failures and successes will help to show, I hope, how possible the acquisition of such distance is.

The books differ somewhat in subject matter and in intended audience. *Writing in the Arts and Sciences*, as the title announces, aims solely to assist students in learning to write for college; after a preliminary five-chapter section on the writing process, Maimon et al. devote the remaining nine chapters to three sections on writing "in the humanities," "in the social sciences," and "in the natural sciences." These chapters explain the kinds of intellectual work that characterize the various disciplines, and explicate the rhetorical conventions that shape the work. The primary audience is, apparently, students at an early stage of initiation into the academic community, such as freshmen uncommitted to a major field of study—but not students at such an early stage that they cannot write Standard English (for example, the book includes no instruction on the formulation of sentences). Given the shape of most college writing programs, however, this omission may not be a "silent" one, as was the omission of training in Standard English in the old composition course; the omission may be based on the assumption that the book will be used in programs in which other courses address problems with Standard English. I might also note here that in my experience, students are more interested in mastering the conventions of Standard English *after* they have become engaged in college intellectual work and see the social necessity of such mastery for further pursuit of their intellectual interests; even assuming then no other "support" courses, Maimon et al.'s omission may be pedagogically well advised.

The title *Four Worlds of Writing* accurately suggests a more ambitious scope. In covering the "worlds" of "private," "public," "college," and "working" discourse, Lauer et al. seem to be trying to include most of the universe of discourse. The audience of writers to whom the book is addressed apparently includes almost anyone who ever wanted to write anything, except for scholarly or highly technical work. That this audience might include those who do not write standard English easily is indicated by the inclusion of a chapter on "editing," which details what are called "conventions" of grammar, punctuation, spelling, and mechanics; also of help to such writers are the "sentence patterns" exercises spaced through the text, and a chapter on sentence combining. Although, if possible, engagement in college intellectual work should come first, this is the kind of instruction in standard English that one hopes the students of Maimon et al. will receive somewhere. This approach to "correctness" has several advantages: it treats Standard English as a condition of prose to be achieved only after careful editing, instead of a condition that "comes naturally"; it treats Standard English as a conventional system of language use preferred by certain discourse communities, instead of the one correct form; it discusses questions of usage and syntax with a minimum of grammar terminology (see O'Hare 1971).

The book's inclusiveness, however, suggests another intended audience. It seems to me that this is a textbook written to promulgate a theory of composition. Such books are not uncommon in a field that, until very recently, received little attention from scholarly publishers; the way to get one's theory out, then, was to write a textbook that embodied it. For example, Young, Becker, and Pike's *Rhetoric: Discovery and Change* (1970), though ostensibly a textbook, has probably been read in many more graduate composition theory courses than undergraduate writing courses. *Four Worlds of Writing*'s similar audience may be indicated in the large number of footnotes in the text that cite scholarly work in composition.

The theoretical project is most clearly revealed in the complexity of the book's scheme. Lauer et al.'s model of composition assumes a writing process, or series of stages in composing, that remains constant whatever the writing task. The writing task is classified, according to discourse theory, in terms of the writer's purpose and the nature of the audience; i.e., different rhetorical strategies are specified as appropriate to each task. *Four Worlds of Writing* is structured so as to guide students repeatedly through a ten-stage writing process that includes several heuristic methods, as they explore eight different writing strategies distributed across the four worlds of discourse. Although the aim is to integrate process theory and discourse theory, the structure turns much more attention onto an anatomy of process. Insofar as undergraduates are the audience for this integration, they are addressed as researchers into their own composing processes; however, I think that many undergraduates would find the writing instructions overdetermined. Although seemingly aimed at a broader audience than *Writing in the Arts and Sciences*, reading *Four Worlds of Writing* requires greater familiarity with academic discourse.

A more serious problem with Lauer et al.'s approach to the writing process is their treating its stages as universally applicable. They do not claim that their model is paradigmatic, but they do assume that such a model will be found. Hence, in spite of their attempt to meld process theory with context-bound discourse theory, their process model tends to float free of circumstances.

Thinking, in other words, is still something one does in isolation—an individualized activity and an ahistorical one.

In contrast, the five-chapter section on the writing process in *Writing in the Arts and Sciences* is not so schematic. Chapter 2 includes the most comprehensive catalogue of heuristic methods I have seen anywhere—and a "catalogue" is what it is. No heuristic is presented as having universal cognitive authority. Each heuristic is demonstrated in use on an academic intellectual problem it is well suited to illuminate. In other words, thinking is bound to the context of academic disciplines. Furthermore, the last three chapters in this section all show how ideas for writing are developed in dialogue with teachers, classmates, and the written resources of the library. These chapters go far beyond introducing the *Reader's Guide to Periodical Literature*; they reveal the sources of academic knowledge in communal intellectual work, thus dispelling the debilitating but persistent myth of individual genius as the key to academic success. To open the doors of the library is to reveal the social rootedness of brilliant individual performances. In short, what Maimon et al. do with the writing process reinforces what they do in the rest of the book with discourse analysis. What Lauer et al. do with the writing process tends to work against what they are simultaneously trying to do with discourse analysis.

Lauer et al.'s treatment of discourse analysis, furthermore, cannot adequately counteract the individualizing and universalizing trends of their process model because it does not deal adequately with considerations of audience. We would expect that it would be in the discussion of audience, if anywhere, that the social circumstances of language use could be recovered. Lauer et al. do seem to talk very frankly about the school situation, using audience analysis techniques borrowed from values clarification to humanize the teacher-student relationship. But the very serious flaw in this approach to audience is that it treats the teacher-student (audience-writer) relationship on an entirely personal and individual basis. Although the authors recognize the institutional framework of these encounters, there is very little critical analysis of this framework, which is to say, little analysis of the function of socially established conventions in shaping language use in the academic community. It is as if Lauer et al. have noticed many of the features of schooling that Bourdieu and

Passeron inspect (1977), without seeing the French theorists' central thesis on reproduction.

For example, here is part of their discussion of the "expository aim" of college research papers: "Research writing sometimes assumes a *pseudo-persuasive aim* [authors' emphasis] when the minimum expectations of the professors are that you will retrieve information familiar to them and organize it in a familiar pattern so that you will persuade them that you understand the subject as they and others like them understand it" (194–195). This, it seems to me, is an accurate characterization of most undergraduate research writing. In noticing the existence of "familiar" information, "familiar" rhetorical patterns, and an audience defined by convention ("they and others like them"), Lauer et al. touch on the boundaries of the territory they ought to explore if they are going to demystify academic discourse. But rather than look at the social context implied here, the authors, in effect, deny its existence in their labeling of this writing as "*pseudo*-persuasive" (my emphasis). They are suggesting that the initiatory interaction between student and teacher that they have just been describing in the research paper is somehow not real.

On the same page, they suggest the equally naive view that actual persuasive writing requires that the audience be convinced of some ideas that it did not previously entertain: that persuasion entails "new" information or a "new hypothesis." This oversimplification is effectively critiqued by Kuhn (1970) in his analysis of the rhetorical element in all "revolutionary" scientific theories—the extent to which a new theory relies for its acceptance on its ability to incorporate and reinterpret previously established beliefs. This is the kind of analysis that reveals the function of "familiarity" in legitimating academic writing. Instead of such analysis, Lauer et al. offer this advice to the student with a "pseudo-persuasive" task: "Even if your professor has only this minimal expectation, you can plan a more meaningful aim. Because research consumes so much time, why not use the opportunity to discover something more valuable to you and your readers than that you know the research process?" (195). Given that the professor is almost always the sole reader of the research paper, and that his or her judgment of how to guide the class determines the paper's value, it is hard to understand who is meant by "your readers" above, and how "something more valuable" will be defined. The students are apparently offered the opportunity to will themselves into a social vacuum. The approach may flatter students' typical complaints about the arbitrary requirements of ivory-tower academics, but the lack of social analysis can lead, it seems to me, only to a quixotic resistance.

When Lauer et al. show how to analyze an academic audience-of-one (professor), the invidiousness of their method is more visible. For example, they quote a student's analysis of the audience for one of his final exams. This particular instructor of criminal justice is described as a black ex-policeman who "doggedly" holds the opinion that most white-collar crime goes unpunished. The student concludes that he should address this audience from the position of a "subordinate" in his exam essay—"which is what I think a student is anyway"—and agree with the instructor's views, which he does agree with, anyway. The authors comment: "[This analysis] suggests that he is intimidated by the examiner and will simply try to agree with the examiner's opinion. It is never a good idea to try to give back to an examiner exactly what he gave you. In the first place, it's impossible. In the second place, it says little to the examiner about you or the subject matter or your command of the subject matter" (253).

The problem with this response is that Lauer et al. conflate the personal and social aspects of the situation because they have no separate conceptual category for social circumstances. It usually *is* a good idea to try to give back an examiner something of what he or she gave you, but exactly how that is to be done is a pedagogical issue of great importance, as Paulo Freire has shown in *Pedagogy of the Oppressed* (1968), when he contrasts "banking education" with education for critical consciousness. Many instructors are "bankers": I have seen the essay exams graded solely on the basis of how many "key words" are present. Also, I would be lying if I did not admit that when I read the more unstructured essay exams I give my literature students, I am more favorably disposed toward those that seem to share my own ethical and political predilections, though not necessarily my esthetic judgments. But all Lauer et al. can do with this student's generalization about being a student (being a "subordinate") is to treat it as a result of the particular instructor's personality (the student is "intimidated").

In analyzing the exam situation, then, the authors are so keen to argue that the student need not regard the instructor as an unimpeachable authority that they almost advise the student to feign disagreement with the instructor's views simply to prove that he is not intimidated. This model of student-teacher relations assumes too readily that students must protect themselves from teachers' assaults. Here, let us suppose, there is a "personal" difficulty between the easily intimidated student and his overbearing instructor. But Lauer et al. can only offer a "personal" solution, the student's self-assertive counterattack. Considering this student-teacher difficulty in its social context, however, we may see the need for a sort of "social" solution, something to "protect" the student besides his own defiance. What he and his teacher need is a conventional system of inquiry that temporarily suspends personalities without suppressing or manipulating them. Such a system exists in the conventions of discourse that constitute intellectual work in the academic community.

Sharing this methodology, student and teacher can investigate such issues as whether most white-collar crime does go unpunished. The student need not feel compelled to believe anything only because the instructor does; at the same time, however, he need not accept Lauer et al.'s hints that the instructor holds his "opinion" because of his race and that he holds it unreasonably ("doggedly"). If the student "gives back" to the instructor the methodology the instructor has been demonstrating, the student acknowledges his social context in the academy; yet he will not have to feel that he is yielding to social restrictions, if, like the instructor, he lets his personal needs and cares determine the experience on which he will employ the methodology.

At the same time, the instructor must think of what he is doing as initiating the student into this critical methodology, instead of subordinating him to the instructor's will. Teacher and student might struggle together to make the classroom intellectually liberating, and to understand the teacher's right to play "examiner," if they discussed what the instructor himself learned when he made the shift in perspective from patrolman to criminologist. It seems to me that Janet Emig (1977) had the exploring of such perspective shifts in mind when she described writing as "a mode of learning." Unfortunately, I find far too little indication in *Four Worlds of Writing* that academic writing can be a mode for exploring perspective shifts and hence attaining a critical distance on experience. Rather, in the authors' analysis of how students should try to satisfy teachers, we are adrift in a world where decisions get made mainly on the basis of their manipulative effect.

Writing in the Arts and Sciences, in contrast, remains "within" the academic discourse community. The method of Maimon et al. is more effective: less elaboration of processes and techniques, and more discussion of the general intellectual purposes of academic writing. Whereas, for example, Lauer et al. provide students with several detailed sets of questions to use in the planning stages of their writing process, Maimon et al. begin by talking about the function of questioning in liberal arts education. Whereas Lauer et al. imply that the use of these heuristics will help students "solve" writing "problems," Maimon et al., even though they, too, speak of "writing as problem solving" (6–7), emphasize that learning academic discourse will be an "unsettling" experience in which students will have to become accustomed to considerable "uncertainty" and to learn the uses of writing "to illuminate ambiguous situations." In short, if Lauer et al. address the student audience as composition researchers, Maimon et al. address them as young initiates into the academic discourse community—a much closer approximation of the students' actual role.

Writing in the Arts and Sciences emphasizes the communal nature of academic work. The "process" chapters, grouped under the heading "Writing to Learn," continually relate the individual student's writing process to other uses of language in academe. Once this communal nature of academic intellectual life is acknowledged, it is easier to explore the conventions that unite the community, and Maimon et al. devote themselves continually to this sort of audience analysis. They begin by explaining that the college writer has to see his or her audience in terms of "the conventions of the discipline." Instead of inspecting a particular instructor's personality, they argue; "It is not sufficient to imagine your instructor as your audience; you must go further and imagine your instructor playing a particular role—representative of scholars in a discipline or representative of people who hold the view opposing the one you are arguing" (8). The salient feature of the instructor's role is practitioner in a particular academic discipline; and the writing tasks are classified by the kind of intellectual work to be performed. Hence, in the three sections on writing "in the humanities," "in the social sciences," and "in the natural sciences," analysis of the writing situation is tied to analysis of the conventions of the academic discourse community.

For example, in discussing the humanities research paper, Maimon et al. explain that although this kind of paper is "bound by quite strict conventions, . . . it is not an empty exercise. The term paper marks a rite of passage in many humanities courses, for you are being asked to perform, in microcosm, the tasks that scholars in the field engage in to produce articles in professional journals" (126). Instead of treating the research paper cynically, as a mindless chore imposed by some martinet, Maimon et al. explain its initiatory function and relate it to the ongoing work in the field. They then go on to explain the nature of the argument as a "reasoned interpretation":

> In a history class you are obligated to back up your interpretation with the kind of evidence that historians will accept. They will not accept as a decisive answer, for example, what Charles II said about his own foreign policy. But historians may disagree on what the answer is, not because it is a mere matter of taste but because the range of facts to be considered in forging an answer is so great. Nor is a disagreement among historians on the subject just a matter of knowledge, of one knowing more about the period than another. The facts known equally to both historians may be open to several equally plausible interpretations. In such a case, there are certainly answers that are plainly wrong—inconsistent with the facts—but several answers that are *reasonable,* worthy of belief [authors' emphasis]. (127)

I have quoted this passage at length because I think it is a very good example of how *Writing in the Arts and Sciences* demystifies disciplinary activity. Note particularly that evidence is treated as something defined by disciplinary conventions ("evidence that historians will accept"); argument therefore cannot involve merely the collecting of facts but more, their selection and interpretation ("several answers that are *reasonable*").

This emphasis on disciplinary definition of evidence can also be found in the chapters on the social sciences. In discussing the case study paper, Maimon et al. (223) admonish the student researcher to "record objectively the details of what you actually see." But they put this seemingly naive recommendation about unfiltered perception in the context of preventing the inexperienced observer from rushing to closure: "If you establish a mindset too early, you may try to fit all of your observations into a pattern that is not really adequate to explain what is happening." Then, instead of pretending that correct observation somehow takes its form from the observed, they recommend "categorizing" observation according to disciplinary concepts: "Do not overlook your textbook as an aid to your vision. . . . If you are writing a case study for a course in early childhood education, you should recall that the authors of your textbook have raised questions about the development of children. They categorize this development into motor, language, social, and cognitive. You should try the same categories" (224). Note that Maimon et al. do not say that children's development *is* divided into four elements; the authors make it clear that these are conceptual frames used by "the authors of your textbook" to "[raise] questions" about children's development. Adherence to disciplinary conventions is recommended without treating those conventions as the product of nature rather than human intellectual activity.

Similarly, in discussing the review paper in the natural sciences, Maimon et al. explain:

> While you should be genuinely curious about your topic, be sure that your curiosity concerns the scientific features of the subject, not the emotional. [In other courses] you can find opportunities to write about the ethical and historical implications of popular topics, but for hard-core science courses, focus on the current state of scientific knowledge in the area defined by your research questions. . . . Topic selection in the natural sciences is based much more on a survey of the literature than on invention devices. (277, 283)

The textbook is, perhaps, less free here from the unexamined expression of disciplinary assumptions, in the designation of "ethical and historical implications" as "emotional" features of a subject, and in the rather self-satisfied labeling of natural-science courses as "hard-core." Nevertheless, "the current state of scientific knowledge" is continually presented as the defining force in scientific intellectual work—not the nature of the observed world.

In contrast, *Four Worlds of Writing* cannot go into such detail about academic intellectual work because only three chapters are given to the "college world." The treatment Lauer et al. give such work, however, makes a revealing comparison with *Writing in the Arts and Sciences.* Instead of seeing it as shaped by disciplinary conventions, they present it as determined either by an individual student's feelings and values or by the structure of a heuristic method that they take to be universally applicable. For example, they quote with approval these notes by a student looking for a "starting point" for a biology research paper.

> I'm very curious about cloning since I saw *The Boys from Brazil* and saw David Rorvik interviewed on *Today.* He claims his book *In His Image* documents how the first human clone was produced. My interest leans toward the current gene transplantation experiments rather than toward research into chromosome structure though I know the one depends on the other. I'm not sure how cloning fits with my value of not messing with nature. (193)

My point is not that curiosity stimulated by popularized, mass-media versions of science is illegitimate; the problem is that Lauer et al. do not give this student much help in moving from this superficial approach toward one with more disciplinary method-ological content. Although in what follows, they do give a lot of advice about doing library research, the sample student paper (239) that finally issues from the project bears a title that accurately indicates its conceptual level: "Engineering Our Own Evolution: The Risks." Here, disciplinary conventions of intellectual work are simply avoided more than they are demystified; the student does not get the benefit of a biologist's view of a controversial subject.

When a heuristic method is used, on the other hand, disciplinary practice is not so much avoided as incorporated into the heuristic without much discussion. In a chapter on critical essays (really literary-critical essays), Lauer et al. give brief definitions of literary terms and then plug them into a modified version of the particle-wave-field heuristic introduced by Young, Becker, and Pike (1970). The very structure of the heuristic is supposed to make it easier for initiates to answer such questions (273) as "Who is the persona in the poem?" and "With what other literature can this poem be compared?" Attention is not called to the communal intellectual work that creates such questions and their currently acceptable answers. Here, *Four Worlds of Writing* operates like a disciplinary textbook that teaches concepts simply by using the disciplinary vocabulary. *Writing in the Arts and Sciences*, in contrast, is more of a "meta-textbook" because it explains the function of disciplinary concepts.

As I noted earlier, of course, we must acknowledge that *Four Worlds of Writing* and *Writing in the Arts and Sciences* do not have exactly the same aim. Lauer et al. place much less emphasis on academic writing; in fact, writing for the "private world" gets the largest number of pages among the four. Also as I noted earlier, they are working from a model of writing that is universalized; that is, the intellectual activity of writing does not change its fundamental nature, whatever the particular writing situation. An opponent to my critique might argue, then, that if we are interested in teaching academic discourse so as to foster critical consciousness, we should prefer *Four Worlds of Writing* for its separation of writing activity and writing context. An opponent might ask whether *Writing in the Arts and Sciences* is really demystifying academic discourse conventions or merely inculcating them.

I hope I have made it clear that *Four Worlds of Writing* is an impressive book, one that does embody much of our valuable new understanding of the writing process. Nevertheless, throughout this essay I have attempted to show what are its limitations, and now is the time to make my own assumptions more apparent. I believe that all writing is context bound, and therefore cannot be adequately described by universalized models. I believe that all academic knowledge is context bound; therefore, the learning situation cannot be adequately described in terms of teachers' and students' personalities. Furthermore, I believe that to neglect the contexts of writing and knowledge is to risk committing a new version of the social injustice attributed to the old composition course. Once, our unexamined stylistic assumptions oppressed students coming from discourse communities at relatively greater remove from academe. Now, our unexamined assumptions about the nature of intellectual work in writing threaten to oppress the same students. If the writing process is understood in terms of a universalized model, students who do not match it risk being seen as cognitively deficient. If the academic situation is understood as a power struggle between personalities, students who either fail or use illegitimate means in the struggle risk being seen as psychologically or socially defective. Ultimately, it seems to me, *Four Worlds of Writing* will be most useful for students who already "know the rules."

Throughout this essay, I have also attempted to show how *Writing in the Arts and Sciences* is more sophisticated about the relationship between discourse, community, and knowledge. It is also true, however, that Maimon et al. certainly do not question that academic intellectual work is worthwhile. They are very aware that the process of joining the academic discourse community is as much social as cognitive, that it is best understood as an initiation, but they do not doubt that this initiation ought to take place. All questions about students' rights to their "authentic voices" or their "own language," as the 1974 College Composition and Communication Conference's declaration has it (Butler et al. 1974), are subsumed, in *Writing in the Arts and Sciences*, in questions about student's intellectual engagement in the academic disciplines. The individual mind and the community's conventions are seen, not in an oppositional, but in a dialectical, relationship.

Thus, our examination of new college textbooks takes us beyond the question of what is happening in composition studies. Because of the centrality of writing to the academic enterprise, we find ourselves examining the worth of academic intellectual work itself when we question the conventions of academic discourse. No one will approve of *Writing in the Arts and Sciences* who thinks that academic work is at bottom worthless. I do not. I believe that the abstracting, formalizing power of academic work enables us to understand our experience in ways not made available by common sense or folk wisdom. We ought not to pretend to give people access to this power by admitting them to college, and then prevent them from really attaining it by not admitting them into the academic discourse community.

It is true that academic knowledge, with its institutionalized power, exerts hegemony over other ways of knowing. We need to reexamine the knowledge the academy disestablishes as well as that which it endorses. But in order to approach this hegemony critically, we must understand how it works, and for that understanding we need to be initiated into the academic discourse community, though we may intend eventually to critique the forms of knowledge which that community offers us.

My position here is profoundly influenced by an analogy with the work of Paulo Freire. It would be presumptuous to say that American teachers and students find themselves in exactly the same situation as Freire's Brazilian associates. Nevertheless, highly relevant to us is Freire's argument linking the acquisition of formal education, if attained with the help of a politically sensitive teacher, to the ability to see one's world as the object of reflection and change. It is this need for "critical distance on experience," or "critical consciousness," that I sensed in the students Lunsford analyzed, and that I do not think is being adequately served by any of the dominant theoretical trends in composition studies today. *Four Worlds of Writing* is cynical about the possibility of attaining critical consciousness in college; *Writing in the Arts and Sciences* is, in contrast, an instrument whereby such critical consciousness might be attained. At least Maimon et al. begin to approach that reflection on the process of knowing—not only the process of writing—for which Freire has called:

> Knowing, whatever its level, is not the act by which a subject transformed into an object docilely and passively accepts the contents others give or impose on him or her. Knowledge, on the contrary, necessitates the curious presence of subjects confronted with the world. It requires their transforming action on reality. It demands a constant searching. It implies invention and reinvention. It claims from each person a critical reflection on the very act of knowing. It must be a reflection which recognizes the knowing process, and in this recognition becomes aware of the *"raison d'être"* behind the knowing and the conditioning to which that process is subject. (1973, 100–01)

If academic discourse constitutes knowledge in the academic community, then that is what we must examine if we are to be reflective in Freire's sense. I have argued that to reflect on the connections between discourse, community, and knowledge should be composition studies' special province (chapter 2, this volume).

The question, when knowledge is power, is: who is to know? Demystifying the conditions of knowing—the conventions of academic discourse—will certainly be a difficult task, and current trends leave uncertain the part college composition studies will play in this task. Process theory has not announced any interest in this task; discourse theory is not bringing to it the necessary political insight. Yet our understanding of the college writing situation has improved tremendously over the past decade. Not to try to push it further will mean that power will remain with those who have relatively easy access to it now. No matter how technically sophisticated, then, writing teachers will find the institutional definition of "service" narrowing in on them again. We will not be able to feel that we are educating for critical consciousness. The initiation that we guide will be empty indeed.

REFERENCES

Bernstein, Basil. *Class, Codes, and Control.* 2d ed. rev. New York: Schocken Books, 1975.

Bizzell, Patricia. "Thomas Kuhn, Scientism, and English Studies." This volume.

Bourdieu, Pierre, and Jean-Claude Passeron. *Reproduction in Education, Society, and Culture.* Beverly Hills: Sage, 1977.

Elbow, Peter. *Writing Without Teachers.* New York: Oxford University Press, 1973.

Emig, Janet. "Writing as a Mode of Learning." *College Composition and Communication* 28 (1977): 122–28.

Foucault, Michel. *The Order of Things.* New York: Random House, 1970.

Freire, Paulo. *Pedagogy of the Oppressed.* New York: Seabury Press, 1970.

———. *Education for Critical Consciousness.* New York: Seabury Press, 1973.

Kinneavy, James *A Theory of Discourse.* Englewood Cliffs, N.J.: Prentice-Hall, 1971.

Kuhn, Thomas. *The Structure of Scientific Revolutions.* 2d ed. rev. Chicago: University of Chicago Press, 1970.

Lauer, Janice M., Gene Montague, Andrea Lunsford, and Janet Emig. *Four Worlds of Writing.* New York: Harper and Row, 1981.

Lloyd-Jones, Richard, et al. "Students' Right to Their Own Language." *College Composition and Communication* 25 (special issue, Fall 1974), 33 pp.

Lunsford, Andrea. "The Content of Basic Writers' Essays." *College Composition and Communication* 31 (1980): 278–90.

Macrorie, Ken. "To Be Read." *English Journal* 57 (1968): 686–92.

Maimon, Elaine, Gerald L. Belcher, Gail W. Hearn, Barbara F. Nodine, and Finbarr W. O'Connor. *Writing in the Arts and Sciences*. Cambridge, Mass.: Winthrop, 1981.

O'Hare, Frank. *Sentence-Combining: Improving Student Writing Without Formal Grammar Instruction*. Urbana, Ill.: National Council of Teachers of English, 1971.

Shaughnessy, Mina P. *Errors and Expectations*. New York: Oxford University Press, 1977.

———. "Some Needed Research on Writing." *College Composition and Communication* 28 (1977): 317–21.

Vopat, James. "*Uptaught* Rethought: Coming Back from the Knock-out." *College English* 40 (1978): 41–45.

Wiener, Harvey. "Administering Comprehensive Writing Programs within Liberal Education." *Forum* 3 (1981): 1–2.

Young, Richard, Alton Becker, and Kenneth Pike. *Rhetoric: Discovery and Change*. New York: Harcourt, Brace and World, 1970.

Academic Discourse and Critical Consciousness: An Application of Paulo Freire

Whether academic discourse can be taught in a liberating way is now an important question for composition teachers, because most college writing programs now have the same official goal: to equip students for performing the writing tasks their college education demands, and the writing tasks they will encounter after college. At most schools, achieving this goal entails instruction in "Standard" English and in academic discourse, which uses "Standard" English. Individual teachers' methods and goals may vary with the particular character of their students, but in general, commitment to the official goal presumes the resolution of an issue that concerned writing teachers not so long ago—namely, the tension between the individual student, with his or her own cultural identity and creative potential, and the conventional requirements of standardized writing instruction. The 1974 declaration by the Conference on College Composition and Communication concerning "Students' Right to Their Own Language" now seems to be a dead letter and, not too surprisingly, the CCCC Executive Board is considering revising it.[1]

The pedagogical innovations of the 1970s have, of course, affected the way composition teachers talk about what they do. In almost every discussion of classroom practice, we ritually reject the sort of focus on "product" that might, for example, examine student papers for their mastery of academic discourse conventions. We call "Standard" English "School" English or "edited" English, so as to display our awareness that this language may not be the student's home language or indeed, that it may not be anyone's native tongue. We have been inclined, I think, too easily to regard the enormous growth of college writing programs in the past decade as a triumph for the "learner-" and "process"-centered pedagogy that is now orthodox. The programs' growth has been deceptive, however. Despite what individual teachers tell themselves about what they're doing, college writing programs have owed their growth to their willingness to serve a rather traditional goal of instruction in "Standard" English and academic discourse. Writing instruction has been institutionalized, through the formation of programs with their own administrators, staff, entrance and exit tests, and battery of required courses, precisely to ensure that this goal is met, since it can no longer be taken for granted as an outcome of college education.

Increasingly, what we find in modern composition theory are attempts to justify these goals to which we find ourselves committed. It is as if we can overrule the students' right to their own language only if we can somehow prove that "our" language—the language of academic discourse—deserves its ascendancy. This desire for justification is one motive, I believe, for current interest in psycholinguistics as a source of theoretical models and research methods for composition studies. In *The Philosophy of Composition*, E. D. Hirsch, Jr., uses psycholinguistics, information theory, and related fields to support his contention that Standard English deserves to be taught because it is cognitively superior to other languages. Hirsch believes that the argument from psycholinguistics raises his definitions of language and pedagogy "above mere ideology."[2] Hirsch resolves the tension between the student's individuality and conventional requirements by arguing that individual potential can only be thoroughly developed through cultivation in the most cognitively rich and efficient means of communication.

A similar kind of argument has been advanced to justify the teaching of academic discourse. In *A Conceptual Theory of Rhetoric*, Frank D'Angelo attempts to establish a structural match or "isomorphism" between modes of discourse and human thought processes.[3] If such an isomorphism exists, then to teach conventional patterns of discourse would be to teaching "thinking"; or to put it another way, the psycho-chemical processes of the brain would be triggered by matching discourse structures, and the student would produce persuasive argument. Such a conclusion lies behind D'Angelo's discussion in the "Implications for Teaching" section of his book. He characterizes the "emphasis on creative expression and on personal writing," the radically innovative pedagogy of the early 1970s, as "the new romanticism" (159). Although the label is faintly derogatory, D'Angelo doesn't attack this widely influential pedagogy. He does suggest that a concern for creativity is better served by his own method. D'Angelo has elaborated his pedagogy in an analysis of discourse patterns he calls "paradigms," such as the "Classification Paradigm" and the "Cause-and-Effect Paradigm," and he argues, "Acquiring, understanding, and using paradigms can help [students] to ascend to higher levels of linguistic and conceptual development."[4]

These "cognitive" defenses of Standard English and academic discourse are inadequate, however, in that they ignore the function of historical context in establishing the privileged language and discourse.[5] They also attempt to detach a student's "creative potential" from his or her particular historical circumstances. Thus, modern composition theories lose the sense of living in a world in which questions of political power are unavoidable. While I hope to recover some of the social aspects of composition in the discussion that follows, I also want to argue that so-called "Standard" English and academic discourse should be taught. But their teaching must be justified in a way that does not obscure the political questions. I will argue that such a justification can be found, at least in part, in the rhetorical practice of academic discourse. In academic discourse, the undeniable tension between the individual and discourse conventions is treated as a source of fruitful dialogue. Writing becomes the means to incorporating individual desires and judgments, but also to moving beyond them into involvement in the life of a community. It may be possible, then, to teach academic discourse in a way that does not conflict with the aim of encouraging critical consciousness, in Paulo Freire's sense.

Freire has linked the acquisition of formal education, if attained with the help of a politically sensitive teacher, to the ability to see one's world as the object of reflection and change. In discussing the efficacy of problem-posing pedagogy for agronomists working in the Brazilian countryside, Freire observes:

> Human beings are active beings, capable of reflection on themselves and on the activity in which they are engaged. They are able to detach themselves from the world in order to find their place in it and with it. Only people are capable of this act of "separation" in order to find their place in the world and enter in a critical way into their own reality. "To enter into" reality means to look at it objectively, and apprehend it as one's field of action and reflection. It means to penetrate it more and more lucidly in order to discover the true interrelations between the facts observed.

> However, the more we observe the behavior patterns and the thought-habits of peasants, the more we can conclude that in certain areas (to a greater or lesser degree) they come so close to the natural world that they feel more *part* of the world than transformers of the world. . . . This nearness which identifies them with the natural world makes the act of "entering into" it difficult for them, inasmuch as the nearness does not allow them to see in perspective that which they "enter into."[6]

In Freire's opinion, education can foster "the act of 'entering into'" one's world.

Many students now come to college in need of this kind of fostering education. Andrea Lunsford has added to our knowledge of where freshmen are, intellectually, with a comparative study of essays by "basic writers" (those judged to be in need of remedial work in composition) and skilled writers. She concludes: "The basic writers I have been quoting, then, seem to represent the egocentric stage of cognitive development and the conventional stage of moral development, to conceptualize and generalize with great difficulty, and, most of all, to lack confidence."[7] According to Lunsford, the basic writers display "the egocentric stage of cognitive development" by their frequent use of the personal pronoun and of evidence drawn from personal experience. Their "conventional stage of moral development" is apparent in their reliance, when asked to make a judgment, on maxims received uncritically from authority. Their inability "to conceptualize and generalize" seems to be a function of their personal focus, in that they rarely try to reason out connections between their own experiences and the lives of others. Lunsford sees that they "lack confidence" when they describe themselves primarily as victims of social forces and divulge many personal fears and anxieties. Although Lunsford asserts that "the basic writers' prose is more vital, more engaging, and more true to their own experience than the impersonal, strangely disengaged prose often produced by our more skilled students," she believes that "the real challenge for us as teachers of basic writing lies in helping our students become more proficient at abstracting and conceptualizing and hence at producing acceptable academic discourse, without losing the directness many of them now possess" (287).

It seems to me that Lunsford's observations can be profitably reinterpreted in light of Freire's analysis. Lunsford's reliance on psychology to explain the basic writers' essays obscures their social dimensions. Basic writers are very much like Freire's peasants. The basic writers cling to a personal perspective because "they feel more *part* of [their] world than transformers of the world." They rely on maxims because they have been subjected to what Freire calls "banking education" in which knowledge has been deposited by authorities in their passive minds.[8] Even so, when seeing themselves as "more or less helpless victims" of advertising, for example, these students may not be revealing their need for psychological counseling, as Lunsford seems to suggest, but rather their emerging consciousness of the attempts made to control them by dominant social groups (Lunsford, 279–80). When Lunsford notes that most basic writers favored capital punishment while most skilled writers opposed it, I find myself wondering whether more of the basic writers come from neighborhoods where violence is a daily possibility (281–82).

It is unlikely that the "directness," or vivid sense of a surrounding world, that Lunsford values in the basic writers' essays can be preserved if their teachers see "abstracting and conceptualizing" as "skills" (implied by the designation of the other group as "skilled" writers) to produce "acceptable academic discourse." Instead of making the necessary movement toward critical consciousness of their world, students are likely to try to leave their precollege experience behind in order to rise to supposedly higher levels of cognitive development and mental health. In attempting to accommodate their writing to academic discourse, students become al-most like learners of a foreign language, which they approximate in their own idiosyncratically logical forms. This is the great insight upon which Mina Shaughnessy's *Errors and Expectations* is based; her pedagogical goal is to give students some control over the process to which they are submitting themselves by making them aware of it.[9] For the unaware, however, as David Bartholomae has shown, slavish imitation of academic discourse is a potent source of confusion in writing, and academic discourse itself comes to seem an obstacle to critical consciousness.[10]

College textbooks begin the process of obfuscation. A textbook, of course, has as its avowed purpose explaining a scholarly discipline to a novice; but typically, textbooks inculcate the discipline as much by immersing the novice in its discourse as by explaining its premises. The opening chapters of most textbooks are characterized by the stating of maxims and the defining of terms; but often, after disciplinary assumptions and vocabulary have been explained once, the textbook discourse proceeds as if its audience is now familiar with them. In the following example from a text on poetry, note that the terms "stanza" and "understatement" are printed in bold type once, when their meaning is established, and are then immediately used as if further elaboration is unnecessary. Note also that the preferred reading procedure is not so much explained as demonstrated to the student, who is implicitly invited to participate in the first person plural pronoun performing the analysis.

> The first **stanza** tells of the rural remoteness in which the *maid* (what are this word's connotations?) *dwelt:* we might notice the past tense, which at first reading merely suggests to us that she used to live there but does not specify the cause of her removal. The second stanza—to which we shall return—offers us a couple of comparisons that suggest certain qualities of the maid. The first line of the third stanza repeats the sense of the first line of the first; but the second word, *lived,* subtly brings out a meaning in the *dwelt,* which it has replaced, and draws our attention, with a sense of shock, to the full significance of the word *dwelt* and its past tense. The power of *dwelt,* when its full significance is revealed, is due to **understatement**; it anticipates and is related to the understatement in the final line, which declares as a climax the meaning of Lucy's death to the speaker.[11]

This passage assumes not only that the student remembers how "connotation" and "speaker" have been defined earlier in the text, but that he or she also already knows the discipline-specific meanings of "climax" and "past tense," which are not defined. There is a kind of presumed inclusion in the discourse community that the textbook is supposed to introduce, a presumption that there extends to suggesting the appropriate emotional reaction to the poem ("a sense of shock" at the maid's being dead).

The sort of introduction to a discipline offered by most textbooks encourages students to believe that what is expected of them in their own writing is a demonstration of familiarity with disciplinary discourse. Students are likely to imitate the disciplinary discourse before they have completely mastered it. For example, Lunsford quotes from one of her basic writers, " 'I would enforce this capital punishment to any extent, here come my explanations' " (282). Lunsford seems to feel that this student's announcement about the explanations reveals arrest at a stage of moral development in which justifications are reified as maxims. It seems to me, in contrast, that the announcement reveals an as yet imperfectly controlled but nevertheless correct sense that a value judgment, such as support of capital punishment, must be supported by reasons or "explanations" in academic discourse. "Here come my explanations" is a bit of the conventional scaffolding the student has used to construct the essay, but the student is still too unpracticed to realize that the scaffolding should be cleared away from the finished product.

Students who have become somewhat more familiar with discourse conventions, however, may overuse them in an attempt to display their fluency. For example, instead of beginning her essay with the statement, "This poem is a sonnet," the student might say, "In this sonnet, the octave builds up a dramatic situation in which the speaker imagines that his lover is unfaithful." To begin "This poem is a sonnet," is to acknowledge one's inferior status as a novice and to imply that the essay's purpose is simply to demonstrate familiarity with basic critical tools. To begin, "In this sonnet . . ." is to imply that, of course, reader and writer know what a sonnet is. Putting herself in a less humble position, this writer can go on to discuss more sophisticated aspects of the poem and to present what looks more like mature work in the discipline. The second formulation, then, shows more sophistication about the rhetoical situation involved in writing school papers. That is, school papers are designed to communicate knowledge about how the student is progressing in the discipline, not about the discipline itself. Teachers may writhe when students ask about a writing assignment, "What do you want?" because the question seems to suggest that all that goes on in the classroom is the students' attempt to placate the teacher's arbitrary demands. The question, however, may be sincerely asked by students who are eager to enter into the discourse community to which the teacher belongs.

Nevertheless, the essay beginning, "In this sonnet . . ." may develop in the direction of jargon. Composition specialists generally define "jargon" as writing that overuses disciplinary vocabulary, abstract words, Latinate words, and elaborate sentence structure, to name some of the characteristics. We expect accomplished writers, on the other hand, to produce these characteristics in moderation: the question then is, how do we decide when they are used too much? I think we react negatively when the paper begins to read like a parody of accomplished academic discourse (asking students to parody academic discourse is a good way to alert them to the dangers of jargon). The jargon-filled essay, it seems to me, usually evokes a certain amount of anger, resentment, or embarrassment in its faculty reader, as opposed simply to a calm judgment of inadequacy. Jargon produces these reactions because it makes the disciplines to which we have committed ourselves look foolish. I would define jargon, then, as writing which seems over-elaborately academic in view of the argument's apparent significance to the writer and to the discipline.

Too often, it seems that students proceed from fluency in jargon in college to more dangerously manipulative discourse in the world beyond college. Academic discourse outside the academy can issue in self-serving corporate policy statements, picayune legal documents, and responsibility-shifting government reports, to name a few examples. An argument's significance to the writer and to the community addressed, which I have advanced above as a test of jargon, cannot be assessed in a rhetorical situation in which motives are predetermined by indoctrination. Academic discourse can only attain this justifying significance, and escape being judged all as jargon, if learning academic discourse can give access to real knowledge, as Paulo Freire has described it in *Education for Critical Consciousness.*

Knowing, whatever its level, is not the act by which a

subject transformed into an object docilely and passively accepts the contents others give or impose on him or her. Knowledge, on the contrary, necessitates the curious presence of subjects confronted with the world. It requires their transforming action on reality. It demands a constant searching. It implies invention and reinvention. It claims from each person a critical reflection on the very act of knowing. It must be a reflection which recognizes the knowing process, and in this recognition becomes aware of the *"raison d'être"* behind the knowing and the conditioning to which that process is subject. (100–01)

It is toward this kind of knowing that Freire wants to move people who are beginning to make the separation between self and world. Of the academic community that would achieve this kind of knowing, Freire says, "Thus, in a situation of knowing, teacher and student must take on the role of conscious subjects, mediated by the knowable object that they seek to know" (101).

Academic discourse must be taught and learned so as to foster this kind of knowledge and this kind of community if its teaching and learning are to foster critical consciousness. But the tendency of college writers toward jargon indicates how infrequently academic discourse is now so taught and learned. Often, to go through college is to be indoctrinated, or as Freire would have it, passively filled with the contents of disciplines. This oppressive kind of knowing is fostered by the attitude that disciplinary content matches or mirrors reality, or, to put it another way, that disciplinary content is empirically true. If that were the case, there would be no need for "searching," "invention and reinvention," and "reflection . . . [on] the *'raison d'être'* behind the knowing and the conditioning to which that process is subject." I believe, however, that a closer examination of academic discourse will reveal that its conventions allow for the activities of self-consciousness that Freire recommends. This flexibility tends to be forgotten when disciplinary practice is not in question and when the academic community is relatively homogeneous.

In times of stability, the academic community comes to resemble Freire's peasant community. We find it hard to achieve separation between, on the one hand, our conceptualizations of the world and our experience in it, and, on the other hand, that reality itself. Changing times have started to awaken the academic community, however; we have fewer and fewer students, for example, who know for sure what past tense is. It is no coincidence that composition studies is now undergoing a profound reexamination of its premises. In order to recover the conceptual flexibility of academic discourse, we have also to reexamine its assumptions concerning how knowledge is obtained and how it is used.

The crucial point here is that knowledge is constituted in academic discourse, not merely communicated by it. Recent trends in the philosophy of science have been especially helpful in revealing the opacity of discourse in the disciplines and the dependence of truth-value on persuasion. Convention-governed rhetorical practice is now seen as the methodology by which competing theories are tested, according to Thomas Kuhn and Paul Feyerabend. Feyerabend, however, evinces a certain nostalgia for positivism in his argument connecting the rhetorical methodology to a loss of confidence in theories as bases for disciplinary activity.[12] Thomas Kuhn, on the other hand, has indicated that it is precisely their generation in community debate that gives new theories legitimate authority. A "scientific revolution" that brings a new "paradigm" to power does not install a dictatorship precisely to the extent that argumentation and persuasion have been constrained by conventional practice and have involved the whole community.[13]

To teach academic discourse as a conventional practice for arriving at a consensus, then, is to make community agreements on what counts as knowledge more open to the kind of examination Freire recommends. Our very examination of discourse, of course, takes place in a historical context circumscribed by tradition and current group and individual needs. Insofar as we can achieve a critical distance on our discourse, however, we achieve a critical distance on our knowledge. Thus, having separated ourselves from the world and our knowing of it, we can reapproach experience to revise our provisional agreements on practice as our circumstances change. Radical scepticism isn't called for here; at any given time, we will have agreement on how community activities should proceed, and we can work together. But if we do not see academic discourse as determined solely by external reality, we will be more free to bring critical consciousness to bear on our decisions about knowledge—what is worth pursuing and how it should be used.

In moving students toward familiarity with academic discourse, then, teachers should emphasize that its conventions are established in use, by consensus of the community this discourse unites. Academic discourse conventions derive their authority more from their status as conventions than from any inherent superiority. The more that "Standard" English is used in academic discourse, for example, the more standard it becomes. Furthermore, since the conventions are shaped by communal practice rather than immutable laws, the rigor of their enforcement varies in different situations. The newly initiated are expected to adhere to the conventions very closely, while well-established community members can treat them more casually and are even expected to flout them periodically in the interests of community health. Finally, and most important, students should be helped to understand that since academic discourse conventions cannot be regarded as absolute patterns of truth, then academic discourse cannot be regarded as simply conveying or communicating truth. Rather, academic discourse establishes a provisional truth through dialogue in the community; academic knowledge counts as knowledge to the extent that consensus can be reached on its value.

The academic community's importance to our culture lies in its ability to be a community with a relatively high tolerance for frequent debate over what the community knows. Like communities defined by a common political or religious belief, the academic community feels more comfortable when virtual unanimity exists; but unlike many other human communities, the academic community has embodied in its discourse the conventions to ensure that dialogue cannot long remain silent. Even in situations when academic discourse is most clothed in authority, as when a teacher lectures, there is still an attempt not only to instruct but to persuade—to persuade that the lecture's area of concern is worth careful attention, that the teacher's approach to it is valuable, and so on. Academic discourse is most commonly engaged in a certain kind of argument, not in confession, prophecy, or decree, as Mina Shaughnessy has recognized in suggesting "such images as the contest or the dispute as acceptable metaphors for writing."[14]

Some of the conventions that enable academic discourse to generate and test knowledge through consensus and debate are: agreement on a standard language, Standard English, as the medium of discourse; familiarity with "common knowledge," or a standard range of literary and historical allusions, terms that have transcended their disciplines, and so on; employment of specialized vocabulary specific to the kind of problem addressed (disciplinary vocabulary); employment of a method for defining the problem to be addressed, a method predetermined by disciplinary practice; employment of a predetermined method for generating and applying evidence; employment of a predetermined method for judging the plausibility of the argument advanced. Members of the academic community win their intellectual freedom by submitting to discourse conventions. The community is continually straining its own bonds of unity by encouraging debate, but its members' training in certain conventions of debate helps in turn to reestablish those bonds.

One rationale for the establishment of a standard language in academic discourse is the "educated ethos" that its use conveys. Standard English may well be a language that nobody speaks, but it is precisely the "School" quality, the "Edited" quality of this English that contributes to its users' credibility. That is, writers who use Standard English fluently show that they have been in school, have learned to take pains with their work—in short, that they have received the training necessary to the academic community's rigorous intellectual tasks. Standard English serves to unite and strengthen our academic community as Latin did for European scholars in the Renaissance. To teach this justification for learning Standard English is, at least, to reveal the social roots of usage conventions. It is assuredly more oppressive to claim that other forms of English are cognitively inferior to the standard form.

If Standard English functions to unite the academic community, then, we can understand why novices are required to produce it more strictly in accordance with usage conventions than mature practitioners are. The notive is initiated into and bonded to the community through the process of her mastery of the community's language. The mature practitioner, on the other hand, more secure in her position, can afford to relax these elementary ties. Indeed, as Joseph Williams has argued, an academic reader's perception of language errors in a piece of writing is a function of the writer's standing in the academic community. Only after sharpening one's critical eye can George Orwell, for example, be detected committing the stylistic sins he inveighs against in "Politics and the English Language." An essay written for a freshman composition class, in contrast, is, almost by definition, a text in which errors will be found.[15]

Attention to deviations from the standard language is also affected, however, by the larger society's view of education's value. When notions of how important education is and who must be educated are relatively stable, language instruction does not need to be obsessively devoted to the extirpation of error; rather, it can be assumed that acculturation in the community's language will proceed "along with" the rest of one's education. When assumptions about education are destabilized, language instruction may tend to focus more on error as the readiest means of maintaining some community coherence. What is now called the "back-to-the-basics" movement is not so much a return to abandoned standards as it is the creation of minimum criteria for community membership during an era of great strain on education. When the group of novices is larger and more culturally diverse than ever before, the pressure on each novice to conform to usage conventions is proportionally greater.

Composition teachers, therefore, now often find themselves in the position of mediators between their students and the rest of the academic community. To the mediator, it often seems that the two groups to whom he or she is responsible have opposed interests: that is, the students want, sometimes unconsciously, to retain their "own" language, and the academy wants, sometimes grudgingly, to assimilate them. It seems to me, however, that the answer the mediator must give to both groups lies in the persuasive power of the "educated ethos." The mediator must convince both groups that the "educated ethos" conveyed by standard language usage is valuable and worth attaining.

Paradoxically, the academy may be the harder of the two groups to convince, since teachers are feeling particularly embattled and denigrated these days. In effect, the composition teacher must convince them that the academy is not, in fact, so intellectually shaky that a split infinitive will topple it. At the same time, students must be convinced that they will gain from their education—or more precisely, they must be persuaded to gain from the education a critical consciousness that can serve the larger society, as well as a set of techniques that can serve their private career goals. Again, to justify learning Standard English on social grounds is less oppressive than to justify it on cognitive grounds, and more conducive to students' retaining their "own" language while learning the standard one; but to teach Standard English in this way is also to prevent what may be a more common problem nowadays, students' eager willingness, while learning Standard English, to throw their "own" language away.

Like Standard English, the "common knowledge" of the academic community can be taught, justifiably, to put students in touch with a conventional means of joining the group. Transdisciplinary allusions signify one's participation in the cultural traditions that matter to the community. To show that one knows these traditions is, then, to establish even more firmly the "educated ethos" associated with the standard language. It is also true that in a period of destablization, community members become acutely sensitive to lapses in novices' familiarity with "common knowledge." For example, one of my colleagues from the Visual Arts Department was really distressed to inform me that a student had identified the man kissing Jesus in Masaccio's "Betrayal in the Garden" as "Brutus." A colleague from the History Department indignantly refused to consider any grade above "F" for a paper in which Abraham Lincoln was mentioned as an influence on the framers on the Declaration of Independence. At the same time, however, reflecting uncertainty about the value of education, both students and teachers sometimes refer to this kind of knowledge as "cocktail party" information; in a similar vein, I recall a *National Lampoon* list of items guaranteed to raise a totally ignorant essay test answer to the "B+" level ("existential despair," "phallic symbol," etc.).[16]

The standard range of allusion cannot in good conscience be

taught as a method of bullshit, of course; but it need not be. "Common knowledge" may look trivial only because it is supposed to be taken for granted. Consider, however, what the categories of such information might be: classical mythology; Bible stories; American history; modern physics; modern psychology; and so on. Not to know this frame of reference is not to know, in a way, who one is as an American. That this holds regardless of one's particular racial or cultural background may be suggested by the urgency with which various previously excluded groups have sought to make their part in the culture "common knowledge." In teaching "common knowledge," we should not aim for strict assimilation; instead, we should make clear both to students and to other teachers that we are committed to the enrichment of the academic range of allusion by reflections of American cultural diversity. At the same time, however, we must insist on every student's right to know the common heritage. For example, on the last night of his debates with Carter, Ronald Reagan described America as a "city on a hill." Surely it would help to assess his presidential possibilities if one recognized here an allusion to a sermon preached by John Winthrop in 1630.[17]

Beyond the standard language and "common knowledge" conventions, however, is a range of discipline-specific conventions whose value is more directly dependent upon the value one is willing to give to a college education. Knowledge of the standard language and "common knowledge" can be acquired outside the academy and can be broadly useful outside the academy. Discipline-specific conventions are academy-specific. It is not within the scope of my essay to undertake a defense of the very existence of colleges and universities as our institutions of "higher learning," and of their subdivision into discipline-related departments. Despite the various social and financial strains on higher education in America today, I do not see its institutional structure as currently problematic.[18] I do think, however, that if one wants to participate in preparing students for disciplinary majors, while at the same time fostering education for critical consciousness, one must continually be asking, out loud, in front of students, why it's worth it to society to create people with disciplinary training.

Speaking very generally, we might say that any community shares—or indeed, exists by virtue of sharing—certain assumptions, protocols, and practices that enable it to deal collectively with its experience in the material world. Speaking more specifically, we might say that the academic community exists in order to deal with particularly complex, detailed, and extensive experience. The assumption that moves our society to support an academic community is fundamentally similar to the assumption that moves Freire to teach peasants to read: experience can be dealt with in a more constructive way, responsive to human needs, insofar as a critical distance on experience can be achieved. The critical distance is established by community protocols; the more rigorous the protocols, the more acute the distance. The academic community, then, undertakes communal thinking projects, as it were, for the larger society. For such projects, conventions that unite people, making them want to work together, and that provide a rhetorical basis on which they can work, are essential. Within the academic community, even tighter unity is achieved in disciplinary subdivisions. The object is not to get people to think alike, but rather to get them to think together about a challenge that has emerged in interaction with the world.

If we see an academic discipline as a group of people working together on a difficult and ongoing project, we can understand how disciplines are constituted by their discourse conventions. Within the group, there must be agreement on what to look at, how to describe it, how to measure it, what to do with it. And, of course, there must be the possibility for debate to change any of these agreements as the group's experience changes. In other words, the formation of knowledge is a social activity. Teachers should take care not to blur this community mission with overemphasis on our popular myths of individual achievement and inborn genius.

Furthermore, even more important from the student's viewpoint, the formation of knowledge is already a social activity—that is, current agreements exist on what to look at, how to describe it, and so on, and people are already working on the basis of these agreements. Therefore, learning an academic discipline is like boarding a moving train. This is why textbooks have the character of assuming participation that I analyzed earlier. We often talk about disciplinary preparation as if it were a matter of a static relationship between individual student and "body" of knowledge: step by step, through "requirements" and "prerequisites," a discrete understanding of the discipline is assembled. This way of talking often leaves students searching for the missing pieces, for the keystone that will suddenly stabilize their understanding. Composition teachers can help students around this barrier to real understanding by emphasizing the rhetorical character of disciplines.

The ability to use disciplinary vocabulary is often the first test of initiation into an academic discipline, as I noted earlier when discussing jargon. Indeed, I have seen papers that a colleague in the Biology Department evaluated simply by circling every instance of disciplinary vocabulary use; the more circles, the better. It is clear, however, from students' persistent struggles with appropriate use of disciplinary vocabulary that the taxonomic or definition-oriented approach of most textbooks is inadequate. A student's misuse of a term can't always be remedied by telling her to "consult the glossary." I think this difficulty arises from the nature of disciplinary vocabulary as a functional vocabulary: it really cannot be understood unless the communal thinking projects it facilitates are also appreciated. Without such appreciation, the risk of degenerating into jargon is increased, according to my definition of jargon writing as that which pursues an argument not important enough to the writer and to the discipline to justify using the disciplinary vocabulary and other discourse conventions.

What I am requiring, in effect, for the understanding of disciplinary vocabulary is an appreciation of the discipline's typical way of approaching experience—its paradigm, to recall Kuhn's term. But I say "appreciation" because I think, since the formation of knowledge is a social activity, that affective as well as intellectual assent is required. In other words, to participate in a discipline's typical way of defining a problem, one must not only be able to see how something could be defined as a problem in such a way, but one must also be willing so to define it, one must see such an address to experience as important.

Composition teachers can sensitize students to the need for understanding disciplinary definition-of-problem through one of our familiar topics, "forming a thesis." Thesis formation is sometimes taught as if the shape of the thesis simply matched the shape of the subject mater, as if the thesis were isomorphic with reality. For example, to write a paper about an embarrassing situation, one might scan one's memory for painful incidents in hopes that an organizing principle would emerge. But I think that students who follow this procedure often say they have nothing to write about. Perhaps, however, the teacher suggests considering the audience when trying to form a thesis. One then might keep one's classmates in mind and find the choice of a situation to write about helpfully constrained by wanting to shock, impress, or charm them. Students have trouble, however, transferring this procedure to courses in which the actual audience will be only the professor reading the paper somewhere else and in which the subject matter resists being shaped like an anecdote. Attention to audience, then, is not a helpful guide to thesis formation unless some attention is given to the audience's conventional expectations. For example, one might write a very good essay on an embarrassing situation if one organized it with the composition course's goal in mind—clear expression, honest voice, concrete details, or whatever. One deduces these goals from the terms of praise and blame the teacher uses, from the reading that is assigned, the essay tasks set, and so on.

In other words, thesis formation should be taught as a function of the disciplinary way of seeing things, whatever the discipline is. This emphasis may help students who are just learning a discipline to concentrate their attention profitably upon their teacher's example as a practitioner of the discipline. I often hear from a beginning literature student, "I've read the story three times and I still don't see anything in it!" These students need to review their class notes and to recall with me where class discussions have led, not to read the story again. For what it is they have to "see," to find in order to write their papers, is not exactly "in" the story, but rather in the disciplinary approach to it that I have been demonstrating. Pedagogy has an affective as well as an intellectual function here. That is, the teacher certainly must be willing to explain the disciplinary approach so that the student grasps it conceptually; but she must also be willing to demonstrate the approach so that the student is drawn to it affectively. It would be impractical to require that the student like his teacher; but I think we undervalue today the importance of his respecting her.

The interrelatedness of discourse conventions is also shown in the way thesis formation is demonstrated: typically, by using a disciplinary thesis to aid in the generation of evidence. What counts as evidence is a matter of disciplinary convention, and so is what counts as enough evidence; I think we err if we suggest that evidence can somehow exist independent of human intellectual activity. It's misleading to speak of "collecting" evidence like shells at the seashore. In many undergraudate writing experiences, both thesis and evidence are, in effect, predicted by the assignment; what we call an "original" thesis and "new" evidence are rarely expected of undergraduates. The point, rather, is to train them to see the world in a particular way.

Evidence is important in academic discourse because "evidence" is what academic discourse makes of experience. In other rhetorical situations, one can convince with personal testimony; in academic discourse, personal experience is controlled by conventions governing evidence, both in order to deal with more, and more complex experience, and also to increase the possibility of persuading others to whom one's personal experience is remote. These conventions govern experiment design, measurement, methodologies for interpreting and reporting results, and so on. I do not mean to argue, for example, that there is nothing "out there" to suggest that smoking cigarettes causes lung cancer; I do mean to argue that the conclusion, "smoking cigarettes causes lung cancer," is the product of disciplinary interaction with what's "out there." The conventions governing evidence do not prevent—indeed, they exist to encourage—the possibility of a new conclusion to become authoritative later on, as our experience changes. The surgeon general did not cite Queen Elizabeth I's warning against tobacco.

Composition teachers, then, should not address questions of evidence without discussing not only the personal vagaries of different audiences but also their conventional expectations. We might pose the problem not in terms of "finding" evidence, but rather in terms of figuring out what can be *used* as evidence. Teaching an acontextual notion of evidence often produces the mechanical essay format of introductory question, list of examples, concluding answer. But this kind of essay will not be read as logically connected according to disciplinary conventions of plausibility—or, as the Yiddish proverb has it, "For example is no proof."

Disciplinary conventions of plausibility are connected to other discourse conventions. Appropriate thesis formation, use of disciplinary vocabulary, and presentation of evidence all affect the judgment of an argument as logical. Evaluations of logic are a function of current disciplinary assumptions and needs. Even if a transcendent, universal form of human logic exists, it will not be found in academic discourse, because the logic of academic discourse is for use. It is conditioned by preceding argumentation, and directed toward circumstantial ends. Again, therefore, composition teachers should not try to present logic acontextually. Students' current inability to develop ideas, in my view, springs more from a lack of appreciation for the social uses of logical argument than from a lack of mental capacity.[19] Discriminations between arguments on the basis of logic, or, as I prefer to call it, plausibility, can still be made: but they must be based more on rhetorical purpose than on formal structure. Thomas Kuhn, among others, has shown us that this is how disciplinary discriminations are made.

Let me restate the picture I am drawing of intellectual activity in an academic discipline. By entering a discipline, one commits oneself to looking at experience in the particular way established by that discipline. One then names one's experience (disciplinary vocabulary), and defines areas of study (disciplinary thesis formation), in accord with the disciplinary view. Through this intellectual commitment, complex and chaotic experience is rendered controllable, at least to some degree (disciplinary evidence), and the community's thinking projects, undertaken ultimately for the good of the larger society, are advanced. As a mature practitioner in the discipline, one also has the responsibility of continually checking the community's activities against experience and, when one deems it necessary, arguing for a change. All of this disciplinary life is constituted in the discipline's discourse.

Room here for critical consciousness is created, first, in our awareness that disciplinary life is rhetorical. While gaining a liberating distance on experience, we are continually brought back to human needs by the necessity of interacting with our colleagues. Hence, we come to see that truth is a matter of persuasion, which is also to say that it has a political dimension. This definition of truth as subject to change is incorporated in the very nature of the academic community, to the extent that this community does live in discourse: textbooks, lectures, tutorials, research notes, scholarly journals and books, debates at professional conventions, and explanatory articles for the general public. In other words, the community is so organized as to be continually providing opportunities for dialogue, not only within itself but also with the larger society. Our frequent complaints about academic isolation should be seen, I think, as a sign of the community's concern for dialogue, a concern that is not so vocally evinced by other tight-knit, powerful communities in our society.

Furthermore, the individual member of the academic community has a degree of personal responsibility for the community's health and life that is relatively large. We bemoan our stratified professional hierarchies; nevertheless, no teacher can satisfy anyone with the claim that he was "just following orders." Joining any community requires some submission to community conventions; on the other hand, no one is autonomous, and the academic community, in effect, requires more freedom of its members than many other communities permit. There is no reason why one's responsibility to check the plausibility of disciplinary practice cannot be informed by one's critical consciousness, though of course, this is not to say that one's persuasive efforts will always be successful. Indeed, it seems to me to be unavoidable that everyone's use of his or her academic training will be informed by his or her whole pattern of personal belief and commitment.

I admit, however, that intellectual training does not automatically produce critical consciousness. I have tried, first, simply to establish that the two are not inimical. The rhetorical basis of the academic community makes it relatively open to dialogue and relatively reliant upon members' individual responsibility. Furthermore, in this situation, what one learns enables one to understand and pursue political issues in a specially rigorous way, even though the academic community sometimes claims to be apolitical and restricts diversity in the politicization of its goals. Insofar as there is tension between conventions and the individual, this is inevitable in any community, and in the academic community, the helps for enduring it and the rewards for enduring it are relatively greater.

Finally, however, I want to argue not just that mastery of academic discourse will not make critical consciousness impossible, but rather that it will foster it. Mastery of academic discourse lets students participate in the community primarily responsible in our society for generating knowledge. Whether they work inside or outside the academic community as adults, this training will enable them to reflect on experience and work for change with some power. Therefore, politically committed instruction in academic discourse can do more for the cause of social justice than simply keeping hands off the students' "own" language. Teachers can make a difference in the effects of current trends in composition instruction.

NOTES

1. Richard Lloyd-Jones et al., "Students' Right to Their Own Language," *College Composition and Communication* 25 (special issue, Fall 1974; includes text of the resolution with rationale and bibliography), 33 pp.

2. E. D. Hirsch, Jr., *The Philosophy of Composition* (Chicago, Ill.: University of Chicago Press, 1977), 4; it is interesting to note that on this same page, Hirsch indirectly attacks opposition he seems to expect from the left by suggesting that his argument shares with Marxism a notion of historical inevitability, while, he claims, avoiding Marxism's errors by resting on more valid facts.

3. Frank D'Angelo, *A Conceptual Theory of Rhetoric* (Cambridge, Mass.: Winthrop Publishers, 1975), 16; further references in text.

4. Frank D'Angelo, "Paradigms as Structural Counterparts of 'Topoi,' " in *Linguistics, Stylistics, and the Teaching of Composition,* ed. Donald McQuade, Studies in Contemporary Language 2 (Akron, Ohio: Department of English, University of Akron, 1979), 50.

5. For an elaboration of this critique, see "Thomas Kuhn, Scientism, and English Studies" and " 'Inherent' Ideology, 'Universal' History, 'Empirical' Evidence, and 'Context-Free' Writing: Some Problems in E. D. Hirsch's *The Philosophy of Composition*" in this volume.

6. Paulo Freire, "Extension or Communication," trans. Louise Bigwood and Margaret Marshall, in *Education for Critical Consciousness* (1969; rpt. New York: Seabury Press, 1973), 105; further references in text.

7. Andrea Lunsford, "The Content of Basic Writers' Essays," *College Composition and Communication* 31, (October 1980), 284; further references in text.

8. Paulo Freire, *Pedagogy of the Oppressed,* trans. Myra Ramos (1968; rpt. New York: Seabury Press, 1970).

9. Mina Shaughnessy, *Errors and Expectations* (New York: Oxford University Press, 1977); see also David Bartholomae's review of this book in *Linguistics, Stylistics, and the Teaching of English* (cited above).

10. David Bartholomae, "Inventing the University," paper presented at the Conference on College Composition and Communication, March 1980, Washington, D.C.; and "The Study of Error," *College Composition and Communication* 31, (October 1980), 253–269.

11. Stanley B. Greenfield and A. Kingsley Weatherhead, "Introductory Essay: The Experience of a Poem," in *The Poem: An Anthology,* eds. Greenfield and Weatherhead (New York: Appleton-Century-Crofts, 1968), xxxi; the poem under discussion is Wordsworth's "She Dwelt Among Untrodden Ways."

12. Paul Feyerabend, *Against Method* (London: Verso, 1978).

13. Thomas Kuhn, *The Structure of Scientific Revolutions,* 2d ed. enlarged (Chicago: University of Chicago Press, 1970). My thinking about disciplinary conventions has been strongly influenced by Kuhn's concept of the "paradigm," or set of assumptions and methods shared by practitioners in a discipline. I have tried to avoid frequent use of the term "paradigm" here, however, both because of the vagueness Kuhn and his critics now detect in it and because of the looseness with which the term has been used in English studies. For a critique from the perspective of philosophy of science, see Margaret Masterman, "The Nature of a Paradigm," in *Criticism and the Growth of Knowledge,* eds. Imré Lakatos and Alan Musgrave (Proceedings of the International Colloquiäm in the Philosophy of Science, 1965; London: Cambridge University Press, 1970), 59–89. For a critique from the perspective of English studies, see my "Thomas Kuhn, Scientism, and English Studies."

14. Mina Shaughnessy, "Some Needed Research on Writing," *College Composition and Communication* 28, (December 1977), 320.

15. Joseph M. Williams, "The Phenomenology of Error," *College Composition and Communication* 32, (May 1981), 152–168.

16. For an interesting discussion of the extent to which liberal learning is constituted by "common knowledge," see William G. Perry, "Examsmanship and the Liberal Arts," in *Examining At Harvard College,* ed. L. Bramson (Cambridge, Mass.: Faculty of the Arts and Sciences, Harvard University, 1963), 125–135.

17. The sermon is "A Model of Christian Charity," preached by Winthrop on board the Arbella as he came over to assume the governorship of the Massachusetts Bay colony. One is led to wonder in what ways Reagan's ship of state is modelled on the Arbella.

18. For a history of American higher education's institutional structure, see *The Organization of Knowledge in Modern America, 1860–1920,* eds. Alexandra Oleson and John Voss (Baltimore, Md.: The Johns Hopkins University Press, 1979).

19. On composition teachers' perceptions of student writing problems, see

Richard M. Bossone and Richard L. Larson, *Needed Research in the Teaching of Writing* (New York: Center for Advanced Study of Education, The Graduate School and University Center of the City University of New York, 1980); respondents to this national survey of elementary, secondary, college, and university writing teachers most frequently cited as a "major problem" in student writing the "inability to develop ideas" (85.8 percent), and the next-most-frequently cited "major problem" was "inability to organize" (68.9 percent) (12).

William Perry and Liberal Education

The work of psychologist William G. Perry, Jr. has attracted much attention recently from college writing teachers who seek a developmental model to inform composition courses and writing-across-the-curriculum programs. To assess Perry's usefulness to writing instruction, I would like first to summarize his work, giving his own interpretation of its significance, and then to say how I think we should, and should not, use it.

After taking a BA in psychology at Harvard College, Perry began his academic career teaching English literature at Williams College. In 1947 he returned to Harvard to head the Bureau of Study Counsel, and there he performed the research that led to the publication of his influential book, *Forms of Intellectual and Ethical Development in the College Years: A Scheme* (New York: Holt, Rinehart, and Winston, 1968). Perry describes how college students pass from childhood to adulthood by moving through nine developmental positions. The shape of this process and the nature of the positions were defined through a series of interviews with Harvard undergraduate men in each of their four years in college.

Perry's nine-position scheme chronicles movement through three world views, "Dualism," "Relativism," and "Commitment in Relativism." The young person typically passes through them in this order, sometimes pausing or back-tracking. Each world view shapes value judgments on religion, politics, family relations, and so on. Drawing on the student interviews, Perry depicts each world view primarily in terms of the young person's attitude toward schoolwork.

The first world view, "Dualism," is characterized by the belief

Reprinted with permission from *College English* 46 (Sept. 1984): 447–54. Copyright 1984 by the National Council of Teachers of English.

that everything in the world can be ordered in one of two categories—right or wrong. These categories are defined by axiomatic statements or "Absolutes," which are possessed by "Authority," adults who have perfect knowledge of the Absolutes. The proper task of Authority is to convey the Absolutes to the ignorant. For the dualist, knowing the world means memorizing the Absolutes and applying them to individual instances. For the student Dualist, education is a process of finding right answers (correct applications of Absolutes), with the help of the teacher (Authority). The student Dualist resists exploring academic problems that have no one right solution, and prefers teachers who supply answers and disciplines in which answers can be securely quantified.

In the second world view, "Relativism," Absolutes either are unknowable or no longer exist. Without them Authority can no longer empower one to categorize the world as right or wrong. In place of these generally applicable standards, selfish interest becomes the basis for each individual's decisions. For the Relativist, knowing the world means devising an individual strategy for survival. For the student Relativist, education is a process of devising persuasive answers, since right answers no longer exist. The teacher judges persuasiveness according to idiosyncratic criteria, not Absolute standards. As the student Relativist learns how to satisfy teachers' demands, he or she enjoys exploring problematic questions and prefers disciplines in which they abound. This student also prefers teachers who do not stand on the (now unfounded) authority of their office but relate personally to the student.

In the third world view, "Commitment in Relativism," the world is still without Absolutes and Authority. Nevertheless, it is not without order, and decisions need not be based on solitary self-interest. For the Committed Relativist, knowing the world means understanding what has been rendered important by one's family, friends, religious and ethnic traditions, and intellectual interests. These priorities derived from social surroundings guide choices about the values that will order one's life, choices that Perry calls "Commitments." As one's Commitments develop, one can make confident judgments of what is better or worse relative to them, while still realizing that other people who have sufficiently examined their values may employ different but valid standards of judgment. For the student Committed Relativist, education is a process of achieving the knowledge necessary for making Commitments. Once Committed to a field of study, this student does not seek right or glib answers; rather he or she tries to start working productively in the chosen field. The teacher is neither Authority nor personal friend during this process, but rather a more experienced fellow worker, or mentor.

Perry does not clearly explain what his developmental scheme describes. Is it a process through which all normal 18- to 21-year-olds can be expected to pass, a process that is automatic, genetically determined? If so, Perry's scheme would extend the developmental scheme put forward for younger children by Jean Piaget. Piaget sees children moving through a series of stages of cognitive activity, from sensori-motor on to formal-operational; this process unfolds independent of a child's particular cultural context. Most researchers in the development of adolescents seek to complete Piaget's scheme, that is, to describe the stages children pass through after puberty; and Perry, too, nods in the direction of Piaget. He suggests that he follows Piaget in the notion that developmental processes repeat themselves on different levels—in other words, that we can expect to find some process in the adolescent analogous to the movement through cognitive stages in the young child.

Perry differentiates his study from Piaget's, however, when he says that *Forms of Intellectual and Ethical Development* focuses on "the level at which a person undertakes the development of his 'philosophical assumptions' about his world" (29). I see two distinctions from Piaget here. First, Perry describes this development as something a person "undertakes"; in other words, it is a process of which the person is conscious and which he or she can guide to some extent. In contrast, Piaget describes cognitive development as unfolding naturally, with only occasional awareness on the child's part that changes are occurring, and without much possibility of anyone, child or observing adult, altering the course of the development. The second distinction follows from this self-conscious aspect of the development Perry describes: what are developed are "philosophical assumptions," not cognitive stages. Philosophical assumptions, I take it, can be examined, revised, and consciously affirmed by their possessor, unlike cognitive stages. Perry puts the phrase in quotation marks to indicate that he does not see the typical undergraduate as a systematic thinker; nevertheless, he wants to use such language because it suggests that the scheme focuses on beliefs consciously held in the mind. The process of developing philosophical assumptions may be analogous to that of developing mature cognitive abilities, but it is not the same kind of process.

But if Perry derives from Piaget only the concept of a developmental process, then what kind of process does Perry's scheme describe? Perry's answer to this question is not clear. I think, however, that in spite of Perry's nod to Piaget, his developmental scheme describes something that does not necessarily happen to all cognitively normal 18- to 21-year-olds. Perry drops many hints that what he is describing is what happens to young people when they receive an education. Furthermore, he suggests that an education-induced developmental process should not be regarded as value-neutral, as we would presumably have to regard a process that unfolded according to some genetic necessity, such as that described by Piaget. Education initiates one into the traditions, habits, and values of a community. Perry's scheme focuses particularly on liberal arts education and the world view it inculcates. Obviously, then, it is possible to pass through the ages of 18 to 21 quite "normally" from the psychological point of view without undergoing this kind of development.

Perry aims in his book to convince us that undergraduates in a liberal arts college do pass through the developmental process he describes, but he also does something more. He tries, I think, to persuade us that this development, although not necessary for normal cognition, is desirable. There is, of course, an implicit argument for the desirability of a developmental process in any work that claims simply to describe such a process. If the process is developmental, then by definition, movement through it must be good and arrest at an early stage bad. The researcher is not supposed to assign such values to the stages being described and therefore is not expected to defend the implicit values. Perry, however, has openly assigned values to his developmental stages: successful completion of a liberal arts education requires moving eventually into the world view of Committed Relativism. Perry must either defend the values or be charged with bias in his research.

Consequently Perry openly states: "The values built into our scheme are those we assume to be commonly held in significant areas of our culture, finding their most concentrated expression in such institutions as colleges of liberal arts, mental health movements, and the like" (45). He understand that these values are "statements of opinion," with which others may differ (45), and that framing these values in a developmental scheme implicitly argues for them by implying that the closer one adheres to them, the more one "grows" (44). But he is unembarrassed at arguing for these values because he believes that they lead ultimately to the truest world view, or as he puts it, "an optimally congruent and responsible address to the present state of man's predicament" (45). Ultimately Perry sees the achievement of this world view as having spiritual significance; he refers several times to his scheme's being a sort of modern-day *Pilgrim's Progress,* and he stresses the courage it takes for young people to win through to the end (37, 44).

Perry's scheme, then, charts the creation of, not just any intellectually and ethically mature adult, but precisely "the liberally educated man," a man (or woman) "who has learned to think about even his own thoughts, to examine the way he orders his data and the assumptions he is making, and to compare these with other thoughts that other men might have" (39). Perry characterizes the adult who cannot be self-reflective in this way as "anti-intellectual," even if he or she is otherwise intelligent (39). To develop this kind of self-reflective intellectual maturity, Perry explicitly recommends a pedagogy of pluralism, which forces students to confront opposing views on an issue, forcing them out of the Dualist world view on into Relativism and beyond. Persuasively arguing for this pedagogy, Perry cites Socrates as its first practitioner and finds an American supporter for it in Henry Adams (35). Pluralism is also the pedagogy of Harvard College. Perry recognizes that its pervasiveness at Harvard has conditioned his research results, but he does not seek to claim universality for his results. Rather, he argues for this particular education-induced development. Let other colleges,

Perry implies, follow Harvard, as they have done in the past, in defining "the very heart of liberal education" (35–36).

Perry does not discuss the place of writing in the development for which he argues. He does not say, for example, that a Dualist student will write a particular kind of essay. Indeed, to determine a student's position in the scheme, Perry looks at nothing other than what the student tells the interviewer about his experiences. From the transcript of the interview Perry derives the student's attitudes toward schoolwork, which serve to characterize the positions in the scheme, as I explain above.

These general attitudes toward schoolwork presumably do inform particular kinds of academic performance, however. In a much anthologized essay Perry has distinguished between the attitudes that produce "cow" writing, or data unorganized by theory, and "bull" writing, or theory unsupported by data.[1] He does not use the descriptive terms from his scheme to characterize "cow" and "bull" writers, but he does connect students' papers with their understanding of academic ways of thinking.

With this indirect encouragement from Perry, many writing teachers have found it easy to match typical kinds of student essays with positions in the scheme. For example, a familiar sort of undergraduate essay is the one without an organizing thesis, the essay that is simply a collocation of facts strung together like beads with connectives such as "another" or "next." Typically, too, this kind of essay is either hypercorrect or fraught with errors that seem to have kept the student's attention fixed on the sentence level, so underdeveloped are the ideas in the whole paper. In place of generalizations from data this paper relies on maxims used so uncritically as to strike us as dreadful clichés. Mina Shaughnessy has found these characteristics in the writing of students at the most "basic" level of approximation to academic discourse.[2] Building on Shaughnessy's work, Andrea Lunsford finds similar characteristics in the essays of some of her Basic Writers.[3] It seems easy to identify such writing as the work of what Perry calls Dualist students, with their belief in unquestionable Absolutes and their view of education as the collecting of right answers.

Much more research is needed, however, before we can use

Perry's scheme to classify kinds of student writing. No doubt there are common kinds of undergraduate essays other than that described above, which seems to fit the scheme so neatly; we do not know whether Perry's scheme can provide an exhaustive explanation of variation in student writing. We should remember that Perry's scheme was based on the experiences of students who were highly successful academically and who were attending one of the most selective liberal arts colleges in the country. Although Shaughnessy and Lunsford, working with students somewhat different from Perry's, found signs in student writing of a development similar to the one he describes (neither of them refers to Perry), we do not know to what extent Perry's scheme can extend its explanatory power across a variety of student abilities, academic preparation, and college experiences. We should also note that Perry provides no timetable for progress through his scheme; nowhere does he suggest that all freshmen can be expected to be Dualists, who then as sophomores and juniors traverse Relativism and achieve Committed Relativism as seniors. The existence of these gaps in our knowledge of the scheme's application to student writing argues against using the scheme to classify student writing in any detailed way.

Furthermore, I would argue that we should not use Perry's scheme as a blueprint for writing curricula. Mechanical applications of Perry's scheme will tend to trivialize it while producing curricula that really tell us nothing new. For example, one freshman composition curriculum based on Perry uses his analysis of Relativism to justify the already familiar recommendation to ask students to read several essays that take opposing views on a controversial issue and then to develop their own argumentative positions.[4] The method is so familiar as already to have been embodied in numberless freshman composition anthologies. Furthermore, because students require prolonged exposure to pluralistic methods in many disciplines, and time to reduce the domain of Dualism, this curriculum does not do justice to the rather elaborate process whereby a student achieves the Relativist world view, according to Perry. Some research has suggested that Dualists make more progress if teachers initially take a nurturing, rather than a challenging, stance with them.[5] Moreover, students who have already achieved

Relativism may not be greatly benefited by lessons in recognizing and arguing from opposing views on controversial issue. Such practice may only entrench them in intransigently held personal views, a mind-set which, according to Perry, often retards students' progress through Relativism to Commitment.

If we agree with Perry that students pass through certain positions on their way to the kind of intellectual maturity valued in liberal arts colleges, it does not necessarily follow that we can get them to progress faster by forcing them to imitate more advanced positions until their brains kick on and hold these positions on their own. We should not, in other words, commit a version of what has come to be known as the "American heresy" with respect to the work of Piaget, that is, the attempt to find ways of moving children faster through the Piagetian levels. Perry's scheme describes the effects of a certain liberal arts curriculum, to be sure—Harvard's—but this does not mean that we can turn the effects into a model of causes for a new curriculum that will perform the same changes more efficiently. To try would be to neglect the emphasis Perry himself places on the function of education as acculturation, not training; inculcation of values, not practice in techniques.

Of what use, then, is Perry's work to college writing teachers? I think his scheme can help us to understand why the differences occur in student writing, even if we cannot apply his classification scheme rigidly. Shaughnessy and Lunsford do not agree on why such differences occur. Shaughnessy suggests that they arise from students' unequal ability to meet the expectations of the academic discourse community. Lunsford argues that the students are at different levels of cognitive development in the Piagetian sense— Basic Writers are "egocentric" (284). Perry's scheme forges a link between these social and cognitive explanations because, as I argued above, he is describing a developmental process that is only analogous to but not identical with Piaget's. Perry's analysis describes the changes in student thinking that result from their socialization into the academic community. The great strength of his scheme is its focus on one important constant in the struggles of all college writers: the intellectual demands of liberal education.

Perry's work should make us realize that as we bring our students through the process of liberal education, we are not simply teaching them to think or to grow up, as we sometimes like to say that we are. Rather, we are teaching them to think in a certain way, to become adults with a certain set of intellectual habits and ethical predilections. We are asking them to accept a certain kind of relation to their culture, from among the range of relations that are possible.

Thus Perry's greatest use to writing teachers is to provide us with a sort of philosophical map of the changes liberal education seeks to induce in our students. Such a map can help us understand that certain typical problems students have with writing in college should be regarded as problems with accepting the academic community's preferred world view, and not necessarily as problems with achieving "normal" cognition. This is supported by the rough match between Perry's scheme and the characteristics Shaughnessy and Lunsford note in the writing of students who are different from those in Perry's research sample.

In short, Perry provides us with a useful picture of the kind of "cultural literacy" required in a liberal arts college. The term "cultural literacy" refers to the objects of knowledge and the ways of thinking that one must master in order to participate in a particular community.[6] Following Perry we come to realize that the academic community requires students to know, for example, not only what Genesis says about the creation of the earth but also what geologists, biologists, and other scientists say about it. A community of religious fundamentalists might require only knowledge of Genesis. Furthermore, the academic community requires students to know how to evaluate competing ideas according to criteria of logical structure, adequate evidence, and so on; this academic way of thinking might not be valued, for instance, in a fundamentalist community in which tradition or the judgment of a revered authority is sufficient to validate arguments.

Literacy in the more usual sense of the ability to read and write is also highly valued in the academic community. Clearly, literacy is not required for participation in every sort of community. Some communities, too, value reading over writing—when there is a sacred text to be chanted, for example. But the academic community places a high value on writing, and Perry can help us see why.

The whole thrust of his developmental scheme is toward an increasing distance on the beliefs of one's childhood. These beliefs can no longer be accepted uncritically as Absolutes, once we realize that well-intentioned people may hold beliefs different from our own. As the pedagogical pluralism which Perry recommends widens the students' perspectives, it also fosters relativism by casting their beliefs into comparative relations with those of others.

Many theorists in composition studies have argued that writing is a unique mode of learning precisely because it fosters this kind of distancing.[7] One's ideas can be more easily examined, critiqued in comparision with other views, and reformulated as they are worked out in written form. Learning to write, then, can be seen as a process of learning to think about one's own thinking, a process which may well be unfamiliar to students in their home communities.

Furthermore, Perry's quasi-spiritual tone should remind us that we tend to invest teaching with moral fervor. I submit that most teachers will recognize in themselves a sort of moral repugnance about bad writing, a feeling that students "ought" to be able to organize and develop their ideas better, even while recognizing that this feeling partakes of the irrational blaming of the victim. Given that we do have this moral investment in the objects of knowledge and the ways of thinking that we teach, it seems hypocritical to pretend that academic activity is value-neutral, that we are merely teaching "thinking," not thinking in a certain way. And it seems more respectful to our students to see what we are doing when we teach as attempting to persuade them to accept our values, not simply inculcating our values.

Is this development desirable? The nature of Perry's scheme makes this question inevitable, fortunately. As in all discussions of cultural literacy the issue is, whose culture will be empowered to set the terms of literacy? Writing teachers are already acquainted with one such discussion in the debate over students' right to their own language. Personally, I believe that the kind of cultural literacy whose development is both chronicled and advocated in Perry's scheme is desirable for all students. But I do not want to begin here the lengthy argument that would be needed to defend that view.

Here I would simply like to make the point that our assumptions about the ends of education are strongly culture bound, as Perry helps us see. Furthermore, Perry gives us a perspective on all college teachers as, in effect, rhetors. To a high degree we persuade students to our values through our use of language, in lectures, textbooks, informal discussions, and writing assignments. Writing-across-the-curriculum programs do not so much create important roles for writing in all disciplines as they render us self-conscious about the role writing already plays. Some college teachers may not be comfortable with the view of themselves as rhetors, preferring to see themselves as investigators, reporters, value-neutral conveyors of truth. Perry's most important contribution to writing instruction may well be the critique he implies of this positivistic view of the teacher's role.

NOTES

1. "Examsmanship and the Liberal Arts," in *Examining at Harvard College*, ed. L. Bramson (Cambridge, Mass.: Faculty of the Arts and Sciences, Harvard University, 1963).

2. Mina Shaughnessy, *Errors and Expectations* (New York: Oxford University Press, 1977), 198–202.

3. "The Content of Basic Writers' Essays," *College Composition and Communication* 31 (1980), 279–283, 285.

4. This experimental composition program was described in a paper presented by Professor Gene Krupa of the University of Iowa at the 1983 Conference on College Composition and Communication. Professor Krupa did not want to draw any conclusions yet about its worth.

5. See, for example, Kiyo Morimoto, "Notes on the Context for Learning," *Harvard Educational Review* 43 (1973), 245–57.

6. For a definition of the term, and an argument in favor of a cultural literacy similar to that in Perry's scheme, see Richard Hoggart, "The Importance of Literacy," *Journal of Basic Writing* 3 (1980), 74–87.

7. See, for example, Janet Emig, "Writing as Mode of Learning," *College Composition and Communication* 28 (1977), 122–28; and Linda Flower, "Writer-Based Prose: A Cognitive Basis for Problems in Writing," *College English* 41 (1979), 19–37.

What Happens When Basic Writers
Come to College?

I wish to propose a hypothesis for researching an answer to this question. For the time being, let me suggest that "basic writers" are those who are least well prepared for college. They may be defined in absolute terms, by features of their writing, or in relative terms, by their placement in a given school's freshman composition sequence, but, either way, their salient characteristic is their "outlandishness"—their appearance to many teachers and to themselves as the students who are most alien in the college community. Currently there are three major ways to describe what happens to these outlanders when they enter college. Each approach tends to focus on one element of basic writers' complex experience. While each approach can give us a valuable partial view of basic writers' experience, I am seeking a more comprehensive approach to frame my research hypothesis.

One of these three current approaches says that basic writers entering college precipitate a clash among dialects. The basic writers are those students who experience the greatest distance between their home dialects and Standard English, the preferred dialect in school. These students feel that if only they could learn to write "grammatically," their problems would be solved. Some teachers agree, saying we should help—or require—these students to learn Standard English. This solution is institutionalized in the composition course requirements at most colleges. Once entangled in these requirements, however, basic writers may wish they could

Reprinted with permission from *College Composition and Communication* 37, no. 3 (Oct. 1986): 294–301. Copyright 1986 by the National Council of Teachers of English.

avoid the demands of Standard altogether—after all, it's only a matter of how they're saying it, not what they say, they feel. Scholars such as James Sledd have argued that the solution is to stop demanding that all school work be conducted in Standard English, and to give these students the option of either learning Standard English, if they so desire, or writing and speaking in school in their home dialects.

We know that all dialects of English, whether Standard or non-Standard, are capable of conveying complex thought. Given this consensus, students and teachers who wonder whether Standard English must be learned are assuming that the issue is whether thoughts, however complex, should be conveyed in Standard or in some other dialect. In other words, the thoughts are supposedly unchanged by the dialect in which they are conveyed. Advocates of requiring the Standard form often argue that although students can think complexly in their home dialects, unfortunately the larger society demands the Standard form and therefore if we wish to enable them to get ahead, we have to enable them to use it. Defenders of home dialects say that forcing students to abandon dialects, even if only occasionally or temporarily, presents such a barrier that students will learn very little while concentrating on the language problem. Hence James Britton, and his American followers such as Lil Brannon and C. H. Knoblauch, would provide many opportunities in school for "expressive" speaking and writing in the students' home dialects as important ways of learning prior to, or perhaps instead of, practice in "transactional" language using the Standard dialect.

A second approach says that basic writers' problem on entering college is that they face a clash, not of dialects, but of discourse forms. The focus here is not mainly on features of language, such as forms of the verb to be, but on features of texts, such as verbal devices used to achieve coherence. Basic writers discover that the ways of organizing information and convincing audiences with which they are most familiar are not the ways of winning arguments in academe, as Mina Shaughnessy has observed. These students do not know what Elaine Maimon calls the "genres" of academic writing, and, as David Bartholomae has shown, they will seek to shape their writing according to discourse conventions more familiar to them from other sources, such as soap operas or grammar-school history lessons on "great men." Basic writers will be puzzled at the unenthusiastic reception afforded such papers by their teachers, especially if they have managed to write them in Standard English!

To what extent are discourse conventions to be regarded as surface features of writing? If they are surface features only, then adherence to discourse conventions would be a matter of pouring thoughts into "formal shells," as Brannon and Knoblauch disparagingly call them. But what if following the conventions actually generates thoughts that would not be accessible without the conventions? If the conventions are seen as surface features, then we get a version of the debate over requiring Standard English: should all students be required to learn such conventional academic genres as the case study or the literature survey, or be allowed to pursue the "same" intellectual work in genres with which they feel more comfortable, such as the journal? Advocates of requiring students to practice academic genres argue that knowledge of them is necessary for success in college; advocates of other forms argue that the criteria for success in college must change.

If, however, the discourse conventions are seen as generating, and not merely conveying, certain kinds of complex thinking, then the "same" intellectual work is not possible in different genres. For example, the journal might be a genre that generates personal connections with classwork, such as expressing religious revulsion for genetic research, but that discourages other kinds of thinking, such as surveying religiously motivated resistance to scientific research through the ages. According to this line of argument, students would need to learn other, more "academic" genres in order to become able to perform more kinds of academic intellectual work. A corollary of this position is that whereas many genres, like the many dialects of English, are equally capable of generating complex thoughts, they are not capable of generating the *same* complex thoughts. Thus students will be thinking in different ways, depending upon the dialect and discourse forms with which they are familiar.

It is a short step, then, from seeing basic writers participating in a clash of discourse conventions to seeing them engaged in a clash of ways of thinking. Basic writers may begin to feel that their problem really is that they're too dumb for college, or that they just can't think the way the teacher wants. Suspecting that perhaps such students really are incapable of college-level thought, researchers such as Andrea Lunsford and Frank D'Angelo have turned to cognitive psychology for models to understand basic writers' intellectual development. In this third approach to understanding basic writers' problems, the developmental schemes of Jean Piaget or William Perry have been used to rank-order student writers, with basic writers placed at the least developed end of the scale. The teacher's task then becomes similar to the therapist's, in seeking ways to correct basic writers' cognitive dysfunctions. Other scholars argue that to use psychological models in this way is to stigmatize basic writers and to ignore the cultural bases of differences in thinking (see "Cognition, Convention, and Certainty," this volume).

I want to find an approach to the difficulties of basic writers entering college that can take into account these differences in dialects, discourse conventions, and ways of thinking. When students see their problem only as one of dialect, they're apt to say, "It's just that I can't talk right!" If they experience the problem as difficulty shaping a paper—what I've called a problem of unfamiliarity with academic discourse conventions—they may not see their problem as having to do with writing at all. They may just complain, "I don't know what the teacher wants." This kind of bewilderment increases if they begin to see their problem as a thinking problem—as I've suggested, this view often leads to a radical loss of self-confidence. When teachers see students' problems in only one of these ways—when they see it as only a dialect problem, or only a thinking problem—they risk similarly narrow views of basic writers' experience.

We can correct this excessively narrow focus through the notion of a language community: that is, a community that coheres because of common language-using practices. Perhaps all communities are in some sense language communities, although social class or geographic proximity, for instance, may also play a part in their cohesion. But the academic community is a community united almost entirely by its language, I think; the academic community is not coterminous with any social class, though it is more closely allied to some than to others. Like any other language community, the academic community uses a preferred dialect (so-called "Standard" English) in a convention-bound discourse (academic discourse) that creates and organizes the knowledge that constitutes the community's world view. If we see the relation between dialect, discourse conventions, and ways of thinking as constituting a language community, then we can no longer see dialects or discourse conventions as mere conveyances of thoughts generated prior to their embodiment in language. Rather, dialect and discourse generate thoughts, constitute world view.

It would not be correct, however, to say that a language community's world view is *determined* by its language, because that would imply that the world view could not change as a result of interaction by the community with the material world, and we know that such changes do occur. In order to participate in the community and its changes, however, one must first master its language-using practices. Thus basic writers, upon entering the academic community, are being asked to learn a new dialect and new discourse conventions, but the outcome of such learning is acquisition of a whole new world view. Their difficulties, then, are best understood as stemming from the initial distance between their world views and the academic world view, and perhaps also from the resistance to changing their own world views that is caused by this very distance.

To understand basic writers' problem in these terms, we need to ask three questions: What world views do basic writers bring to college? What is the new world view demanded in college? And do basic writers have to give up the world views they bring to college in order to learn the new world view?

The first of these questions has not yet been answered, as far as I know. We do not know much about the world views basic writers bring to college. Demographic information, on race or income for example, cannot lead to a satisfactory answer because there is no widely accepted model of the American class structure to which world views could be linked. Assumptions about "working-class" world views help to explain the school difficulties of certain groups of students in the research of Basil Bernstein in England, for example, and Pierre Bourdieu and Jean-Claude Passeron in France. We cannot make similar assumptions because, unlike the European researchers, we cannot identify a working class securely enough to be able to form hypotheses about its world view and so to test whether basic writers belong to this group. Some American researchers have argued that we should see basic writers as the products of an oral culture, so that differences of world view become differences between "literacy" and "orality" (see Ong, Farrell). Such analyses seek to attend to what the European researchers call class differences, in that oral culture seems to occur more frequently in certain social groups. The orality/literacy dichotomy, however, eventually flattens out class differences on behalf of the two main categories. Hence the variety of basic writers' cultural backgrounds and the differences in world views arising from this variety are not taken into account.

We will find it hard to assess the difficulty of acquiring the academic world view until we know how different it is from basic writers' home world views. Even though we cannot now say how great the difference might be, since we do not know enough about basic writers' original world views, basic writers' "outlandishness" in college strongly suggests that the difference is great and that for them, to a much greater degree than for other students, acquiring the academic world view means becoming bicultural. We do not know how difficult it is to become bicultural, although evidence exists that this is possible (see Fishman). If with great effort students can acquire the academic world view without having to give up their original world views, we do not know what benefits motivate them to make the effort, although there is some evidence that such benefits exist (see Patterson, Hoggart).

Perhaps we could get a better idea of what benefits are to be derived from acquiring the academic world view if we knew just what that world view is. I think we do have a good start on an answer to the question of what world view the college demands, in the developmental scheme of William Perry. I have argued that this scheme is culture-bound (see "William Perry and Liberal Education," this volume). In other words, it anatomizes an "intellectual and ethical development" that results from four years in an American liberal arts college, not a genetically determined growth process. Furthermore, Perry happened to perform his research at Harvard, a college of long-standing and far-reaching influence in American academic life. Hence the world view Perry describes can be taken as hegemonic, as the "target" world view toward which basic writers are urged, to a greater or lesser degree, everywhere.

I do not wish to summarize Perry's entire scheme, partly because space is limited and partly because, since we cannot assume that basic writers are coming into the process from the same sort of cultural background as Perry's research subjects, we have no reason to assume they will go through the same stages on their way to the final developmental position. I will attempt, however, to summarize that final position as the one at which basic writers must eventually arrive, if they are to succeed in college, however they get there.

Perry finds that the young men who have completed the process he describes see the world as a place in which there are no "Absolutes," no standards of right and wrong that hold good for all times and places. They feel that anyone who still sees the world as governed by Absolutes is epistemologically provincial. The liberal arts college, instead of accepting such naive dependence on Absolutes, requires the comparative study of ideas as the only way to choose among competing standards, to arrive at an informed judgment. Perry states that the essential component in the world view of the "liberally educated man" is the willingness "to think about even his own thoughts, to examine the way he orders his data and the assumptions he is making, and to compare these with other thoughts that other men might have" (39). The outcome of his deliberations is that he chooses to make "Commitments" to certain ideas, projects, and people, Commitments which will order his adult life.

On what basis are these Commitments made? Perry implies that their content will be strongly influenced by the allegiances students bring with them to college, to a particular religion, for example. At the same time, however, their form will be influenced by academic standards of logic, evidence, and so on. Hence the adult Commitment to a religion is a decision to build an area of meaningfulness, through participation in a group that shares one's sense of what is important, in a world which Perry apparently sees as essentially without intrinsic meaning. While Perry certainly does not wish to suggest that liberal arts education is destructive of religious faith, he implies that that faith will never be the same again—that after one has fully entered into the academic world view, one cannot willfully return to a world view constituted by Absolutes when one worships. The young men who have completed the process Perry describes see themselves as having accepted the individual responsibility of constructing meaning in their world, while acknowledging that this responsibility can only be accomplished through participation in like-minded groups, religious, political, and so on.

If Perry is right, then the academic world view makes a strong bid to control all of a student's experience. The student is asked to take a certain distance on all of his or her Commitments, to weigh them against alternatives, and to give allegiance only as a result of a careful deliberative process. In this sense, the academic world view cannot coexist peacefully with another world view in which standards for commitment are different—for example, one in which a father is authorized to make his children's choices. Perry implies that if one's precollege world view includes seeing one's father's decisions as law, then one should certainly take one's father's wishes into account when determining adult Commitments. But one cannot both follow one's father's decisions unquestioningly, and yet weigh them as only one factor, however important, in one's own decision-making process.

It seems, then, that biculturalism is likely to be very difficult when the academic world view is one of the world views involved, because the academic seeks to subsume other world views to which the students may retain allegiance. The privileged position of the academic world view in society makes it seem an even more domineering partner. In other words, basic writers may feel that they are being asked to abandon their less prestigious, less socially powerful world views in favor of the academic. Richard Rodriguez is one former basic writer who has written of the pain his conversion to the academic world view caused him, with its attendant estrangement from home.

It could be argued, however, that the home world view, especially if it is associated with a social group of relatively little power, has a better chance of surviving if some who hold allegiance to it are also sufficiently familiar with the academic world view to wield power in the larger society. They will be able to argue for the preservation of the language and culture of the home world view, for example, by making persuasive arguments to school administrators for bilingual education programs and by organizing political action to convince the larger society of these programs' value. But what is to prevent these academically successful students from going on simply to secure their own financial advantage, forgetting about their home communities? Although such aspirations are certainly legitimate, their pursuit will not necessarily foster preservation of the home language and world view.

According to Perry's understanding of the academic world view, true mastery of it is the preventative against simply self-serving behavior. The student seeking to make Commitments, in Perry's sense, cannot operate autonomously because to make a Commitment is to connect with other people, with like-minded groups. To put it another way, the student seeking to make Commitments comes to value his or her connections with like-minded groups precisely because the student realizes that only through such connections can Commitments be realized.

There is nothing in the Perry model to suggest that such a student *must* make a Commitment to the like-minded group of his or her own home community. This student will probably have other groups from which to choose in making Commitments, such as those associated with his or her profession. But the Perry model does suggest an economy of Commitments, a desire not to sever connections with any group to which one might potentially make a Commitment and, moreover, a desire particularly to foster Commitments that preserve integrity—in both the senses of honor and of coherence—in the individual's life, such as to a religious faith, or to a home culture that differs from the dominant one of the larger society. Thus, if we believe Perry, there is grounds for hope that the student who masters the academic world view will for that very reason wish to preserve his or her ties to the home community, and so to preserve its language and world view, whatever estrangements may have occurred on the way to this mastery.

I would like to conclude by suggesting that we need a study of basic writers similar to that conducted by Perry—a series of interviews to tell us how they mediate between their home cultures and the academic culture as they move on through their college educations. Perry's scheme can suggest the kind of developmental process such research would seek, although we would have to be careful not to assume that this test group will go through the same positions as Perry's Harvard students. Such a study would help to answer the other two questions I raise above: we would get a better idea of what world views basic writers bring to college, and we would hear what they themselves think about the cost of acquiring a new one. I suspect that they will not find the comparative, deliberative stance of the academic world view as hard to accept as Perry's more sheltered students do. The basic writers already know that their home communities' standards are not the only ones possible—they learn this more immediately and forcefully when they come to college than do students whose home world views are closer to the academic, when they experience the distance between their home dialects and Standard English and the debilitating unfamiliarity they feel with academic ways of shaping thoughts in discourse. I also suspect that they will find the stakes for accepting this world view higher than the stakes were for Perry's students—given the greater difference between this world view and their precollege world views, basic writers have more to lose in modifying their earlier world views. But precisely because of the hegemonic power of the academic world view, my hypothesis is that they will also find its acquisition well worth the risks.

BIBLIOGRAPHY

Bartholomae, David. "Inventing the University." In *When a Writer Can't Write*. Ed. Mike Rose. New York: Guilford Press, 1986.

Bernstein, Basil. *Class, Codes, and Control*. 1971; rpt. New York: Schocken Books, 1975.

Bizzell, Patricia. "Cognition, Convention, and Certainty: What We Need to Know about Writing." This volume.

———. "William Perry and Liberal Education." This volume.

Bourdieu, Pierre, and Jean-Claude Passeron. *Reproduction in Education, Society, and Culture*. Beverly Hills, California: Sage, 1977.

Britton, James et al. *The Development of Writing Abilities (11–18)*. London: Macmillan Education, 1975.

D'Angelo, Frank. "Literacy and Cognition: A Developmental Perspective." In *Literacy for Life: The Demand for Reading and Writing*. Eds. Richard W. Bailey and Robin Melanie Forsheim. New York: Modern Language Association, 1983.

Farrell, Thomas J. "IQ and Standard English." *College Composition and Communication* 34 (December 1983), 470–84.

Fishman, Joshua A. "Ethnocultural Dimensions in the Acquisition and Retention of Biliteracy." *Journal of Basic Writing* 3 (Fall/Winter 1980), 48–61.

Hoggart, Richard. "The Importance of Literacy." *Journal of Basic Writing* 3 (Fall/Winter 1980), 74–87.

Knoblauch, C. H. and Lil Brannon. "Writing as Learning through the Curriculum." *College English* 45 (September 1983), 465–74.

Lunsford, Andrea. "The Content of Basic Writers' Essays." *College Composition and Communication* 31 (October 1980), 278–90.

Maimon, Elaine. "Maps and Genres." In *Composition and Literature: Bridging the Gap*. Ed. Winifred Horner. Chicago: University of Chicago Press, 1983.

Ong, Walter J., S. J. *Interfaces of the Word*. Ithaca, New York: Cornell University Press, 1977.

Patterson, Orlando. "Language, Ethnicity, and Change." *Journal of Basic Writing* 3 (Fall/Winter 1980), 62–73.

Perry, William. *Forms of Intellectual and Ethical Development in the College Years: A Scheme*. New York: Holt, Rinehart and Winston, 1968.

Rodriguez, Richard. "The Achievement of Desire: Personal Reflections on Learning 'Basics.' " *College English* 40 (November 1978), 239–54.

Shaughnessy, Mina. "Some Needed Research on Writing." *College Composition and Communication* 28 (December 1977), 317–20.

Sledd, James. "In Defense of the *Students' Right*." *College English* 45 (November 1983), 667–75.

Composing Processes: An Overview

What Is "Composing"?

Composition scholars agree that the composing process exists or, rather, that there is a complex of activities out of which all writing emerges. We cannot specify one composing process as invariably successful. Current research in the field is beginning to draw a detailed picture of these composing processes.

"Composing" usually refers to all the processes out of which a piece of written work emerges. During composing, the writer may spend some time musing, rereading notes or drafts, or reading the texts of others, as well as actually putting words on the page herself. In composition research, "writing" usually refers precisely to the scribal act. One focus of composition research examines the extent to which composing occurs during writing, as opposed to the composing that takes place while other tasks, such as those I just listed, are being performed.

Simply to acknowledge that composing processes exist is something of a gain for modern composition studies. My undergraduate students would like to deny this premise: they prefer the fantasy that when they finally become "good writers," they will be able to sit down at the desk and produce an "A" paper in no more time than it takes to transcribe it. Nor are my students alone in this fantasy of instant text production. It is part of a more general notion in our culture, a sort of debased Romantic version of creativity wherein verbal artifacts are supposed to be produced as easily and inevitably as a hen lays eggs. This more general fantasy affects Americans'

Reprinted with permission from Anthony Petrosky and David Bartholomae, eds., *The Teaching of Writing* (Chicago: University of Chicago Press, 1986).

judgment of political orators, for example; we value as "good speakers" those who can think on their feet, apparently producing eloquence in no more time than it takes to utter the words.

The classical rhetoricians knew better. Greek and Roman teachers of effective writing and speaking elaborated a five-stage composing process: invention, or finding ideas; arrangement, or putting the ideas into persuasive order; style, or dressing the ideas in persuasive language; memory, or memorizing the text of the speech thus prepared; and delivery, or delivering the speech with the most effective use of voice, gesture, and so on. No one supposed that brilliant orators simply opened their mouths and let it flow.

Many of my students, however, have not encountered anything like the classical composing process in school. Until very recently, most language arts instruction in American schools had lost a sense that composing requires complex processes. Instead, students brought their finished products to the teacher for correction and evaluation. The composing of these products was something students had to manage on their own. Whatever processes they used remained a "black box" to the instructor: the assignment went in at one end, and out came the final paper at the other.

Given that classical rhetoric did emphasize process, how is it that we have inherited such a product-oriented pedagogy? The history is too long to recount here in detail, but let me summarize by saying that over the centuries rhetoric was shorn of four of the five classical stages of composing. In the Renaissance, Ramist rhetoricians, because they sought to develop a purely objective discourse in which to conduct the researches of the new science, redefined invention and arrangement as matters of logic. Rationality, rather than persuasiveness, would be the new standard for judging the soundness and order of ideas. Much later, as English departments were formed in late nineteenth-century American colleges, their avowed focus on literature—on texts to be read—made the study of memory and delivery unnecessary (these elements continued to be studied in the departments of speech which, not coincidentally, split off from English departments at about this time).

As a result of these changes, the study of rhetoric came to focus on only one stage in the classical composing process: style. The tasks of the English department were to analyze the style of canonical literary works, for the purpose of interpreting these works' enduring human values; and to analyze the style of student essays, for the purpose of correcting their errors and encouraging the writers toward the beauties discovered in the canonical works. From the students' viewpoint, the English department thus devoted to the study of style certainly encouraged the fantasy that there are no composing processes. Only finished products were treated in class, whether the accomplished works of literary masters or the mediocre ones of the students themselves. Evidently one could not learn how to compose more effectively, since this was never taught. Evidently one either possessed the inborn ability to produce good texts, or one was out of luck: a cat can't lay eggs.

Rediscovering Composing

Dissatisfaction with this product-centered pedagogy has arisen periodically at least since the early twentieth century in the Progressive Education movement. But a surge of interest in composing developed in the 1960s. It probably received its single greatest impetus from the change in the school population that began to be evident at that time. To summarize this change crudely: more and more students were unable to bring to their teachers essays that needed only stylistic revision. More and more students were producing essays full of errors that were supposed to disappear in the earlier grades and of ideas so ill considered as to call into question the students' cognitive development. Drastic action seemed called for to help these student writers to improve.

It was largely in response to the perceived new needs of students—and teachers—that composition studies began to emerge in the 1960s as an area of specialization within English studies. Literary critics, too, were dissatisfied with the New Criticism's focus on style and began the theoretical debates over a replacement paradigm that have continued to the present. The entire discipline of English studies, in other words, has been undergoing some radical changes. But while literary scholars have focused on problems of reading literary texts, composition scholars have turned to examining writing, the process of composing texts, and particularly the texts of student writers and others who are not literary masters.

Most of the research that shapes our current knowledge of composing has been published since 1970. Composition specialists in the 1960s saw themselves primarily as teachers of writing, not as researchers. Nevertheless, their work has strongly influenced current research, not only in what it tells us about composing but also in the professional agenda it establishes for composition studies.

These first of the modern scholars in composition found themselves at odds with the academy from the beginning. Many academics (not to mention administrators and parents) assumed that the solution to the problem of student writing was simply to correct the ever-more-numerous errors, until by dint of the drill students finally learned not to splice commas, split infinitives, and so on. This assumption informed many early professional decisions made by senior academics about their colleagues in composition. For instance, if teaching grammar need be the only content of the writing class, writing teachers would not require advanced academic training. It became customary (as it still is to this day) to staff the bulk of a school's writing courses with teachers reassigned from other disciplines, voluntarily or not, with graduate students, or with people no longer actively seeking terminal degrees and teaching part-time by choice or necessity. These writing teachers found themselves garnering little professional respect, except, perhaps, that due the person who undertakes a necessary but unpleasant job that nobody else wants. Their senior colleagues assumed, moreover, that there was no serious scholarly work to be done in the field of composition studies, so that the way to professional advancement lay in escape from the writing classroom.

But writing teachers became increasingly convinced, on the basis of their classroom experience, that the initial assumption on the need for grammar drills simply was wrong. Attending closely to the problems students had in writing their papers, rather than merely to the problems that appeared in their finished products, writing teachers became convinced that students needed a better understanding of the whole process of working on a piece of writing, to give adequate time to the task and to make the time spent more productive. To gain this understanding, writing teachers began to work through this process along with their students and to try to determine what contributed to a successful, or unsuccessful, writing process.

Some early fruit borne by such study was the model of composing introduced by Gordon Rohman and Raymond Wlecke.[1] Rohman and Wlecke found that successful college-level writers typically traverse three stages in composing: pre-writing, writing, and editing. Most significant here is the concept of "pre-writing," that is, idea-generating activities that provide essential preparation for drafting. This was perhaps the first intimation that we needed to study a whole complex of composing processes, of which the actual writing of the paper was only one. Moreover, Rohman suggested that pre-writing activities such as journal keeping and meditation could be taught—that composing processes, rather than grammar drills, could become the actual content of the writing course.

Some academics opposed such activities, however, on grounds that they were not likely to foster the writing of good academic expository prose. This objection was met with even stronger resistance from writing teachers. During this same era, the academy itself began to seem discredited, in the eyes of many students and teachers, by political developments in the nation at large. For one thing, the academy was reluctant to incorporate new methods of responding to these developments, preferring its traditional subjects and methods of inquiry. For another, this reluctance was seen as enforcing discriminatory social sorting, with white middle-class men being educated for positions of power and all others being disenfranchised. Academic expository prose, the mastery of which was a prerequisite for traditional academic work, was implicated in the indictment of the academy as an institution of political oppression.

Hence, many writing teachers came to argue that students could not write good academic expository prose because academic expository prose was bad in itself—it was verbose, indirect, and impersonal to the point of hypocrisy. Instead of forcing students to master it, and the concomitant complexities of formal Standard English, writing teachers began to believe that they should be helping students to free themselves from its baleful influence if ever their writing were to improve. Students should forget their anxieties about correctness, stop trying to sound like someone else, and work to discover and refine their own personal, authentic writing styles.

The study of composing thus came to serve the liberation of each student's personal style, a way of writing that would clearly and sincerely convey her perspective on the world, as uniquely valuable as the student's own humanity. As I have tried to suggest, a combination of professional and historical circumstances made the development of a pedagogy of personal style something of a political crusade for many writing teachers. By fostering students' own styles, instead of forcing conformity to an oppressive institutional standard, writing teachers could feel they were making their own contribution to the reform of oppressive academic and political institutions.

Since the standard for judging a personal style could come only from within the student, who alone could certify its ability to represent her perspective on the world, the pedagogy of personal style aimed mainly to remove barriers to students' perceptions of what they had achieved in their writing. Close-reading, a technique of literary New Criticism, in which many writing teachers were trained, could be adapted for this purpose. Working as a group, teacher and students focused on student writing as the principal text for the course, and by detailed analysis helped each student writer to see whether her choice of words adequately expressed her thoughts. Given the original political agenda of personal-style pedagogy, this process typically worked to eliminate oppressive vestiges of academic writing. A student's personal style was to be characterized by comfortable use of the first person; by focus on a topic the student knows at first hand, typically personal experiences rather than academic subjects; and by exposition relying far more heavily on a detailed account of the writer's perceptions and feelings than on analysis and generalization. Peter Elbow's influential textbook, *Writing Without Teachers,* emphasizes the open-endedness of the composing processes necessitated by the search for a personal style.[2]

The pedagogy of personal style thus established that composing processes are complex and often lengthy and, hence, that a substantial phenomenon exists for scholarly study. The Rohman-Wlecke model of composing has been faulted for its linearity, that is, for assuming that the successful writer typically moves through the composing process without backtracking or omitting any stage. But, in general, personal-style pedagogy, with its emphasis on rewriting, encouraged the view of composing processes as recursive, which has been confirmed by contemporary research.

In addition to these influential assumptions about composing, personal-style pedagogy helped shape contemporary research through its assumptions about what should go on in the writing classroom: that students and teacher should democratically discuss each student's work, with the teacher acting not as authoritative director but as knowledgeable collaborator and with the goal being each student's accomplishment of self-selected writing tasks. Students should not be sidetracked in their search for personal styles by emphasis on standards of correctness set by others, such as the rules of formal Standard English. The teacher's main function, in addition to participating in the class writing workshop, should be to protect students from the academy's oppressive requirements.

Since the great majority of composition scholars have adhered at some time to personal-style pedagogy, it is not surprising that its pedagogical assumptions, as well as its assumptions directly bearing on composing, have influenced our sense of what research projects are worth undertaking. Moreover, this influence is not pernicious, both because all research can only occur under the guidance of assumptions and because these assumptions have guided us toward some fruitful research. It might not be too much to say that we owe all our current knowledge of composing to the early decisions of beleaguered composition scholars to resist the pedagogical agenda being set for them by senior academics, namely teaching grammar, and to seek a pedagogy more responsive to student needs. This pedagogy, in helping students develop their personal styles, brought their composing processes into the classroom and hence into the domain of scholarly inquiry. Moreover, the emphasis of this pedagogy on the personal, on the creative power of the individual writer's mind, helped to legitimate voices silenced in the traditional English classroom, voices of women, ethnic minorities, and other oppressed groups, and so did help to make the academy more responsive to contemporary political issues.

Under the influence of personal-style pedagogy, the first school of thought on composition research, which continues to flourish, encouraged the study of what goes on inside the individual writer's head. Such research is now often referred to as cognitive analyses of composing, because it has borrowed some methods and assumptions from the social sciences. The work of this school has been valuable, as I will explain below; unfortunately, however, until recently, composition research was limited to work in this school by personal-style pedagogy's assumptions about the individual nature of writing ability.

The problem was—and still is, to some extent—that personal-style pedagogy sees the political conflict in schools as between an oppressive institution and individual creative talents. In this view, what the student writer needs to do is to strip away all "outside" influences, such as academic standards of correctness, in order to get down to the thoughts and language that are uniquely, authentically hers. The kind of first-person narrative elicited in personal-style classes was assumed to be such "authentic" writing. The problem with this assumption, however, is illustrated by the fact that this "anti-academic" writing is actually a well-recognized belletristic essay style in itself, as exemplified in writers such as George Orwell and E. B. White, favorites for personal-style classroom reading. To heighten the irony, this style comes much more easily to white middle- and upper-class students than to others, thus preserving in personal-style pedagogy the very social discrimination it sought to combat.

What this example illustrates, however, is not the culpability of writing teachers for failing to free themselves from class-based attitudes, but rather the impossibility of doing so. No one uses language autonomously. One's speaking, reading, and writing are always shaped by one's social and cultural background and by the political relations this background creates with audiences of similar or very different backgrounds. This shaping is as much a matter of what the writer knows as of what she does. For example, a student may fail to produce an acceptable personal-style essay because she comes from a social group that does not value the sort of intense introspection such an essay calls for. Hence, she may either be simply too unfamiliar with introspection to produce it, or too wary with classmates (and teacher) from other social groups to produce it for them to read. As I have argued elsewhere, research into the social and cultural contexts from which the writer's knowledge comes and in which she is addressing an audience is as necessary to our understanding of composing as is research into what goes on in the writer's head.[3] Recently, more research into these contexts of composing has been forthcoming, as I will explain below.

Cognitive Analyses of Composing

The contemporary moment of research on composing may be said to begin with the work of James Britton and Janet Emig. Working independently, but aware of each other's work, Britton and Emig developed strikingly similar pictures of students' composing processes. Perhaps the greatest insight they share is that composing processes vary with the kind of writing the student is doing. Britton distinguishes three kinds: "poetic," which produces literary artifacts; "expressive," in which the student explores a subject and her own feelings about it, for an audience of herself or an intimate friend; and "transactional," in which the student seeks to convey information or argue for a position, for an audience of the teacher in the role of examiner.[4] Emig names two kinds of writing: "reflexive," very similar to Britton's expressive; and "extensive," very similar to Britton's transactional.[5] Britton and Emig agree that student writers' composing processes typically are most truncated and least successful in transactional/extensive writing and most elaborated and most successful in expressive/reflexive writing. Britton and Emig conclude that students should be offered far more opportunities in school for expressive/reflexive writing.

Britton and Emig formed these conclusions about composing by looking at student work, not literary masterpieces. Britton and his colleagues read about 2,000 essays by British schoolchildren between the ages of eleven and eighteen. Emig interviewed eight American high school seniors while they composed and produced a case study of one of these writers. This methodology has been widely influential, without being followed to the letter. Although not all researchers base their conclusions on a sample of student essays or on case studies, there is general agreement that composing is best investigated by looking at writers at work.

Emig's and Britton's conclusion, that students need more opportunities in school for expressive/reflexive writing, has also been widely influential, even when their terminology is not used. Indeed, this conclusion formed one of the assumptions of the pervasive pedagogy of personal style. The work of Emig and Britton was thus welcomed because it appeared to provide empirical justification for personal-style pedagogy's political indictment of academic writing. Britton and his colleagues, however, do not see the conflict in terms of academic writing versus individual styles, although their language is sometimes misleading. Rather, it is a battle between the language-using practices of the privileged social class and those of other social classes attempting to gain legitimacy in school. The underlying political agenda of Britton et al. is thus much more radical than that of personal-style pedagogy, calling for a class-based reversal of what constitutes good style rather than for a democracy of styles.

Preferring a focus on the personal, American composition research developed first along lines indicated by Emig, to explore what goes on in the individual writer's head. Some researchers have attempted to make the examination of working writers more rigorous by borrowing methodology from the social sciences. Composition scholar Linda Flower and her colleague, cognitive psychologist John R. Hayes, have pioneered the use of protocol analysis, a cognitive psychology research technique, for studying composing. Flower and Hayes ask writers to describe their thought processes aloud while they are composing. The transcript of what they say is the protocol, which the researchers then analyze for regular features of a composing process.

The Flower-Hayes model divides composing into three main parts: one, the "task environment," subdivided into "rhetorical problem" and "text produced so far"; two, the "writing process," subdivided into "reviewing" (further subdivided into "revising" and "evaluating"), "translating," and "planning" (further subdivided into "generating," "goal-setting," and "organizing"); and three, the "writer's long-term memory." "Task environment" encompasses the immediate context of a composing situation, such as a school assignment for which a written product must be completed; "long-term memory" encompasses the larger social context for composing to be found, for example, in the writer's knowledge of genre. In the Flower-Hayes model, however, these contexts of composing are treated largely as a ground or frame for the main area of interest, namely the "writing process" (note the much greater number of subdivisions in this part of the model). "Writing process" encompasses activities taking place inside the writer's head.[6]

The most influential arguments propounded in the Flower-Hayes model are, first, that the writer can "access" task environment and long-term memory and switch from one writing subprocess to another at any time while composing: in other words, the composing process typically is recursive, not linear. For instance, the writer typically does not plan first and, that done, go on to write without ever reconsidering her plans. Second, although there is no single natural order in which composing activities do or should occur, there is a sort of natural relationship among them such that some activities are, or should be, subordinated to other activities: in other words, the composing process typically is hierarchical.

The Flower-Hayes model seeks to be comprehensive, that is, to describe all possible composing behaviors, although Flower and Hayes have been careful to point out that not every act of composing will—or should—employ every possible behavior. But in spite of this model's important arguments, which I just mentioned, it can be critiqued precisely on grounds of its claim to comprehensiveness. The problem is that some composition specialists have been prompted by this claim to attempt to explain the differences between successful and unsuccessful writers in terms of how fully they make use of the cognitive activities described in the model. Such research might lead to use of the Flower-Hayes model as a Procrustean bed for students' necessarily diverse composing processes.

For example, some researchers influenced by the Flower-Hayes model have argued that poor writing results from neglecting the recursive quality of the composing process, as did the poor writers in Pianko's study who failed to pause for reflecting on what they were writing.[7] Other researchers have held that poor writing re-

sults from misranking activities in the process hierarchy. The poor
writers studied by Sondra Perl accorded inordinate importance and
time to editing for errors in grammar, spelling, and mechanics.[8]
The single most important factor in successful writing, Perl has
argued, is to allow for the recursive quality of composing by rereading the text as one produces it and waiting for a "felt sense" of
structure to emerge and guide planning.[9]

The new importance given to the recursive quality of composing
has led some researchers to focus exclusively on revision. Nancy
Sommers has argued that the whole composing process, rightly
understood, is a process of revision in which the writer does not
simply polish her style but, more important, develops her ideas.
"Revision" comes to mean the whole complex of activities of rereading, evaluating, and making small-scale and large-scale changes in
the text as one produces it. Unsuccessful writers, Sommers argues,
do not so understand revision, saving it for the end of the composing process and using it only to make small-scale changes such as in
word choice.[10] It follows that the most effective writing pedagogy
will be that which creates a climate for continual revising in the
classroom, as described, for example, by Lil Brannon.[11]

Interest in revision and a desire to correct some problems with
protocol analysis by adapting Emig's case-study method for research on composing have led researchers such as Carol Berkenkotter[12] and Mimi Schwartz[13] to follow the progress of a single text
through multiple revisions. This research has emphasized that successful writing, whether by accomplished professionals or beginning students, emerges from recursive composing processes. There
must be adequate time for rethinking; a willingness to respond to
hunches, word associations, and other seemingly random techniques to trigger revision; and a recurring strong sense of the audience for whom one is writing.

Schwartz, Donald Graves, and others have argued that these
factors influence revision even in very young children's writing.[14]
Children have a natural proclivity for composing, according to
Glenda Bissex and other researchers into the genesis of writing
ability.[15] Graves argues in his influential book *Writing: Teachers
and Children at Work* that it is vitally important for schools not to
stifle children's natural desire to write by constraining them with

assignments they are not interested in and intimidating them with constant corrections.[16] Rather, children should be given many opportunities to write on topics they choose and offered help with any aspect of composing only when such help seems necessary to the successful completion of a particular writing project and when it can be offered in such a way as not to make the child feel that she is no longer in control of her own writing. Although Shirley Brice Heath, David Olson, and others have argued that students' readiness to develop their writing in school is greatly influenced by their social and cultural backgrounds, most researchers into children's writing agree that Graves's pedagogy is the most helpful for all students.[17]

It is interesting to note how these various kinds of cognitive research on composing, like the work of Britton and Emig, echo some assumptions of personal-style pedagogy. The work of Pianko, Perl, and Sommers leads to the conclusion that something very like personal-style pedagogy is still the best: the main classroom activity is group revision of student texts, students rewrite to achieve their own expressive goals rather than to satisfy academic requirements, and any insistence on formal correctness is taboo. Graves recommends a similar pedagogy for elementary-school children, with the additional personal-style assumption that the resources they will call on in writing are mainly innate abilities, not knowledge gained in school. Thus, the kind of pedagogy emerging from current cognitive research on composing is open to the same objection that was leveled against personal-style pedagogy, namely, that this new pedagogy does not lead to mastery of academic writing. Personal-style pedagogues, as I noted earlier, were inclined to answer this charge by arguing that mastery of academic writing was undesirable anyway. Those advocating the new pedagogy, however, generally argue that it offers the best route to eventual mastery of academic writing and any other kind of writing the student chooses to do. This view is still open to debate; we have no research evidence that students educated according to this pedagogy develop into more accomplished academic writers than those educated by other means, though the student excerpts typically quoted in works advocating this pedagogy suggest they are accomplished at other kinds of writing. The fact is, however, that curricula designed according to this pedagogy generally do not teach academic writing directly, whatever abilities may be expected of students afterwards.

Research on the Social and Cultural Contexts of Composing

Although, as I suggested earlier, the first contemporary school of thought on composition research focused on the individual writer's mind, more recently a second school has developed to research the social and cultural factors that influence the individual writer's performance. These researchers have been motivated in part by a reluctance to accept the conclusion, forced by personal-style and cognitive-based analyses of composing, that differences in individual performance are due to differences in individual talent. This reluctance sprang from the scholars' observation that performance differences seemed to correlate with social groups; it seemed logical, therefore, to assume that social and cultural, as well as individual, factors influence composing. Moreover, poor performance seemed to correlate with relatively less privileged social groups. Retaining a sympathy with these groups consistent with some assumptions of personal-style pedagogy, these scholars wished to save them from the stigma of personal failure and to seek a pedagogy specific to their needs.

For many of these researchers, mastery of academic writing has become once more an acceptable goal of composition pedagogy, but not as it was traditionally taught. Once, the course teaching academic writing simply laid down its laws, and those who would not or could not conform simply left the academy. Now, composition scholars seek to serve these students particularly—the ones who have trouble mastering academic writing—so as to give them equal access to the knowledge generated and maintained by the academy. Some scholars may hope that, if academic writing is still a weapon of political oppression, students who master it may be able to turn the weapon against the oppressors. At any rate, many students are now asking for help in mastering academic writing, and writing teachers are responding, just as we responded fifteen years ago when they asked for help in mastering nonacademic, personal styles.

Another influence on the interest in social and cultural contexts of composing has been the new interest in classical rhetoric among composition specialists. Classical rhetoric began to be recovered for English studies in the 1960s, when new collections of original classical texts became available and E. P. J. Corbett's influential *Classical Rhetoric for the Modern Student* suggested contemporary pedagogical applications.[18] At first, classical rhetoric's most important contribution was its multistage composing process, particularly its emphasis on invention, which reinforced the movement in personal-style pedagogy to develop "pre-writing" or idea-generating techniques.

The classical model of composing has been faulted on grounds of excessive linearity. C. H. Knoblauch and Lil Brannon have blamed classical rhetoric, not as recently rediscovered but as embedded in American schooling since the nineteenth century, for influencing teachers to vitiate new pedagogical techniques, such as those encouraging personal style, by inserting them into a curriculum dominated by this linear model of composing.[19] In this way the techniques became mere moments in a rigid progression of stages of composing, rather than, as they should be, periodically useful tools in an open-ended and recursive process. But there is more to the story of classical rhetoric's relevance for the modern student.

As composition specialists have begun to turn to research on the contexts of composing, they have become aware that perhaps the most important contribution of classical rhetoric is precisely its focus on context. Classical rhetoric assumes that the function of writing is not to express oneself but to effect change in the human community in which one lives. Hence, the ability to suit one's style to the particular audience, rather than addressing all in one "personal" register, becomes art, not hypocrisy. Classical rhetoric invites discussion of the social and political uses of writing in ways that personal-style pedagogy, for all its political agenda, never could.

As composition specialists' interest in the contexts of composing has emerged, two seminal theorists have been Ann Berthoff and Mina Shaughnessy. They take two very different approaches, without much reference to each other, but both insist on the crucial connection between individual writer and "outside world." Berthoff has made this point in the strongest terms: human beings use language to make sense of themselves and their world.[20] Hence, if we want to understand composing, we must look at that world with which the writer is in a dialectical relationship, as well as at the writer's individual talents. Berthoff does share some assumptions with personal-style pedagogy concerning all students' innate meaning-making powers. But because she also looks at the context of composing, the world in which and on which they work, she realizes that student writers can be taught to make more personally satisfying use of their meaning-making powers in language—that is, she favors a more directive pedagogy than the personal-style, one that offers what she calls "assisted invitations" to composing. These "invitations" aim not to liberate student writing from the influence of others' styles, but to make students constructively self-conscious about the resources available to their own writing in their society's repertoire of styles. For example, instead of merely keeping a personal journal, Berthoff's students might be encouraged to maintain a "double-entry notebook" in which they periodically reread and critique their own earlier observations. Thus they are made students of their own language-using practices.

While Berthoff's approach is intended, I believe, to be universally applicable, that is, to describe the universal human experience with making meaning in language, Shaughnessy confined her study specifically to the academic community.[21] In her analysis of successive drafts of papers by extremely unskilled college writers, Shaughnessy has found attempts at meaning making where there appears to be no order at all. She understands the composing process as a socialization process, in which gradually bringing one's writing into line with the discourse conventions of one's readers also brings one to share their thinking, their values, in short, their world view. Shaughnessy has argued that student writers are least successful when most ignorant of academic discourse conventions: how the academic audience evaluates evidence, what allusions strike it as elegant, what personae it finds credible, and so on. Shaughnessy has suggested a philosophical critique of personal-style pedagogy in her repudiation of the "honest face" persona for student writers. Nowhere, including the academy, does clear, sincere self-expression win assent unaided.

Shaughnessy's work gave composition specialists a new perspective on student writing problems. Her analysis allowed us to retain the best element of personal-style pedagogy, namely, its sense that students' relationship with the academy is agonistic and requires our mediation if social justice and common humanity are to be served. But she also allowed us to step back from the position that bad student writing is caused by the imposition of bad academic standards on natural creativity. Rather, if no writing is autonomous, if all writing is situated in some language-using community, then bad student writing, according to Shaughnessy, should be understood as the output of apprentices or initiates into the academic community. The pedagogy they need is not one that excoriates academic discourse, but rather one that mediates their introduction to it while remaining respectful of the language-using practices they bring to school.

Research into the social, cultural, and political influences on composing, particularly as they bear on students attempting to master academic writing, has taken several directions, exploring writing across the curriculum, basic writing, collaborative learning, and reading/writing connections. Questions which remain problematic for this research include the extent to which social, cutural, and political factors determine composing as opposed to merely influencing it, and the pace at which students should be urged toward mastery of academic writing. Assumptions from personal-style pedagogy can be seen playing their part in this school of research, as much as in the cognitive research that this school often seeks to correct or oppose. For example, recommendations for workshop classrooms in which students pursue self-selected writing goals often emerge from this research, as my brief overview will show. Nevertheless, the emphasis on contexts of composing is an essential and unique contribution.

Writing across the curriculum began as a pedagogical movement in Great Britain in the late 1960s. It was fostered by James Britton, Nancy Martin, and their colleagues in response to the discovery, made in the course of their composing process research, that students wrote very little outside the English classroom. Believing that students would write better if given more opportunities to write in school, particularly opportunities for expressive writing, the British researchers pubished a series of pamphlets explaining how to integrate expressive writing into a wide range of academic disciplines. In effect, these pamphlets argue for teaching a composing process which would begin with expressive writing, for example in class journals, and only later issue in finished academic essays. The British researchers envision a classroom in which much student writing and talking do not issue in finished work at all, but are nevertheless essential for their heuristic value.[22]

Toby Fulwiler[23] and Lil Brannon and C. H. Knoblauch[24] are among the American composition scholars who have adapted for American colleges the work of Britton et al., which is aimed at elementary and secondary level students. In arguing for the efficacy of a journal-centered composing process in college-level academic disciplines, these proponents of writing across the curriculum have focused the British methods more directly toward the production of finished essays, while maintaining that better papers grow from personal interest in the topic that students develop through their journals. This pedagogy, too, has argued that student composing processes may be idiosyncratic and no single composing process can be assumed to be successful for everyone.

Other American work in writing across the curriculum moves away from this focus on the individual writer to look more directly at the academic context and its demands. Composition scholars such as Elaine Maimon have sought to respond to Shaughnessy's call for a taxonomy of academic discourse conventions.[25] Maimon's focus is not merely on formal features of texts, such as laboratory report format. Rather, she analyzes the intellectual framework suggested by the laboratory report and asks: What do the discourse conventions reveal about how scientists define and interact with the world? What kind of thinking does this kind of writing ask students to do or actually make them do as they write? Maimon's work suggests that there may be epistemological constraints on composing. A writer's varying degrees of success with different kinds of writing may not be due to a simple dichotomy of personal writing (good) versus academic writing (bad). Rather, the different kinds of thinking demanded in different disciplines may cause the student's composing process to vary as a function of the different distances between these ways of thinking and that with which the student is originally comfortable.

Thus these two different approaches to writing across the curriculum typically lead to different pedagogies. The journal-centered approach, once again, endorses something very similar to personal-style pedagogy. The classroom is a workshop, students generate their own writing topics and stylistic goals, and emphasis on correctness is avoided. The teacher is likely, however, to encourage writing projects that involve something like traditional academic inquiry—for instance, a topic requiring library research. Moreover, it is not unusual for such a writing course to be linked with a course in some other discipline, so that the students prepare their papers for that course with the aid of the journal-centered pedagogy of the writing course. Typically, however, journal-centered pedagogy spends relatively little time on formal academic expository writing.

In contrast, the approach centered on academic discourse conventions gives first priority to mastery of academic writing and the formal Standard English it employs. Students may well be encouraged to begin from journals and other forms of pre-writing associated with personal-style pedagogy, but they will be urged along more quickly to the production of finished academic essays. Students will be helped to meet academic English standards in the final stages of composing, on grounds that to do so is to observe what counts as polite behavior in the community they are seeking to enter. The classroom atmosphere is likely to be more directive, with the teacher actively seeking to explain academic writing conventions and to demystify the kinds of thinking they make possible.

The academic context has particularly marked effects on students who are least familiar with its discourse conventions and ways of thinking—the students known as "basic writers" who are at the very beginning stages of being able to produce successful academic writing. Much research on the composing processes of basic writers has focused on the extent to which their difficulties are due to the academic context. Mike Rose has argued that a truncated or blocked composing process can result from overly rigid internalization of advice given in writing instruction, rather than from some deficiency in the student's innate ability to compose.[26] David Bartholomae, extending the work of Shaughnessy, has explained the discourse of basic writers as an approximation of the academic discourse whose conventions and world view are unfamiliar to them, rather than merely as a tissue of errors.[27] These readings of the work of basic writers suggest that their composing processes must include a considerable amount of trial-and-error experimentation as they gradually discover how to use academic discourse for their own purposes.

Teaching academic discourse to basic writers has become a particularly sensitive issue because their difficulties with academic writing tend to be a function of the social distance between the academy and their home communities. That is, basic writers typically come from less privileged social groups, where the language-using practices are most unlike those of the academy, which reflect the practices of the privileged groups in our society. Hence, basic writers appear to be in more danger than others of being alienated from their home communities by mastery of academic discourse. Literacy researchers Walter Ong[28] and James T. Farrell[29] have argued in favor of such alienation or assimilation, on grounds that the ways of thinking enabled by the language-using practices of such students' home communities are cognitively inferior to those of the academy. Other scholars, however, see such arguments as unjustly enforcing the social privileges of academic writing.[30] We do not know whether academic ways of thinking are in fact cognitively different from, or superior to, those of other communities; nor do we know to what extent assimilation is unavoidable for basic writers.

As research on writing across the curriculum and on basic writing has emphasized students' adapting to new ways of thinking, many composition researchers have been led to focus on the extent to which learning to compose is a socialization process, a process of initiation into the discourse community's world view. Such a focus immediately brings to the foreground the extent to which composing is a collaborative process. More broadly, the ways we "compose" experience are culturally conditioned. More particularly, all writers are influenced in their composing processes by other writers, other writing, more experienced mentors, and so on. For the student, these are the influences of academic discourse, teachers, and peers. Kenneth Bruffee, a specialist in the "collaborative learning" of writing, has explored these influences and concludes that students who understand something of the academic world view and its discourse are often more effective than teachers in mediating other students' introduction to the academy.

Bruffee has developed a method of training students to tutor their peers that helps them all to become conscious of what they already knew about academic discourse and to improve their knowledge through attention to their own composing processes. Bruffee's writing workshop resembles the personal-style classroom in procedure, with the difference that the main goal is not discovery of one's inmost honest feelings, but rather articulation of a public voice that will allow participation in the academic intellectual community.[31] The greatest contribution of work on collaborative learning is to emphasize that composing is always in some sense a social process.

Intellectual socialization may be accomplished not only by interacting with people, but also by encountering the writing of others. Thus research on connections between reading and writing also speaks to our knowledge of composing processes. That the writer must be able to read her own text while composing it, we know from such work as that of Sommers and of Flower and Hayes. But Anthony Petrosky and Mariolina Salvatori have suggested that the ability to read the works of others also affects a writer's composing process. Petrosky argues that the successful reading of a literary text is a "transaction" in which the reader must work to make the text meaningful in terms of her own experience, a view influenced by reader-response literary theory. Writing from these perceived correspondences between personal and literary experience helps student writers to elaborate their composing processes where improvement is most needed: in the linking of adequate illustrations to the generalizations that frame their arguments.[32] Similarly, Salvatori has argued that student writers develop intellectually more complex composing processes as they learn to link moments of reading comprehension into larger patterns of meaning and to relate these in turn to their own experience for comparison or critique.[33] In effect, for these researchers, the texts of others become collaborators in the students' composing processes, stimulating critical reflection on composing in much the same way as do peer tutors or the conventions of academic discourse itself, self-consciously viewed.

What We Know: Curricular Implications

We know that the act of composing through writing is a complex process. Although we are beginning to identify characteristic moments or stages in this process, we cannot say exactly what are the relationships of these stages one to another. We can say that we know such relationships exist, that is, the composing process is hierarchical, and also that they are not necessarily ordered serially, that is, the composing process is recursive. We cannot say that there is one composing process invariably successful for all writers, for all purposes. Rather, we know that composing processes vary both as the same writer attempts different kinds of discourse and as different writers attempt the same kind of discourse, and that such variations may be necessary to success in composing. The current state of our knowledge of composing permits the limited generalizations that successful composing results more often from attention to the thinking required by a piece of writing than to its adherence to standard conventions of grammar, spelling, and so on; and that successful composing results more often from a process that allows for rereading, rethinking, and rewriting than from one in which time limitations or other pressures force a rush to closure. I believe that we can also conclude—although this is perhaps more debatable—that "successful" composing results in writing that participates actively in the language-using practices of a particular community, without slavishly imitating them.

This limited understanding of composing processes nevertheless permits some broad recommendations on curriculum. First, learning to write requires writing. Students cannot be expected to master such complex processes if they only practice them two or three times in a school term, or without a teacher's guidance. It follows, then, if students are to be writing frequently and receiving frequent responses from the teacher, that classes in which writing is taught (whether in English or some other discipline) must be kept small. The teacher must be able to get to know the students in order to respond consistently to the thinking they develop in their writing. Moreover, if the emphasis in writing is to be on developing thinking, it follows both that the curriculum should be structured to encourage recursive composing processes and that institutionalized testing of student writing should not set a counteragenda for the writing class, such as mastering a certain number of features of formal grammar.

But in this small class in which students are writing and rewriting frequently, what should they be writing? What should the classroom activities be? These questions, it seems to me, are more open to debate. Some answers can be found in the Position Statement on teaching composition promulgated by the Commission on Composition of the National Council of Teachers of English.[34] This document suggests that students should be encouraged "to make full use of the many activities that comprise the act of writing," presumably including various pre-writing and editing techniques as well as the actual drafting of papers. The document also states that writing assignments should reflect the wide variety of purposes for writing, including expressive writing, writing across the curriculum, and writing that would have a place in "the world beyond school." The writing classroom, according to the document, should be organized as a workshop in which students write for each other, as well as for the teacher, and in which writing is used as "a mode of learning" rather than merely "reporting on what has been learned." To accomplish these ends, class size should not be larger than twenty students, and student writing should be the principal text. Tests should allow students "to demonstrate their writing ability in work aimed at various purposes" and should encourage the development of students' self-critical abilities.

The recommendations on class size, testing, and teaching a full range of composing activities, which would necessitate much attention to substantive revision, may be the most politically sensitive of the recommendations, since they at once ask the public for more money for education (more teachers to keep class size small) and deny the public the kind of testing in writing skills that it seems to desire. Yet current research suggests that it is essential to implement these recommendations if student writing is to improve.

It is not equally evident, however, that for good writing to ensue students must always write for each other and make their own writing the principal text. If the curricular goal is to foster mastery of academic discourse, such a classroom organization will not be very productive unless many of the students have already achieved the desired goal and so can teach the others. But it appears that today's students typically do not have enough prior knowledge of academic discourse conventions to help each other to mastery of them. More guidance from the teacher and more reading materials that illustrate and elucidate these practices may be needed (without, however, returning to the traditional, authoritarian classroom).

The Position Statement may be recommending what amounts to a personal-style classroom because the value of this approach is widely acknowledged among composition specialists, while the goal of mastering academic discourse is more problematic. The Commission also finesses the issue of academic discourse by taking a pluralistic view of the kinds of writing assignments it recommends, all the way from personal-style pedagogy's favored expressive writing to some kind of business or technical writing (for "the world beyond school"). In fact, there is no consensus on what kinds of writing students should be doing. Recent anthologies of college student writing, published as textbooks, suggest that personal-style essays still enjoy an edge; indeed, if they did not, there would be no point in publishing such anthologies.[35] But, as I suggested earlier, various kinds of academic writing are mounting a strong challenge. I believe, however, that it is salutary for teachers and students to discuss the problem of what constitutes "good" writing. Thus there is no way to escape the fact that course content choices, with the kinds of writing they valorize, will have political consequences with which we must deal.

Indeed, perhaps the most important conclusion to be drawn from this overview of research on composing is that research results alone not only should not dictate a curriculum, they cannot dictate it. Notice how persistently composition researchers have interpreted their results in light of personal-style pedagogical assumptions, whether about classroom organization or political agenda. But we could not do otherwise. Scholars writing up their research, like students struggling with their first essay assignments, must work within the language-using practices of a particular community, which are in turn shaped by its social, cultural, and political circumstances. The challenge is to be an active participant, to change the community in light of the values that make one's commitment to education professionally and personally meaningful.

NOTES

I would like to thank Bruce Herzberg and David Bartholomae for their careful reading of drafts of this essay.

1. D. Gordon Rohman, "Pre-Writing: The Stage of Discovery in the Writing Process," *College Composition and Communication* 26 (May 1965): 106–12.

2. Peter Elbow, *Writing Without Teachers* (New York: Oxford University Press, 1973).

3. Patricia Bizzell, "Cognition, Convention, and Certainty: What We Need to Know about Writing," this volume.

4. James Britton, T. Burgess, N. Martin, A. McLeod, and H. Rosen. *The Development of Writing Abilities (11–18)* (London: Macmillan Education, 1975).

5. Janet Emig, *The Composing Processes of Twelfth Graders* (Urbana, Ill.: National Council of Teachers of English, 1971).

6. Linda Flower and John R. Hayes, "A Cognitive Process Theory of Writing," *College Composition and Communication* 32 (December 1981): 365–87.

7. Sharon Pianko, "A Description of the Composing Processes of College Freshman Writers," *Research in the Teaching of English* 13 (February 1979): 5–22.

8. Sondra Perl, "Composing Processes of Unskilled College Writers," *Research in the Teaching of English* 13 (December 1979): 317–36.

9. Sondra Perl, "Understanding Composing," *College Composition and Communication* 31 (December 1980): 363–69.

10. Nancy Sommers, "Revision Strategies of Student Writers and Experienced Adult Writers," *College Composition and Communication* 31 (December 1980): 378–88.

11. Lil Brannon, Melinda Knight, and Vera Neverow-Turk, *Writers Writing* (Montclair, N.J.: Boynton/Cook, 1983).

12. Carol Berkenkotter and Donald Murray, "Decisions and the Planning Strategies of a Publishing Writer, and Response of a Laboratory Rat—or, Being Protocoled," *College Composition and Communication* 34 (May 1983): 156–72.

13. Mimi Schwartz, "Two Journeys Through the Writing Process," *College Composition and Communication* 34 (May 1983): 188–201.

14. Donald Graves, "An Examination of the Writing Processes of Seven-Year-Old Children," *Research in the Teaching of English* 9 (Winter 1975): 227–41; Linda Leonard Lamme and Nancye M. Childers, "Composing Processes of Three Young Children," *Research in the Teaching of English* 17 (February 1983): 31–50.

15. Glenda L. Bissex, *Gnys at Work: A Child Learns to Write and Read* (Cambridge, Mass.: Harvard University Press, 1980).

16. Donald H. Graves, *Writing: Teachers and Children at Work* (Portsmouth, N.H., and London: Heinemann Educational Books, 1983).

17. Shirley Brice Heath, *Ways With Words: Language, Life, and Work in Communities and Classrooms* (Cambridge: Cambridge University Press, 1983); David R. Olson, "The Language of Instruction: The Literate Bias of Schooling," in *Schooling and the Acquisition of Knowledge*, eds. Richard C. Anderson, Rand J. Spiro, and William E. Montague (Hillsdale, N.J.: Lawrence Erlbaum Associates, 1977), 65–90. For a dissenting view, see Margaret Donaldson, "Speech and Writing and Modes of Learning," in *Awakening to Literacy: The University of Victoria Symposium on Children's Response to a Literate Environment: Literacy before Schooling*, eds. Hillel Goelman, Antoinette A. Oberg, and Frank Smith (Exeter, N.H., and London: Heinemann Educational Books, 1984), 174–84.

18. Edward P.J. Corbett, *Classical Rhetoric for the Modern Student*, 2d edition (New York: Oxford University Press, 1971).

19. C. H. Knoblauch and Lil Brannon, *Rhetorical Traditions and the Teaching of Writing* (Montclair, N.J.: Boynton/Cook, 1984).

20. Ann E. Berthoff, *The Making of Meaning: Metaphors, Models and Maxims for Writing Teachers* (Montclair, N.J.: Boynton/Cook, 1981).

21. Mina P. Shaughnessy, *Errors and Expectations: A Guide for the Teacher of Basic Writing* (New York: Oxford University Press, 1977).

22. Nancy Martin, ed., *Writing Across the Curriculum: Pamphlets from the Schools Council/London Institute of Education W.A.C. Projects* (Montclair, N.J.: Boynton/Cook, 1984).

23. Toby Fulwiler, "The Personal Connection: Journal Writing Across the Curriculum," in *Language Connections: Writing and Reading Across the Curriculum*, eds. Toby Fulwiler and Art Young (Urbana, Ill.: National Council of Teachers of English, 1982), 15–32.

24. C. H. Knoblauch and Lil Brannon, "Writing as Learning Through the Curriculum," *College English* 45 (September 1983): 465–74.

25. Elaine Maimon, "Maps and Genres: Exploring Connections in the Arts and Sciences," in *Composition and Literature: Bridging the Gap*, ed. Winifred Bryan Horner (Chicago: University of Chicago Press, 1983), 110–25.

26. Mike Rose, "Rigid Rules, Inflexible Plans, and the Stifling of Language: A Cognitivist Analysis of Writer's Block," *College Composition and Communication* 31 (December 1980): 389–400.

27. David Bartholomae, "The Study of Error," *College Composition and Communication* 31 (October 1980): 253–69.

28. Walter J. Ong, "Literacy and Orality in Our Times," in *Composition and Literature: Bridging the Gap*, ed. Horner, 126–40.

29. James T. Farrell, "I.Q. and Standard English," *College Composition and Communication* 34 (December 1983): 470–84.

30. See rebuttals to Farrell by Karen Greenberg, Patrick Hartwell, Margaret Himley, and R. E. Stratton in *College Composition and Communication* 35 (December 1984): 455–77.

31. Kenneth A. Bruffee, "Collaborative Learning and the 'Conversation of Mankind,'" *College English* 46 (November 1984): 635–52.

32. Anthony R. Petrosky, "From Story to Essay: Reading and Writing," *College Composition and Communication* 33 (February 1982): 19–36.

33. Mariolina Salvatori, "Reading and Writing a Text: Correlations Between Reading and Writing," *College English* 45 (November 1983): 657–66.

34. Commission on Composition of the National Council of Teachers of English, "Teaching Composition: A Position Statement," (Urbana, Ill.: National Council of Teachers of English, 1983). I should note that as a member of the commission, I participated in the drafting of this document and endorsed its publication.

35. See, for example, William E. Coles, Jr., and James Vopat, eds., *What Makes Writing Good: A Multiperspective* (Lexington, Mass. and Toronto: D. C. Heath and Co., 1985); Nancy Sommers and Donald McQuade, eds., *Student Writers at Work: The Bedford Prizes* (New York: Bedford Books of St. Martin's Press, 1984).

Foundationalism and
Anti-Foundationalism in
Composition Studies

"Social" seemed to be the key word at the 1985 Conference on College Composition and Communication. Many of the papers presented there analyzed the discourse conventions that a particular social context inculcates in participating writers. Other papers sought to detail the pedagogy that would enable student writers to make informed choices among the discourses appropriate to different contexts, without enforcing any one choice as the best. The recurring references to the social indicated the great degree to which composition studies is coming under a truly rhetorical theory of language and knowledge, one that sees all language-using practices as determined by social consensus.

In taking this social turn, composition studies is moving in concert with recent developments in philosophy, literary theory, and the human sciences. In all of these disciplines, questions are being raised about any theory of language that claims to transcend social contexts—and about the educational authority of such a theory. In the terminology of philosopher Richard Rorty, "foundationalism" as a theory of language and knowledge is under attack everywhere, and "anti-foundationalism" is carrying the day.[1]

A persistent problem in composition studies, however, suggests that we have yet to confront the full implications of our anti-

Reprinted with permission from *Pre/Text* 7, nos. 1–2 (1986): 37–56.

foundationalism, no matter how much we talk about the social. This is the problem of defining academic discourse and deciding how—or whether—to teach it. It is a central problem not only for composition studies but for all the disciplines currently engaged in a rhetorical critique of their assumptions about language and knowledge, for, as Rorty has shown, academic discourse has been the principal means of establishing and disseminating foundationalist attitudes. Yet academic discourse cannot simply be set aside. We know this in composition studies because we are continually being urged, by administrators, colleagues, parents, and students, to teach academic discourse. The discourse persists because none of us knows any other way to talk about, that is to conduct, the intellectual work of the academy.

Many of us in composition studies have been seeking a way out of this dilemma, that is, seeking a way to teach academic discourse without fostering foundationalism. In general, these efforts focus on teaching students to analyze academic discourse as socially constituted. This procedure is supposed to undermine the foundationalist authority of the discourse, both by showing students that it has been made by human beings and can be changed by human beings, rather than owing its form and function to some transcendent source; and by encouraging students to believe that the same method they use to analyze and demystify academic discourse can be used on any other discourse they encounter. Students are thus supposed to be able to resist the dominance of the academic and all other discourses at will, simply by employing the analytic method that will reveal the discourse's social construction.

The danger inherent in this approach to academic discourse is that it places too much reliance on the method of analysis as a way of getting a critical distance on the discourse. Students who have mastered the method are thus presumed to be autonomous agents in the universe of discourse, capable of making individual choices about which discourses they will or will not participate in, solely on the basis of their own desires. Scholarly work urging this kind of pedagogy often concludes with a panegyric to the "empowerment of the individual student" or some such phrase, which actually means that at the point the students have mastered the method of analysis, we can leave them to their own devices. We need ask no more questions about how they will fare in a world of contesting discourses.

Stopping the argument at this point, I fear, means leaving out of consideration the cultural and political forces whereby one discourse asserts power over another; and consequently, the circumstances that make students from some social groups better able to "choose" certain discourses than are students from other social groups. What we are doing is turning our anti-foundationalism back into foundationalism, according to the terms of the current debate on the consequences of literary theory in which Stanley Fish has extended Rorty's analysis of the promulgation of foundationalism in academic discourse.[2] I would like to use this debate to shed light on the problem I am identifying in composition studies.

Let me begin by explaining the use I wish to make of Rorty's terminology. When I refer to "foundationalism," I wish to focus precisely on the beliefs that an absolute standard for the judgment of truth can be found, and that employment of this standard in evaluating knowledge enables the individual mind to transcend personal emotions, social circumstances, and larger historical conditions, and to reflect critically on them. Typically the foundationalist advocates a candidate for the position of absolute standard of truth, supporting this candidate with demonstrations of how its employment produces self-evidently "objective" (impersonal, asocial, ahistorical) judgments in some currently controversial area of knowledge. According to Rorty, this rhetorical strategy is what has kept philosophy in business all these years. The same might be said for the theoretical branch of any discipline, for these all are influenced by the foundationalism spreading outward from philosophy.

"Anti-foundationalism," I take it, includes the belief that an absolute standard for the judgment of truth can never be found, precisely because the individual mind can never transcend personal emotions, social circumstances, and historical conditions. Far from being adventitious, these are seen as totally constitutive of both the individual mind and any standard of judgment the mind can formulate. Hence any argument promoting a candidate for the position of absolute standard should be scrutinized to reveal the personal, social, and/or historical interests it serves, interests that are likely to center around the controversial area of knowledge the standard is supposed to adjudicate. The rhetorical strategy of revealing such interests has typically been employed by Marxists and other historically minded critics in all disciplines.

Literary theorists have recently been occupied with just such a project, revealing the interests that underly the critical theories that have been dominant. No new critical theory has emerged as paradigmatic, in place of those that have been displaced by such critique, but there is a tendency for the method of analysis itself to fill the authoritative role previously occupied by a foundationalist theory. Anti-foundationalist analysis of social context itself is presumed to liberate us from that context. Stanley Fish has argued that when this happens, anti-foundationalism slides back into foundationalism. The tendency, in other words, is to hope that by becoming aware of the personal, social, and historical circumstances that constitute our beliefs, we can achieve a critical distance on them and change our beliefs if we choose. In encouraging this hope, anti-foundationalism is setting up its method in place of the absolute standards of judgment it debunks. That is, it is promising that employment of the method will confer objective mental powers very similar to those that were supposed to be conferred by the absolute standards. This is what Fish calls the "theory hope" of anti-foundationalism.

I would now like to examine two instances of this anti-foundationalist "theory hope" in composition studies. One arises in the analysis of academic discourse informed by literacy theory, which argues that mastery of academic discourse confers objective mental powers. A second instance is the analysis of academic discourse informed by work in writing across the curriculum, which argues that the study of the concept of discourse confers objective mental powers. Both of these scholarly efforts claim to be anti-foundationalist in their emphasis on the social nature of language and knowledge. But they ultimately fall back into foundationalism in their promise of objective mental powers to those who accept their analysis. I wish to critique these efforts both because they promise these powers and also because they use this promise to screen out of consideration the personal, social, and historical interests that center on the teaching of academic discourse.

II

I would like to look first at the analysis of academic discourse in terms of literacy theory. In general, literacy theory assumes that decisive changes occur when individuals and societies acquire literacy. Social scientists who study literacy, such as Deborah Tannen, Shirley Brice Heath, Sylvia Scribner, and Michael Cole, tend to focus on changes that occur within individuals, changes in the ways they think and interact with the world, but also to consider these cognitive changes as conditioned by the social contexts in which literacy is used.[3] In contrast, humanist scholars who study literacy, such as classical philologist Eric Havelock and literary critic Walter Ong, tend to focus on the changes that occur within discourse—stylistic changes—and to infer from the discourse the cognitive and cultural changes that can be expected to accompany it.[4] This is what Ross Winterowd has termed the "literalist" approach to literacy.[5]

Perhaps because they begin at a further remove from the social than do social scientists who study literacy, humanist literacy theorists have a greater tendency to dichotomize nonliterate and literate states of being, rather than to describe a "continuum of orality and literacy" (Tannen) or "multiple literacies" (Scribner and Cole). The humanists also have a greater tendency to reify the two states into all-embracing conceptual universes of orality and literacy (Ong), mind-sets that totally determine cognitive and cultural activities. This humanist literacy theory has been the most influential version in composition studies, not too surprising when one considers that its literary antecedents are closer to our own disciplinary roots than are the social sciences.

What Thomas J. Farrell and other composition scholars have done with humanist literacy theory is to overlay its characterization of orality and literacy on, respectively, the discourse of beginning student writers and mature academic discourse.[6] Farrell contends that like oral discourse, the written discourse of beginners is agonistic, paratactic, episodic, and stocked with evidence from personal experience or from maxims. In contrast, like literate discourse, academic discourse is impersonal, hypotactic, linear, and stocked with evidence from experimental data or from bibliographic research. Farrell concludes that if oral discourse equals beginners' discourse, and literate discourse equals academic discourse, then when beginners master academic discourse we can expect them to experience the same cognitive changes that humanist literacy theory attributes to the move from orality to literacy.

Like literacy theorists, Farrell is careful not to valorize literacy over orality in any absolute sense, but rather, to argue that we must look at the uses of discourse in particular social contexts. If our pedagogical goal is to help students survive in the academic context, then we must see to it that they master academic discourse. Farrell defends this goal on grounds that the mastery of academic discourse confers advantages both in the kind of cognition it makes possible and in the practical opportunities it affords (for success in school, the professions, etc.).

Farrell's argument is anti-foundationalist in its emphasis on the constitutive power of discourse. He assumes that all students are born with basically the same potential for academic work. The systematic poor performance of certain groups, then, must be due to some difference created by their discourse. It follows that if these groups can be taught to use another discourse, their thinking, their very constitution as individuals will change. Teach them academic discourse, and they will become capable of academic thought. This is an unexceptionably anti-foundationalist position, however much one may take exception to specific elements in Farrell's pedagogical program.

Farrell contradicts this implicit acknowledgement of the constitutive power of discourse, however, in his foundationalist assumption that mastery of academic discourse confers objective mental powers. If we accept Rorty's analysis, then although masters of academic discourse believe that they possess objective mental powers, they cannot in fact possess them. Yet in Farrell's description of academic discourse, foundationalist values of impersonality, "logical" organization, and empirical evidence are put forward as desiderata. If students master academic discourse, they will then be capable of detached analysis of experience. It seems that for Farrell, discourse is constitutive of individuality only until one masters academic discourse; such mastery then enables one to rise above all discourses through analysis—that is, through the use of objective mental powers.

For Farrell, then, academic discourse is cognitively superior to all other discourses precisely in its ability to confer the power to analyze, and so to escape, all other discourses. This is an instance of Fish's anti-foundationalist "theory hope." That Farrell is ultimately heading for such a position may be anticipated by his silent conflation of literate discourse and academic discourse. Here he is simply following his sources in humanist literacy theory. We know from social science research that some literate discourse is not characterized by hypotaxis, linearity, and so on. But academic discourse is so characterized; these are the characteristics of foundationalism that Rorty situates in the academy. If humanist literacy theorists are describing a discourse with these characteristics, then, it must be academic discourse they are describing, and not literate discourse in general.

Pretending that this local discourse, the academic, is the only literate discourse is foundationalist in that it tends to put the authority of academic discourse above debate, to set it up as an absolute standard of cognition. If we do not know that there are other literacies in society, then we cannot ask why this particular literacy, as opposed to the others, has gained ascendance in the academy. If we do not ask this question, then we also screen out questions about the personal connections students have to other discourses, the social contexts in which other discourses are appropriate, and the historical conditions that give cultural powers to some discourses and deny it to others. In short, we screen out precisely the kinds of question that anti-foundationalism is moved to ask.

Moreover, leaving out anti-foundationalist questions leads to the assumption that students are autonomous with respect to the social uses of the discourse—as if they could choose to enter into the contexts in which the discourse is dominant, or make other choices. On the contrary, an anti-foundationalist understanding of discourse would see the student's way of thinking and interacting with the world, the student's very self, as fundamentally altered by participation in any new discourse. These will not be changes the student can erase at will. Also, the ability to participate in a new discourse will change the student's relationship with other discourses—particularly in the case of academic discourse. Because academic discourse is identified with social power, to show familiarity with it can mean being completely alienated from some other, socially disenfranchised discourses. Thus the student's new ability to participate in academic discourse will condition his or her opportunities to participate in other discourses, and make some life paths more attractive than others. This constraining effect of the mastery of academic discourse is not acknowledged by humanist literacy theorists.

III

The second kind of analysis of academic discourse that I want to discuss is emerging from work in writing across the curriculum. Composition scholars in this area have assumed, like those who study literacy theory, that it is desirable for students to master academic discourse. The reason, however, is not to be found in characteristics of the discourse itself. Rather, mastery is advocated merely because academic discourse is the discourse of the community in which teachers and students find themselves. If students are to participate productively in this community, they must master the discourse, whatever it may be.

Mina Shaughnessy was among the first to call for a "taxonomy" of academic discourse, and I have attempted to answer this call in some of my own work.[7] But the problems that arise when humanist literacy theory attempts to find an invariant set of characteristics for literate discourse suggest that it is less important to find such a set if the characteristics are not expected to confer any great cognitive or social benefits in and of themselves. That is, even if we could produce Shaughnessy's taxonomy, we should not assume that we could induce mastery of academic discourse simply by teaching the characteristics. What is needed is more in-depth study of the social contexts in which academic discourse is used. Such study would focus more on the discourses peculiar to individual academic disciplines than on some overarching or generic academic discourse, mainly because the disciplinary discourse community would be easier to delineate for study than the larger academic community.

Fortunately, much writing-across-the-curriculum work has pursued such study, focusing on the discourse of particular academic disciplines, such as the natural sciences; and on particular discourse media, such as the class journal, that may be prevalent across disciplines even if there is no cross-disciplinary academic discourse.[8] This willingness to look at what is there in the academic discourse community, to study particulars, has made scholarship in writing across the curriculum curiously like some social science research in literacy. Writing-across-the-curriculum scholarship often reads like an ethnography of the academic discourse community.

This scholarship tends to draw more on literary theory than on the human sciences for its explanatory concepts, however, and to maintain a largely textual focus, which is not surprising in view of the fact that most of the scholars were originally trained in English studies. Such work is valuable for the hints it gives of what the unique contributions of humanist scholars might be to discourse analysis, if not the reification of an Ong or Havelock. For example, Elaine Maimon has argued that the analysis of academic discourse should be informed by the literary-critical concept of genre. Academic discourse media, such as the laboratory report in the natural sciences, can be analyzed and classified in the same way as types of poems. The outcome of such study should be, not merely a catalogue of the parts of different academic discourse media, but an enlarged concept of generic variability, going beyond the literary canon in its applicability to all discourse.[9] More work is needed here before a humanist discourse theory is clearly delineated.

Other scholars in writing across the curriculum agree with Maimon that the most important thing for students to master is not necessarily academic discourse itself, but rather the concept of discourse, the idea that language use in any social context is formed into a regular discourse by the collaborative efforts of the people who have worked and are working in the discourse. Scholars disagree, however, on how this concept of discourse may best be taught. Whereas Maimon tends to draw most of her illustrations from academic discourse, Toby Fulwiler, C. H. Knoblauch and Lil Brannon, among others, are more willing to let students supply their own illustrations from whatever discourses are familiar to them.[10] This approach is aimed at stressing the collaborative nature of discourse, as students must make their examples intelligible to one another.

All this work in writing across the curriculum is anti-foundationalist in its emphasis on the social generation of academic discourse. Academic discourse is not presumed to have any advantages that guarantee its privileged position, other than the social antecedents that led to its dominance. Moreover, academic discourse is not presumed to be fixed in some final form, but rather to be reshaped constantly as people use it to do intellectual work together. Academic discourse is thus not presumed to be an authoritarian set of rules to which students must submit, but a changing practice that they have the chance of influencing even as it influences them. And because of all this emphasis on the social nature of the discourse, anti-foundationalist kinds of questions about personal, social and historical connections between academic and other discourses are quite congenial to writing-across-the-curriculum work.

The danger of Fish's anti-foundationalist "theory hope" arises, however, to the extent that we assume that understanding the concept of discourse will enable students to analyze any discourse they encounter, so they can participate in it or escape its influence, as they choose. In other words, we must be wary of assuming that the method of analysis conveys the same objective mental powers the foundationalist derives from an absolute standard of judgment.

There is, perhaps, less danger here than in the literacy work that we will regard the students' choices among discourses as none of our business, once they have mastered the academic discourse. Writing-across-the-curriculum work focuses precisely on the students' degree of familiarity with disciplinary discourses, as witness, for example, David Bartholomae's work on the "interlanguages" that result while students are inventing their own understanding of the university community.[11] Hence we notice immediately how students differ in this regard, and how these differences may be traced to the other, non-academic discourses with which they are familiar. Moreover, since students' familiarity with academic discourse can be expected to change as they move through school, we notice differences in these changes, again related to students' other discourse resources. That is, we are studying the way the whole process of schooling is shaped by differences between academic discourse and the other discourses the students bring to the academy.

But often, writing-across-the-curriculum scholars respond to these differences by setting up simple oppositions between academic discourse and other discourses. Mastery of the socially privileged academic discourse may indeed threaten students with cultural assimilation and the loss of their native discourses. Some scholars hope to combat this threat by allowing the students' other discourses to speak beside or within academic discourse, or even to undermine it. An important motive of the pedagogy that encourages collaborative student work is to foster such a plurality of discourses.

For example, Brannon and Knoblauch would have students shape their writing through dialogue with classmates, weighing their own interests against what engages their classmates. In theory, such a pedagogy does not rule out academic discourse any more than any other discourse, if a student wishes to use it and can get his or her classmates to understand it. In practice, however, since most college students are not familiar with academic discourse, their writing is more likely to employ the non-academic discourses with which the students are familiar. Thus such a class will generate much writing that does not participate in academic discourse. Brannon and Knoblauch are well aware that this is the likely outcome of the collaborative course they recommend; this outcome is what is supposed to save the students from simple assimilation into the academic discourse community.

Moreover, students are supposed to be saved from assimilation not only because the class allows them to use their own discourses within the academy, but also because, through the interpersonal dynamic of the collaborative classroom, it teaches them something about the nature of discourse itself. A student is constrained from writing in a discourse no one else in the class knows because the collaborative classroom situation requires that each student enable the others to understand his or her work. From this experience the student learns that no matter how universally human the subject of his or her paper seems, the student's thoughts and feelings about this subject will not be conveyed unless the discourse is accessible to the readers. Thus the student learns that discourse itself is a collaborative project, that effective writing is always created by negotiation between the exigencies of writer, reader, and subject addressed. This understanding of discourse presumably saves the student from assimilation because he or she can use it to analyze any other discourse he or she encounters, including the academic. In other words—once again—a method of analysis confers foundationalist objective mental powers, this time through the opposition of academic and non-academic discourses.

As Stanley Fish has pointed out in a critique of the work of Peter Elbow, the collaborative classroom also verges into foundationalism in its concept of individuality.[12] Elbow assumes that the ability to analyze discourses entails not just the ability to discuss stylistic choices but also the ability to question the feelings and thoughts that are realized in the discourse. It is unexceptionably anti-foundationalist to assume that participation in a discourse shapes feelings and thoughts as well as style—indeed, this is what it means to say that we as individuals are constituted by our discourse. But where Elbow goes wrong, according to Fish, is in his belief that the collaborative analytical method can liberate students from discourse's constitutive power—that when students are allowed to speak for themselves, in a pluralistic, non-authoritarian classroom, each will learn to examine his or her beliefs in light of those advanced by others. Elbow assumes that students are at bottom selves independent from what those selves happen to believe at the moment—so that under pressure from the group, an individual self can step away from a belief, examine it, and change it. This is another version of foundationalist objective mental powers.

To review, then: much writing-across-the-curriculum work seeks to give students control over academic discourse by teaching them how to analyze any discourse. Some of this work adopts a pedagogy that focuses primarily on examples of academic discourse to illustrate the concept of discourse. This pedagogy aims forthrightly at mastery of academic discourse as a desirable goal. Other work adopts a pedagogy that focuses primarily on examples of non-academic discourses, discourses chosen by the students themselves, seeking to illustrate the concept of discourse through the opposition of academic and non-academic discourses. This pedagogy admits mastery of academic discourse as a desirable, but deferrable, goal. In both cases, the work appears anti-foundationalist in its emphasis on the constitutive power of discourse. In both cases, however, the work slides into foundationalism in its hope that an understanding of the concept of discourse, however acquired, can somehow liberate students from the constitutive power of the discourses in which they participate.

British work in writing across the curriculum makes an instructive comparison here, because it is much more likely to acknowledge the function of social class in determining who is familiar with what discourse. The conflict between students' discourses and academic discourse is seen as enforced by social and historical elements that encompass the academic setting. The conflict is thus not imagined as susceptible of resolution via mastery of the ability to analyze discourse, an academic ability.

The British pedagogical approach, too, sets up oppositions between academic and non-academic discourses, favoring the latter by, for example, allowing students to submit as "research papers" transcripts of interviews with relatives about their family history along with the students' own reflections about what learning this history has meant to them. Peter Medway shows, however, that by accepting such work he is not really granting legitimacy within the academy to non-academic discourses; nowhere else but in his classroom is such work accepted.[13] Rather he is just allowing students to learn something in the terms of their own, social-class-based discourse. Very often, one thing they learn is that they don't want to have anything to do with academic discourse. They leave school. Thus, indeed, they escape the threat of assimilation. But also, insofar as Medway was able to determine by keeping in touch with some of his students after they left, they escape any possibility of changing their disenfranchised social status. This leaves British writing-across-the-curriculum work confronting the necessity for a larger, political resolution of the conflict among discourses, a necessity that the American work is able to avoid through a foundationalist faith in individual objective mental powers.

IV

Fish concludes his critique of anti-foundationalism by arguing that anti-foundationalist "theory hope" is unavoidable. No matter what our theory, we will talk as if it conferred objective mental powers. Even if we do not believe that our theory grants access to standards of judgment that are transcendent and absolute, we still must believe that our theory informs a method for making judgments that confers something like objective mental powers. We must act as if we believe that our theory enables us to organize and evaluate experience. Indeed, we could not act at all if we did not believe this. If we are trying to be anti-foundationalist, of course, we will argue that we believe objective mental powers are impossible and the social context cannot be escaped. Fish shares this anti-foundationalist belief but says that it doesn't make any difference in our discourse because we will still inevitably talk as if we have objective mental powers that enable us to analyze the social context.

I read this as Fish's version of the argument that academic discourse cannot be simply set aside, because it is the only way we know how to talk about, that is to perform, academic intellectual work. Thus no theory can achieve transcendence of, and explanatory power over, the discourse in which it is framed. Any academic theory, in literary criticism or any other discipline, will inevitably partake of at least some of the characteristics of foundationalism because these characteristics are those of the academic discourse in which the theory is framed, tested, and established.

Fish's analysis at first seems to reify academic discourse into an all-embracing, totally determining mental universe, in much the same way that humanist literacy theorists treat their versions of orality and literacy. If academic discourse is so monolithic, then Fish's analysis seems to lead to the conclusion that cultural assimilation is inevitable for all who master it. Participation in academic discourse transforms a person into a clone of all the other participants in the discourse. A person cannot attempt to change academic discourse from within by reference either to some empirical reality or to some objective method of analysis, because any reference incorporated into academic discourse will inevitably be transformed into terms acceptable to the discourse. It seems to be impossible to change the discourse.

Yet we know that change does occur in academic disciplines, not only in the objects of study but also in the methods and theoretical assumptions that direct study. How does such change occur, if we cannot attribute it to the self-evident persuasive power of transcendent theory or objective method? This is an urgent question for scholars in all the disciplines currently undergoing an anti-foundationalist critique. Scholars whose anti-foundationalism persuades them that change is needed in their disciplines' foundationalist assumptions find, if they accept Fish's argument, that their anti-foundationalism would also seem to suggest that change is impossible. The turn to the "social" in these disciplines is motivated by an attempt to answer the question of how change occurs. Thomas Kuhn's work has been such an important catalyst in this turn because Kuhn explains change in the sciences—supposedly the most empirical and methodologically rigorous of disciplines—as occurring rhetorically.[14]

Fish and Rorty both subscribe to Kuhn's version of how change occurs; Fish's argument does not after all compel such a totalizing conclusion as first appears.[15] Kuhn, I take it, is no idealist. He sees an academic discipline as a discourse community leading an ongoing life in interaction with a changing material world. There is an external reality, in other words, that impinges on the work of the community. But this reality does not erupt directly into the community; it can only be perceived in terms of the community's discourse. Hence what the community "knows" is never some truth external to its own discourse; it knows only what it can frame, test, and establish in its discourse.

Change in the discourse begins when change in the material world impinges more frequently or urgently than before. Such change in the material world might be, for example, change in the capabilities of scientific instruments, the personal motives of researchers, the institutional structure of the discipline, or the form of government in the society that encompasses the academy. These impinging changes in the material world, however, must first find some embodiment in the existing discourse before they can affect it. Kuhn's notion of rhetorical changes is precisely that process whereby the embodiment in the community's discourse of such material changes is debated. Scholars gradually work out a way of talking about these new elements in their work. The way that most scholars find persuasive and useful becomes incorporated into the discourse of the community—in other words, the discourse changes to include it. Scholars who cannot accept these changes find themselves excluded from the discourse.

Kuhn, Fish, and Rorty disagree about the degree to which disciplinary discourse is open to change. Kuhn tends to dichotomize discourse into the "normal," in which no change is contemplated, and the "revolutionary," in which the process of change is consciously experienced by the community. Kuhn suggests that the overwhelming majority of discourse in the academy is "normal"—indeed, that it must be if any intellectual work is to be accomplished. Scholars cannot be forever debating over their objects of study, methods, assumptions, etc. It follows for Kuhn that in normal discourse, change is actively discouraged. The magnitude of the disjunction between disciplinary discourse and external reality that is needed to induce change, for Kuhn, is indicated by his choice of the political metaphor of revolution to describe it. Such changes occur only rarely.

Both Fish and Rorty, it seems to me, are more alive than is Kuhn to the political implications of his metaphor. Hence both Fish and Rorty see normal discourse as less monolithic. Fish and Rorty compare an academic discipline to the society at large. There is an established political order—the normal discourse—but always at the same time, alternative orders—the revolutionary discourse—subversive to varying degrees of the established order. In society, subversive orders continue to speak in spite of the established order's attempts to suppress them. Indeed, the act of suppression becomes creative of subversive orders as these are granted recognition by the very act of suppression, and as they define themselves in response to this suppression. Similarly in academic discourse, various revolutionary discourses are always calling for a hearing even when normal discourse holds sway. A vigorous attempt to suppress a revolutionary discourse is often a good sign that this discourse is about to be taken seriously as a candidate for incorporation into a new normal discourse. For Fish and Rorty, then, not only is change always more immanent in academic discourse than it is for Kuhn, but also the process of change itself is more political. There are more opportunities for groups of scholars to challenge the dominance of the normal discourse, but such a challenge can only be mounted through group work.

Fish and Rorty both call, in effect, for anti-foundationalists to redirect their energies: stop attacking foundationalism. According to

Rorty, the project of sniffing out foundationalist assumptions in every area of academic work only gives spurious life to these assumptions, which have been effectively discredited.[16] According to Fish, we can never entirely extirpate them anyway—to believe we can do so is to perpetuate a foundationalist assumption! Rather, we should acknowledge the implicit pluralism of academic discourse, the continual presence within it of both normal and revolutionary strands. Then our task as anti-foundationalists should be to contribute to this pluralism, to increase the scope of academic discourse. Fish and Rorty suggest that this may be accomplished by foregrounding the personal, social, and historical interests in academic discourse, which are ruled out by foundationalism. Clifford Geertz, who has noted a similar pluralism as the distinguishing feature of "the way we think now" in the academy, suggests that a similar purpose of enlarging the discourse may be served by undertaking the ethnographic study of the academic discourse community itself.[17]

Given these developments in the intellectual history of our times, it is not surprising that theorists in both literary criticism and composition studies are attempting to reclaim rhetoric as their master discipline. Rhetoric is the study of the personal, social, and historical elements in human discourse—how to recognize them, interpret them, and act on them, in terms both of situational context and of verbal style. This is the kind of study one has to perform in order to effect persuasion, the traditional end of rhetoric. As the academy settles into the new directions indicated by our social turn, the disciplines of letters—in which we might include philosophy, theology, history, speech communication, and the other languages, as well as the branches of English studies—will study what the social turn means for all disciplines' understanding of discourse itself. This project sorts well with the classical injunction that the rhetorician above all needs broadly humanistic learning, needs to be a "cultured" person, in order to perform the kinds of analyses that lead to identifying the means of persuasion.

What does this all finally mean for the pedagogical question with which I began, namely, how or whether to teach academic discourse? For one thing, it means that all students must master academic discourse if they are to participate in the academic community. Moreover, I think it means that we cannot demystify academic discourse for students, cannot teach them to analyze it, until they already understand something about it from trying to use it in imitation of experienced practitioners, such as their professors. In other words, mastery of academic discourse must begin with socialization to the community's ways, in the same way that one enters any cultural group. One must first "go native," as Kuhn puts it in describing adjustment to a new disciplinary discourse. We must not assume that our analytic method can enable students to skip this step.

As students move on through school, they become capable of applying rhetorical analysis to the knowledge of discourse they have already gained. This sequence—acquiring knowledge and then acquiring a method to analyze and evaluate this knowledge—is the sequence that is typically followed in all academic disciplines. There may be good reason for preserving it even after we abandon the foundationalist assumptions about the nature of knowledge that used to sanction it. That is, we no longer believe that the knowledge actually does exist in some way prior to the discourse, with its embedded theoretical and methodological assumptions. But precisely because we believe that the discourse constitutes the knowledge, we can argue that beginning one's initiation into the discipline with some acquaintance with its knowledge is a good route to familiarity with its discourse conventions and assumptions.

But what provision can we find in this pedagogy for the students whose initial contact with academic discourse seems to present no choices other than deracination from a home discourse community or expulsion from the academic community? The short answer to this question is that scholars must simply acknowledge political activity as a professional responsibility. This political activity may focus on the larger social arena in which, for example, government funding for education is discussed. But it may also focus within a particular university, on questions such as what high schools receive heavy recruiting attention, what areas of concentration are available within majors, what faculty attitudes are communicated to students about academic support services, and so on.

Some forms of political activity, particularly on campus, have traditionally been regarded as appropriate professional concerns— but as essentially secondary ones. Any academic who makes such concerns a first priority is likely to be regarded as second-rate. The assumption is that this person must not be engaged in any worthwhile scholarly work, or he or she would not have the time for such peripheral matters. I am calling for a change in the way we weight such activities in evaluating professional competence. For example, a program that trains graduate students to teach writing should be treated as equal in professional importance to published scholarship, to be evaluated on its own merits; there are good programs, and bad books. Such a change in the definition of professional competence would, I think, constitute an enlarging of the scope of academic discourse, such as Fish and Rorty call for. Political activity that changes the nature of the discourse and the institutions whereby the discourse is preserved and promulgated will do more for social justice in educational opportunity, I think, than simply allowing alternative orders or revolutionary discourses to speak in isolated classrooms.

The greatest obstacle to my recommendation, I believe, is the enduring anti-intellectualism of the American academic. I do not refer to attitudes that are expressed within the disciplines themselves. We American academics are anti-intellectual precisely in our reluctance to emerge from our respective disciplines, to act as intellectuals in the larger community of the whole university and the whole society. So many academics prefer to call themselves poets or farmers or anything that can be presumed to be divorced from academic ratiocination. The traditional devaluing of political activity springs from a reluctance to display academic thinking in any way outside the academy. But I will not try to analyze American anti-intellectualism now. I simply say that we must overcome this particular version of bad faith if we are to acknowledge the full implictions of the social turn in the humanities, and to help students from a culturally diverse and far from classless society enter the academic discourse community. We must stop seeking a theory that would enable us to screen out these concerns. Let us embrace rhetoric.

NOTES

1. Richard Rorty, *Philosophy and the Mirror of Nature* (Princeton, 1979).
2. Stanley Fish, "Consequences," *Critical Inquiry* 11 (March 1985): 433–58.

3. Shirley Brice Heath, *Ways with Words: Language, Life and Work in Communities and Classrooms* (Cambridge, Great Britain, 1983); Sylvia Scribner and Michael Cole, *The Psychology of Literacy* (Cambridge, Massachusetts, 1981); Deborah Tannen, "The Oral/Literate Continuum of Discourse," in *Spoken and Written Language: Exploring Orality and Literacy,* èd. Deborah Tannen (Norwood, N.J., 1982).

4. Eric Havelock, *The Literate Revolution in Greece and Its Cultural Consequences* (Princeton, 1982); Walter J. Ong, S.J., *Orality and Literacy: The Technologizing of the Word* (New York, 1982).

5. Ross Winterowd, "The Politics of Meaning: Scientism, Literarism, and the New Humanism," *Written Communication* 2 (July 1985): 269–92.

6. Thomas J. Farrell, "I.Q. and Standard English," *College Composition and Communication* 34 (December 1983): 470–84; see also Frank J. D'Angelo, "Luria on Literacy: The Cognitive Consequences of Reading and Writing," in *Literacy as a Human Problem,* ed. James C. Raymond (University, Alabama, 1982).

7. Mina Shaughnessy, "Some Needed Research on Writing," *College Composition and Communication* 28 (December 1977): 317–21; Patricia Bizzell, "College Composition: Initiation Into the Academic Discourse Community," this volume.

8. Toby Fulwiler and Art Young, eds., *Language Connections: Writing and Reading Across the Curriculum* (Urbana, Ill., 1982); Charles Bazerman, "The Writing of Scientific Non-Fiction," *Pre/Text* 5 (Spring 1984): 39–74.

9. Elaine Maimon, "Maps and Genres," in *Composition and Literature: Bridging the Gap,* ed. Winifred Bryan Horner (Chicago, 1983).

10. C. H. Knoblauch and Lil Brannon, *Rhetorical Traditions and the Teaching of Writing* (Montclair, New Jersey, 1984).

11. David Bartholomae, "Inventing the University," in *When a Writer Can't Write: Studies in Writer's Block and Other Composing Process Problems,* ed. Mike Rose (New York, 1985).

12. Peter Elbow, *Writing Without Teachers* (New York, 1973); Stanley Fish, "Remarks" (paper, Yale Conference on Collaborative Learning, 1984).

13. Peter Medway, *Finding a Language: Autonomy and Learning in School* (London, 1980).

14. Thomas Kuhn, *The Structure of Scientific Revolutions,* 2d edition, enlarged (Chicago, 1970).

15. Richard Rorty, "Philosophy Without Principles," *Critical Inquiry* 11 (March 1985): 459–65.

16. Richard Rorty, "Deconstruction and Circumvention," *Critical Inquiry* 11 (September 1984): 1–23.

17. Clifford Geertz, "The Way We Think Now: Toward an Ethnography of Modern Thought," in *Local Knowledge: Further Essays in Interpretive Anthropology* (New York, 1983).

What Is a Discourse Community?

The concept of "discourse community," though now widely used in composition studies, has not been defined authoritatively—that is, in such a way as to win assent from all composition researchers and scholars of rhetoric. In the absence of consensus, let me offer a tentative definition: a "discourse community" is a group of people who share certain language-using practices. These practices can be seen as conventionalized in two ways. Stylistic conventions regulate social interactions both within the group and in its dealings with outsiders; to this extent "discourse community" borrows from the sociolinguistic concept of "speech community." Also, canonical knowledge regulates the world views of group members, how they interpret experience; to this extent "discourse community" borrows from the literary-critical concept of "interpretive community." The key term "discourse" suggests a community bound together primarily by its uses of language, although bound perhaps by other ties as well, geographical, socioeconomic, ethnic, professional, and so on.

This tentative definition of "discourse community" will not, I suspect, provide an infallible test for determining whether a given social group constitutes a discourse community. The recent work of John Swales (1987), which I will discuss below, can aid us here in emphasizing the crucial function of a collective project in unifying the group, some work in the world its members could not accomplish on their own. But we need to go further toward acknowledging that discourse community membership implicates people in *interpretive* activities.

Dealing with the interpretive world views fostered by discourse communities also creates problems for the field of composition studies itself, considered as a discourse community. For one thing, we are struggling to define legitimate professional activity for participants in our field—to establish the stylistic conventions and canonical knowledge appropriate to a composition studies discourse community. For another, we are struggling to develop pedagogies that can initiate undergraduates into academic discourse, and graduate students into the disciplinary discourse of our field, without too forcibly imposing upon them academic and disciplinary world views.

Concerning the first of these problems, Bruce Herzberg (1986) has observed that although the concept of "discourse community" is not clearly defined, it is the "center of a set of ideas" including: "that language use in a group is a form of social behavior, that discourse is a means of maintaining and extending the group's knowledge and of initiating newcomers, and that discourse is epistemic or constitutive of the group's knowledge" (1). Not everyone using the concept of "discourse community" assents to all of these ideas. Each scholar tends to favor the elements that seem to lead composition studies in the direction he or she wants the field to go. The idea that language use is social behavior has been used to point to the social contexts of writing. Scholars who favor this reading of the concept of "discourse community" seek to ally composition studies with the social sciences. Attention to the way discourse confers authority on knowledge and its possessors has prompted study of discourse conventions, the "rules of the game" for winning authority. Studying these rules requires ideologically informed stylistic analysis (of the sort performed in defining "interpretive communities," for example). Hence this focus reaffirms the ties between composition studies and literary criticism. Alternately, to look at discourse as epistemic is to examine the role of rhetoric in canon formation, interpreting "canon" in the broadest postmodern sense to refer to all kinds of signifying "texts." Put another way, the question is: "What can we know?" This is essentially a philosophical concern. Hence efforts to establish an authoritative definition of "discourse community" can be understood as a struggle over whether the disciplinary definition of composition studies will most closely approach the social sciences, literary studies, or philosophy.

This struggle makes it difficult for us to attend to the changes in thinking we are inducing in graduate student initiates into the composition studies discourse community. Such changes can be profound and painful. We would, I suspect, prefer to believe that our discourse community does not entail a world view. Similarly, we would prefer to believe that our efforts to initiate undergraduates into the academic discourse community are without prejudice to whatever world views they bring with them.

The overarching methodological issue here is precisely how to study a discourse community's power to constitute world view. We may perhaps begin to get at this element of the "discourse community" concept by studying the value contradictions that arise when discourse communities overlap. Such study could profitably unite composition researchers of a social-science orientation and rhetoric scholars of a literary-critical or philosophical bent, provided all are willing to attempt ideological self-consciousness.

Such an "interdisciplinary" project within a discipline of composition studies could not be undertaken in hopes of transcending world views, however. The problems I have noted above probably cannot be solved, but they can be addressed. If we come to seek critical self-consciousness about the ideologies of our own and other discourse communities, we must also be careful not to let the ambiguous word "critical" cover over an important argument. When "critical" is used in composition studies, as in the term "critical thinking" for example, it seems to mean something like "analytic" or "self-conscious in an academic, self-questioning way." The word carries no explicit political meaning, yet it evokes political connotations, both through the everyday sense of "critical" as meaning "attacking something," and through the use in composition studies of the term "critical consciousness," which means using literacy education to foster Christian Marxist political ends, as its originator Paulo Freire (1968) has defined it. Hence we may say that we are encouraging our students to be "critical" of language-using practices, without specifying any political agenda for such criticism, and yet with hope that the word's political undertones will prevent our pedagogy from being taken as one of indoctrination. The argument about whether education can be "critical" in the Marxist sense needs, on the contrary, to be aired.

Working with a tentative definition of "discourse community" as a group sharing language-using practices, I will look at Swales's important emphasis on the group's project orientation. With the help of Carol Berkenkotter and her colleagues (1987), and of Bruce Herzberg I will consider how the limitation of Swales's work—the difficulty of attending to discourse communities' world views—also poses problems for composition studies as we train our graduate students for our discourse community and initiate undergraduates into the larger academic discourse community. With the help of literary critic Jane Tompkins (1986), I will suggest that attending to contradictions may, if not solve our problems, at least give us a way of "doing composition studies" that is theoretically satisfying and politically responsible in the face of pluralism both among scholarly orientations within our field, and among interpretive world views of students entering the academy.

Discourse Community as Project Site

In his recent work the applied linguist John Swales seeks to determine whether a given social group is a discourse community by testing the group against six criteria. These criteria emphasize that for Swales, a discourse community is a social group using language to accomplish work in the world—the context of appropriate social behavior provides cues for how best to employ the discourse conventions to accomplish this work.

Swales suggests that discourse communities vary in the degree to which they demand a major lifetime commitment to their work, personal involvement or care for the work, and rigid adherence to discourse conventions. But, he says, any discourse community should meet the following six criteria:

1. There must be some common, public "goal" the group seeks to accomplish, some work the participants are trying to perform together.
2. There must be some discursive "forum" accessible to all participants; oral, visual, and or/print media may be involved.
3. The group must use its forum to work toward its goal by "providing information and feedback."

4. The group develops expectations for how productive exchanges of information should proceed, which is to say that the group shares discourse conventions or "genres."

5. The group's discourse not only is thus specialized, but exhibits a tendency to become increasingly specialized; there is "an inbuilt dynamic towards an increasingly shared and specialized terminology."

6. There must be a "critical mass" of experts in the group at any given time: people who are intimately familiar with the specialized genres with which the group seeks to accomplish its goals and who thus can initiate novices. The "survival of the community depends on a reasonable ratio between experts and novices" (2–3; I have quoted key terms and phrases).

Thus we see that for Swales, the concept of "discourse community" is useful to explain how a social group employs discourse to coordinate complex activities, to work together on very large, long-term projects. Entering a discourse community means signing on for the project. True, if we examine a discourse community according to Swales's criteria, we will be looking primarily at its stylistic conventions. But at least Swales suggests that there is much to gain by submitting to the requisite stylistic indoctrination: access to work one could not accomplish individually. Swales also allows that people commonly belong to several discourse communities and have varying degrees of commitment to them, so that one allegiance need not totally dominate a person's life.

I would question, however, whether Swales's account acknowledges the power of discourse communities to shape world views. He emphasizes the element of choice in community membership, suggesting that one cannot be a member of a discourse community of which one is unaware. As a social scientist, Swales needs for people to be able to give testimony about their discourse community memberships so he can study them, testimony people could not give if they did not know they belonged. Hence for Swales (as for scholars in composition studies), defining the entity denoted "discourse community" sets his disciplinary research agenda. Indeed, Swales tells us that he has developed his "discourse community" heuristic to solve what he calls the "café owner problem" for his graduate students. People who manage small restaurants obviously have much in common, at least as far as their daily business tasks are concerned, but, wondered the graduate students, do they therefore comprise a discourse community? Applying his heuristic, Swales now can say that they do not, for café owners have no discursive forum for the sharing of information.

Even if there is no *Café Owners' Newsletter,* however, I suspect that this social group is a discourse community. Whether they realize it or not, its members may share the social-class-based or ethnically based discursive practices of people who are likely to become café owners in their neighborhood. They may all use similar discourses when talking to their employees or when buying their supplies. By treating the discourse community as essentially a stylistic phenomenon, Swales delimits the object of study for his graduate students in such a way as to leave out larger socioeconomic and cultural elements—that is, those elements that most forcefully create world views in discourse.

Bird watchers and philatelists are Swales's prime illustrations of his concept of "discourse community." Hobby groups are engaged in such casual projects that it appears ridiculous to consider their discourse as constituting a world view. Yet I would contend that this superficial triviality is misleading. The bird watcher or philatelist participates in a discourse that encourages a certain kind of thinking—collecting and classifying discrete bits of information as represented by stamps or bird sightings. When such a hobby becomes a consuming passion, there may even be an "inbuilt dynamic" for this habit of mind to shape many areas of the hobbyist's experience—indeed, this is a tendency that comic literature has exploited.

Moreover, I suspect that not everyone is equally likely to become a bird watcher or a philatelist. Socioeconomic and cultural factors shape the hobby group discourse community in terms of who has the requisite leisure time and disposable income to participate. Even more interesting from the epistemic point of view is the question of whose prior social experiences predisposes him—or more rarely, her—to the collecting and classifying habit of mind. Ultimately, discourse community membership probably affects a person's world view in ways of which the person must remain unaware on a daily basis, in order to participate comfortably in the community's work.

World View in the Composition Studies Discourse Community

If we acknowledge that participating in a discourse community entails some assimilation of its world view, then it becomes difficult to maintain the position that discourse conventions can be employed in a detached, instrumental way. If we acknowledge that participating in the academic discourse community entails a world view, then we discover that the ways in which we establish authoritative or canonical knowledge are problematic. We are involved in some contradictions (see Harris 1987).

One contradiction concerns conflicting goals for college writing programs. On the one hand, we know that most institutions support these programs in order to initiate students into the academic discourse community, to "prepare" them for all the other written work they will do in school. Many of us can assent to this goal insofar as we would like to help our students stay in school. But, on the other hand, we do not always assume that social justice will be adequately served merely by the students' staying in school. We are sometimes influenced by a Marxist view of the school as a site for indoctrination in the dominant culture and rationalization of its inequalities, a view to which many of us were persuaded by our own experiences as students in the 1960s. To the extent that we see school this way, we hope that initiation into academic discourse will not mean total assimilation. We don't want students to forget the insights into inequality that many of them bring to school, from experience in other communities. In short, our dilemma is that we want to empower students to succeed in the dominant culture so that they can transform it from within; but we fear that if they do succeed, their thinking will be changed in such a way that they will no longer want to transform it.

Another contradiction involves the discipline of composition studies itself—if it is a discipline. On the one hand, composition studies is coalescing into an ever-more-coherent discourse community. As our conferences, journals, and graduate programs proliferate, we engage in ever more self-study to articulate the accepted modes of research and scholarship in our field. We feel that this process is beneficial in part because it sets professional standards, the absence of which can be very costly in terms of individual career development. For example, Stephen North prefaces an overview of composition studies (1987) with an anecdote that describes his motive for undertaking the study: North's graduate student failed his Ph.D. oral exam because he could give no account of the field as a whole. We also value disciplinary self-study because it brings various subgroups into productive dialogue, as Charles Bazerman proposes to do at a "Research Network" workshop before the 1988 Conference on College Composition and Communication. We don't intend that we all should be doing the same kind of work, but that we all can agree on how the work contributes to a complete picture of the objects of study in composition studies.

Obviously this is a project in creating canonical knowledge. Yet we are troubled by the issues of inclusion and exclusion that canon formation always raises. We want to be an academic discipline, yet we want to be unlike any other academic discipline in that we neither rule out nor require any form of knowledge or methodology. I believe that this eclecticism springs from a deep conviction that to create canonical knowledge is to participate in the processes of domination exercised by the culture we want to resist. Perhaps because composition studies has been marginal and politically powerless in the academy for so long, we are reluctant to truncate the criticism of inequalities in our own interests as well as in the interests of our students.

We often look for a way out of these contradictions by claiming that we are producing and conveying value-neutral methods of analysis, an exploratory discourse if you will, that constitutes no world view. This is to say that we wish to identify all discourses but our own as epistemic. This claim takes a slightly different form when applied to our work with undergraduates than when applied to our work in scholarship and professional development. As applied to undergraduate teaching, Bruce Herzberg (1986) has called this rationale the "Myth of the Gatekeeper":

> According to this myth, the community of writing instructors stands at the entrance to the fortress of college education. . . . Therefore, we believe, we have a special opportunity and responsibility to influence our students' relation to the academy at large. . . . For many students,

the knowledge they seek is indeed locked away in a forbidding fortress to whose rooms they have no key. (9)

Herzberg points here to the metadiscursive or "preparatory" function of writing programs to which I alluded earlier, but—tellingly—he characterizes it as a myth, a story that has some function in the world but is not a report on the world. In short, he suggests, we should not think of ourselves as merely proferring a key to entering students, certainly not a key to all mythologies. Because Herzberg views all discourse as epistemic, he argues that insofar as writing instruction initiates students into academic discourse, it provides not simply access to knowledge but knowledge itself, which is to say academic ways of thinking. To believe we have not affected our students' thinking profoundly is to fall into what Stanley Fish calls "anti-foundationalist theory hope" (see chapter 10, this volume).

Graduate programs in rhetoric can present the same kind of problem, when we assume that the scholarly and pedagogical methods we teach there are equally amenable to any politically interested end. For example, Carol Berkenkotter, Thomas N. Huckin, and John Ackerman (1987) have used the concept of "discourse community" to investigate the changes a graduate student made in his writing style in response to his professors' expectations. "Nate" gradually abandoned a style characterized by frequent use of the first person, widely varied sentence length, vivid and colloquial language, etc., in favor of more distanced, formal academic discourse. Berkenkotter and her colleagues argue that this movement should not be seen as Nate's victimization by professorial bullies. Rather, Nate's understanding of the audience for whom he was writing was shaped intertextually, through his entire new experience of talking and listening to fellow graduate students and professors and reading a range of scholarly works presented by his professors as constituting canonical knowledge in the field.

Nate wanted to grow as a teacher and student of composition, so he signed on to work in a community devoted to composition research. But Berkenkotter et al. provide information to suggest that the change Nate underwent is more far-reaching than a change in his style, that entering this discourse community required him to change his thinking about composition studies in radical ways. For one thing, the program Nate joined promotes a particular orientation toward composition studies. It is the graduate program at Carnegie Mellon University where, as Berkenkotter et al. note, a social-science-oriented form of academic discourse is preferred. For another thing, Nate himself is not an academic innocent; he took an M.A. in English before coming to Carnegie Mellon, and taught composition for six years. Berkenkotter et al. point out that Nate's problem in learning to write for his graduate professors should be conceptualized as a clash among discourse communities, not the inscription of academic discourse on an otherwise blank slate.

Nate's own initial orientation toward composition studies is suggested in several ways. For example, the style Nate abandoned is probably not nonacademic, but rather a kind of writing encouraged in certain school writing courses, those informed by what James Berlin (1987) has called expressivism. Expressivists encourage the use of the first person, vivid language, etc. That Nate was initially an expressivist is further suggested by the topic he chose for one of his first graduate research papers: "How and Why Voice Is Taught: A Pilot Survey" (15). "Voice" is a concept associated with expressivism, and in this paper Nate alluded to such well-known expressivists as Donald Murray, Ken Macrorie, and Peter Elbow (15–16). The change in Nate's style is accompanied by a change in his sense of what should be studied, as reflected in the title of the paper he wrote after eighteen months in the Carnegie Mellon program: "Toward a Generative Computer Environment: A Protocol Study" (22).

Of course, it is as difficult securely to infer changes in world view from stylistic changes as it is to separate thought and style. The evidence presented by Berkenkotter and her colleagues does not prove conclusively that the Carnegie Mellon program altered Nate's world view, and indeed, it was not the primary purpose of their research to investigate world views. Nevertheless Berkenkotter et al. speculate that Nate was not "transformed" by his experience, in the sense of being made to abandon all previous academic discourse community allegiances in order to enter the subgroup of social-science-oriented composition researchers. As Swales's work would

suggest, Nate simply enlarged his repertoire of community memberships, integrating when possible and adapting when necessary.

But Berkenkotter and her colleagues caution that the process of
learning a new community's discourse conventions may not occur
without conflict. They conclude with a quote from Nate that suggests painful struggles in his process of entering this discourse
community: "I just need to do it if for no other reason than that you
have to know something from the inside before you can fairly criticize it" (30). Nate expresses a sense that there may be something to
criticize in his new community, and a hope that he retains sufficient
autonomy to criticize it. These feelings render all the more poi-
gnant the concluding questions of Berkenkotter and her colleagues:
"How, for example, do the sociopolitical constraints that govern the
'manufacture of knowledge' in composition studies affect a graduate
student's choice of research program? To what extent are the issues
that concern composition teachers subsumed by the agendas of
mentors as they join powerful research enterprises, such as the one
we studied here?" (30).

I would argue that we must acknowledge conflict as a frequent
and perhaps inevitable concomitant of discourse community interactions, whether we focus on undergraduate students' entry into
the academic discourse community or graduate students' entry into
the subcommunity of our field—which in turn has different theoretical orientations nested within it, as we have seen.

Recognizing the Political Interests of Discourse Communities

If discourse communities entail world views, then conflicts can
arise when discourse communities overlap. Both within a society
and within a person who has multiple discourse community memberships, the resolution of such conflicts requires the exercise of power.
The struggle among discourse communities can thus be seen as a
political struggle. Socially privileged discourse communities tend to
win such battles; but this does not mean that they are absolutely
impervious to challenge. The current canon debate in literary studies illustrates some successful challenges. Literary theorist Jane
Tompkins has examined how such challenges proceed.

Tompkins has defined herself professionally as what I might call a "counter-critic"—that is, someone who questions the dominant literary canon. Tompkins's questions have often come from a feminist perspective, but recently (1986) she explored the implications of her position as one who wished to question the racism of the dominant canon. She tells us that in order to prepare for teaching a course in colonial American literature, she read widely in literary and historical documents on the relations between Native Americans and European immigrants to North America. Initially she hoped that this research would enable her to tell the "true story" and counter the racism and ethnocentrism of Puritan accounts, which are the only ones regarded in the dominant literary canon.

But as she read, Tompkins encountered stories of Native American behavior that irresistibly prompted her to think of them as savages. She was particularly moved by the story of a Comanche captive, a young white girl who was awakened each day with a burning stick thrust into her face—which eventually burned her nose off. As a result of such stories, Tompkins came to feel a sharp conflict between her moral repugnance at racism and her moral repugnance at casual torture. This conflict demonstrated that her initial aim, to get the "true story" that would defend Native Americans against European racism, was mistaken. The Native American side of the story, Tompkins now sees, must be regarded as just as politically interested as the European version, insofar as it is embodied in discourse that constitutes the Native American world view, which may value individual life differently than Europeans do. (Be it noted that Tompkins's problematic example was a white-authored captivity narrative; the Native American "text" here should perhaps be regarded, in Foucaultian fashion, as the body of the captive.)

But if all positions must be interested, then no position can be condemned as interested from a disinterested vantage point; interests can be attacked only in terms of other, opposing interests. In short, Tompkins now says that she was mistaken to think that any amount of research could given her an unassailably disinterested position. This does not mean her research was a waste of time. In the absence of unassailable positions, arguments about whose knowledge is more legitimate must be pursued reasonably—or as I would say, rhetorically. To make a reasonable argument, one must strive to be well informed. Tompkins says:

> I must piece together the story of European-Indian relations as best I can, believing this version up to a point, that version not at all, another almost entirely, according to what seems reasonable and plausible, given everything else that I know. . . . If the accounts don't fit together neatly, that is not a reason for rejecting them all in favor of a metadiscourse about epistemology; on the contrary, one encounters contradictory facts and divergent points of view in practically every phase of life, . . . and one decides as best one can given the evidence available. (118)

I would add that being well informed does not entail just collecting evidence, but listening to the contradictions that arise from membership in various discourse communities. In the case of Tompkins, it is possible to think of her as participating in several specialized discourse communities that are subgroups in the larger "counter-critical" one questioning the dominant canon; here the relevant subgroups are those of feminist discourse and racially sensitive discourse. It's probably not a coincidence that the white character in Tompkins's most shocking "Indian" story is a female. It's as if while doing her racially motivated research, Tompkins heard a voice from feminist discourse rendering this captivity narrative particularly problematic. If the captive had been male, she might not have noticed the cruelty, by her own standards, of his treatment, at least not noticed it enough to interrupt herself in her antiracist research for reflection on the interested nature of all such accounts.

Tompkins treats the presence of contradictory accounts and conflicting positions as normal. The "everything else that I know," the knowledge she uses to make decisions, is full of contradictions and conflicts. The important point here is to see the presence of conflicts not only as normal—indeed, as inevitable if we normally belong to several discourse communities, each with its own canonical knowledge—but as positively an advantage. The more conflicts, the more input from discourse communities at cross purposes, the more chance for an interested critique of one discourse community from another to be sparked. We simply have to accept that there can be none other than interested critiques.

If contradiction has heuristic value, then we can regard each individual as a unique resource for originating what can become collective political action for the transformation of inequalities. I would venture to say that each individual embodies a unique collection of interests, the product of his or her unique combination of life experiences. Each collection of interests raises possibilities for generating that dialectic of conflicting positions from which arises the dynamic for change.

As long as human beings are masses of contradictions, then, the power of a discourse community, no matter how culturally dominant, can never be total. Someone will always be ready to exercise what David Bartholomae has called a "rhetoric of combination" (1985), bringing oppositions into jarring contact that generates a new idea. As he wittily demonstrates, anything can be related to anything else in terms of an interested viewpoint. Thus I might even wish to argue that healthy discourse communities, like healthy human beings, are also masses of contradictions. The presence of the contradictions, though of course not all can be attended to at every moment, helps to ensure the community's viability in the face of changing demands from other discourse communities and changing conditions in the material world. Therefore, we should accustom ourselves to dealing with contradictions, instead of seeking a theory or pedagogy that appears to abrogate them.

Appendix: Canonical Knowledge in the Composition Studies Discourse Community

I have suggested that we might begin to think of composition studies as an "interdisciplinary discipline," a discourse community that coheres comfortably to address the project of understanding writing, a project shared by composition researchers oriented toward the social sciences and rhetoric scholars oriented toward literary studies and philosophy.

This would mean that part of the body of canonical knowledge in composition studies would be social-science influenced: for example, sociocognitive research on composing processes; ethnographic research on writing in natural settings (in and out of the academy); sociolinguistic research on language variety; work using the orality/

literacy model to study ancient rhetoric and modern newcomers to literacy; and more.

Also, canonical knowledge would include scholarship influenced by literary studies: for example, studies of premodern rhetorical treatments of style and their effects on discursive practices, especially the nonliterary; contemporary academic discourse conventions and genres; discussions of theoretical connections between rhetoric and postmodern literary theories; and more.

Moving from literary criticism to literary theory brings us to a third element in canonical knowledge, namely work with a philosophical orientation: for example, scholarship on premodern rhetoric emphasizing theoretical (philosophical) implications; historiographic studies; ideological analyses of the discursive practices of various social groups; and more.

Some of all this research and scholarship would have pedagogical implications and some would be directed explicitly to improving the teaching of writing. Knowledge of pedagogy, where appropriate, thus also becomes an important part of canonical knowledge in composition studies. Composition studies may indeed be distinguished among academic disciplines for our serious interest in pedagogy. At the same time, the richness of research and scholarship in the field as I have sketched it above suggests that one's projects need not be solely devoted to, or judged by, their pedagogical applications.

It follows from this outline of composition studies that graduate work leading to an English degree concentration in the field should be diverse. Probably the student should be introduced to all the elements of canonical knowledge, social scientific, literary, and philosophical, and their pedagogical applications, while choosing to specialize in one area. This training argues for a diverse graduate faculty and graduate course offerings, perhaps not to be encompassed by the Department of English alone at all institutions. We can accommodate the richness of research and scholarship in composition studies if we expect no less in preparing graduate students for this field, than has been customary in preparing degree candidates in English literature. This might mean, for example, "introductory" courses in three of the four areas outlined above plus a cluster of courses in the area of concentration, amounting probably to at least half the course work of a student who will receive a Ph.D. in English. Our collective effort to define such curricula might help to curb eclecticism and theoretical shallowness in some of our scholarship.

REFERENCES

Bartholomae, David. 1985. "Wistful and Admiring: The Rhetoric of Combination." In Donald A. Daiker, Andrew Kerek, and Max Morenberg, eds., *Sentence Combining: A Rhetorical Perspective.* Carbondale, Ill.: Southern Illinois University Press.

Berkenkotter, Carol, Thomas N. Huckin, and John Ackerman. 1987. "Social Contexts and Socially Constructed Texts." Paper presented at Conference on College Composition and Communication, Atlanta, Ga. Published as "Conventions, Conversation, and the Writer: Case Study of a Student in a Rhetoric Ph.D. Program." *Research in the Teaching of English* 22 (Feb. 1988): 9–14.

Berlin, James. 1987. *Rhetoric and Reality.* Carbondale, Ill.: Southern Illinois University Press.

Bizzell, Patricia. "Foundationalism and Anti-foundationalism in Composition Studies." This volume.

Freire, Paulo. 1970. *Pedagogy of the Oppressed.* Trans. Myra Bergman Ramos. New York: Seabury.

Harris, Joseph. 1987. "The Idea of Community in the Study of Writing." Paper prepared for Pennsylvania State University Summer Conference on Rhetoric, State College, Pa. Published in *College Composition and Communication* 40 (February 1989): 11–22.

Herzberg, Bruce. 1986. "The Politics of Discourse Communities." Paper prepared for Conference on College Composition and Communication, New Orleans, La.

North, Stephen. 1987. *The Making of Knowledge in Composition.* Montclair, N.J.: Boynton/Cook.

Swales, John. 1987. "Approaching the Concept of Discourse Community." Paper prepared for Conference on College Composition and Communication, Atlanta, Ga.

Tompkins, Jane. 1986. " 'Indians': Textualism, Morality, and the Problem of History." *Critical Inquiry* 13 (Autumn 1986): 101–119.

Arguing About Literacy

Arguments about literacy typically take the same form. One kind of literacy holds a commanding position, that which comprises the ways of using language valued by the academy and the upper social classes with which it is associated. The dominance of this academic literacy is challenged by people who have made their way into the schools but whose native tongues are at a relatively greater remove from the academic dialect, whose preferred modes of developing ideas conflict with the linear logic and impersonal posture of academic debate, and whose cultural treasures are not included in the academic canon. These challenges of academic literacy typically come from social groups at some remove from the upper classes— that is, from the lower classes, foreign born, nonwhite, and/or female.

Although they have won some battles, these oppositional forces seem to have lost the war. For example, on the college level they have effected change in isolated instances: perhaps through instituting a pluralistic method of holistic essay exam scoring that avoids penalizing nonstandard dialect writers; perhaps through getting selections from "minority" artists included in reading anthologies. But the requirement that students master academic literacy in order to continue their educations is still institutionalized in the great majority of writing programs in this country (see Applebee; Baron; Finegan).

Yet this view of the monolithic power of academic literacy is misleading, and itself politically oppressive. I suspect that historical study of academic literacy would show the steady influence of oppositional forces for change. The academic literacy that is now required of American college students is, I suspect, more pluralistic than that enforced at the turn of the century. It is not my purpose to prove this here; because I think of myself professionally as a supporter of the opposition, I certainly do not mean to suggest that no further change is needed. I simply wish to suggest that change is possible; indeed, this possibility is implied by the argumentative tack typically taken by defenders of the status quo, of academic literacy as it is presently constituted.

Typically, people arguing this position have sought to draw attention away from the social class basis of academic literacy. Rather, they have sought arguments that rest on some supposedly transcendent standards, standards preserved above the merely political. Such "foundationalist" arguments, as contemporary philosophers and literary theorists have taught us to call them, aim to end debate, and with it, the embarrassing questions about who holds the political power to decide what constitutes good language use.

In this essay I examine some of these apolitical arguments for the academic status quo. First I discuss arguments adduced from social science research in what I might call literal literacy, that is, the study of what happens when people who were previously completely illiterate learn elementary reading and writing. We rarely see such people in American colleges. Then I look at work on socalled cultural literacy, most notably that of E. D. Hirsch, Jr., which seeks to be more responsive to the actual situation in our colleges by posing the "literacy problem" in terms of competing bodies of knowledge, but which nevertheless attempts to resolve debate in a way that conceals political implications. Finally I argue for a view of literacy—and thus implicitly defend a way of arguing about literacy—that is based on a properly rhetorical understanding of history and knowledge.

II

Social science research in literacy assumes that some kind of decisive change takes place when individuals and societies acquire literacy. Jack Goody summarizes these changes as "the move from myth to history, from magic to science, status to contract, cold to hot [an allusion to Lévi-Strauss's 'raw/cooked' distinction], concrete to abstract, collective to individual, ritual to rationality" (3). Yet the social science approach to literacy is not as dichotomizing as Goody's characterization suggests. Social science research tends to focus on how these changes occur within individuals, changes in the ways they think and interact with the world, but also to consider these cognitive changes as conditioned by the social contexts in which literacy is used. Hence there is no monolithic concept of what happens when any individual or society, regardless of the historical circumstances, acquires literacy. Social science research in literacy is moving toward a more pluralistic view of "multiple literacies" (Scribner and Cole) or a "continuum of orality and literacy" (Tannen; see also Heath).

Research on literacy, however, has come into the debate on college reading and writing by way of the work of humanists who study literacy, such as classical philologist Eric Havelock and literary critic Walter Ong. In examining changes attendant upon literacy, humanists tend to focus on the changes occurring within discourse—stylistic change—and to infer from the discourse the cognitive and cultural changes accompanying it. Humanists tend to dichotomize nonliterate and literate states of being, and to reify the two states into all-embracing conceptual universes of orality and literacy (see Ong).

Among literacy scholars, the humanist position is called the "Great Cognitive Divide" theory of literacy. According to this theory, an oral culture, in which speech is the sole medium of verbal exchange, is characterized in its verbal style and in its thinking by parataxis, the simple juxtaposition of ideas; by concrete imagery that appeals to the senses and the emotions; by ritualized references to authority in the form of proverbs, epithets, incantations, and other formulae, and by an agonistic posture in disputation.

According to the humanists, this "orality" can be changed only through mastery of alphabetic literacy, in which symbols are assigned to phonemes rather than to syllables or whole concepts. Alphabetic literacy is more "efficient" than nonalphabetic systems because a much smaller number of symbols represents a much greater number of words, with much less ambiguity, thus enabling more people to master the system more quickly, and allowing textual content to be more varied without the need to codify it in orthodox formulae for easy recognition. Hence alphabetic literacy gives rise to the following characteristics of style and thinking: hypotaxis, the subordination of one idea to another in logical hierarchies; generalizations that appeal to reason and text-assisted memory for validation; and a dialectical relation to authority, encouraging the ongoing, disinterested criticism of ideas.

Humanists argue that the single set of changes they see as characteristic of all literacy is always attendant upon the acquisition of literacy and is independent of social variables. They assert that the change from oral thinking to literate thinking can be achieved only through acquisition of alphabetic literacy, and that it is always achieved when alphabetic literacy has been acquired. These two assertions, however, have not been confirmed among variously literate contemporary peoples. Social scientists describe a wider variety of changes than do humanists and link particular changes to features of the particular social situation in which literacy is used. Some forms of alphabetic literacy do not convey all the cognitive changes associated with "Great Divide" literate thinking (see Heath); and some forms of nonalphabetic literacy do encourage some aspects of literate thinking (see Scribner and Cole).

This is not to say that social science scholarship on literacy has disproved the humanist "Great Divide" idea. Rather, the conflict between social scientists' and humanists' findings suggests that they are not looking at the same data. Specifically, social science research has found that the changes accompanying literacy most closely conform to the humanists' expectations when the literacy has been learned in a Western-type secular school. This match suggests that the orality/literacy dichotomy of the humanists has been derived from studying a subset of all possible literate texts, namely those texts that reflect the kinds of thinking induced by academic literacy.

Typically, however, humanist literacy scholars do not acknowledge their conflation of literacy and academic literacy. Thus not only do they reduce all possible cognitive gains attendant upon literacy acquired in various social circumstances to the narrow set of abilities associated with academic literacy, but they also foster arguments that any cognitive gains to be had from any kind of literacy are available only from mastery of academic literacy.

Such arguments have been used in aid of requiring students to learn Standard English because this dialect is preferred in academic literacy. Thomas J. Farrell argues native speakers of Black English score lower than whites on IQ tests and do poorly in school because Black English is essentially an oral, not a literate, language. These students' difficulties would be remedied, he claims, by teaching them Standard English; mastering the copula and other elements in the grammatical "alphabet" of Standard English would automatically enable them to think "literately"—that is, in ways sanctioned by academic literacy. In making this argument, Farrell ignores the fact that the Black English-speaking students he is discussing are not in fact totally illiterate—for example, they read well enough to take the tests upon whose results Farrell's case depends so heavily. Farrell does not recognize the existence of any literate abilities here because the students have not mastered the literate abilities that count for him, namely those associated with academic literacy.

III

The concept of "cultural literacy" has emerged as a corrective to "Great Divide" literacy theories. This concept suggests that all literacy is in fact cultural literacy—that is, that no symbol system in and of itself induces cognitive changes. A cultural context is necessary to invest the features of the system with meaning, to give them the significance that then induces changes in thinking. An alphabet, or a standard grammar, does not somehow structurally force changes in the user's mental apparatus. Rather, such changes flow from the cultural significance attached to mastering the alphabet or the grammar—the kinds of knowledge and social roles open to those who have achieved mastery and so on.

The development of E. D. Hirsch's thought on literacy illustrates how the need for a concept of cultural literacy arises. Hirsch's first major contribution is *The Philosophy of Composition* (1977). Here, like other defenders of the status quo, he attempts to resolve the debate over what should constitute academic literacy by establishing a definition that transcends social contexts and the local ideological agendas to which they give rise. "An authentic ideology of literacy," Hirsch claims, "inheres in the subject itself, and should guide our teaching of it" (xiii).

Hirsch deduces his "privileged ideology" of literacy from psycholinguistic research on memory and information processing, which he interprets as describing the characteristics of an ideally efficient language. He asserts that these characteristics may largely be found in formal written Standard English. Hirsch thus suppresses ideology both in the reasons he gives for teaching Standard English and in the results he hopes to gain from such teaching. He argues in favor of requiring all students to master Standard English because of its cognitive status as the most "communicatively efficient" form of the language. And his predictions of cognitive gains from mastery, like the arguments of humanist literacy scholars for alphabetic literacy, attribute these gains to the formal structure of the symbol system—like the alphabet, Standard English is more "efficient"—rather than to any contextual influences.

Moreover, Hirsch seeks to require mastery not merely of Standard English, but of a particular style of writing Standard English, a style encapsulated in the maxims of Strunk and White's well-known manual, *The Elements of Style*, which he recommends. His argument for the cognitive superiority of a clear, concise style of Standard English, like the humanists' argument for the cognitive characteristics of literate style, fails to notice that this style is socially situated. Hirsch's preferred verbal style, and the humanists' literate style, both appear upon further analysis to be the preferred style and thought patterns of academics, not necessarily of all literate people. In short, Hirsch's candidate for privileged ideology of literacy is not as context-free as he claims: it is an academic ideology of literacy.

Many critics have noted problems with the theory of literacy Hirsch defends in *The Philosophy of Composition* (see Bizzell and Herzberg). So has Hirsch. In this book, Hirsch defines a concept of "relative readability" that, he claims, enables him to measure the communicative efficiency of any text. He received a grant from the National Endowment for the Humanities to test the applicability of this concept. His experiments changed his mind. Hirsch and his associates at the University of Virginia "systematically degraded" academic texts (selections from Will and Ariel Durant, Bruce Catton, and others) to render them more difficult according to the standards of relative readability (Hirsch 1980, 38–42). They then asked different groups ("literate adults" (38), community college basic writing students, and others) to read either the degraded text or the original and to answer some comprehension questions.

Hirsch expected to find, of course, that the original texts, those that rated higher in relative readability, would generate better comprehension scores than the degraded texts. Instead, test results were unpredictable—until Hirsch realized the comprehension scores were tied more closely to the readers' prior knowledge of the subject discussed in the reading selection than to the stylistic features of the selection. If prior knowledge, which is conditioned by the reader's social background, affects readability, then social context in general must affect literacy in general much more than Hirsch had thought when he wrote *The Philosophy of Composition.*

Hirsch has explicitly rejected what he calls the "formalist" bias of his book in his essay "Cultural Literacy" (161). He abandons a "Great Divide" approach to literacy in defining "cultural literacy" as "the translinguistic knowledge on which linguistic literacy depends. You can't have one without the other" (165). He argues that "without appropriate, tacitly shared background knowledge" no audience can understand a text, whether the text is an astrophysics journal or a daily newspaper (165). Hirsch uses the term "canonical" to refer to this necessary knowledge, thus suggesting it is essential not only to reading comprehension, but also to membership in the social group that constitutes the audience for the text that the knowledge renders intelligible. Any audience, whether for an astrophysics journal or a daily newspaper, will have its canonical knowledge that, as a common possession of the group, helps the group to cohere, to distinguish itself from others, and to exclude or initiate outsiders.

To this point, Hirsch's "cultural literacy" position sorts well with the social science approach to literacy. Hirsch suggests that different audiences have different bodies of shared knowledge that enable them to read the texts of their group. In other words, he is describing multiple literacies, and his notion of canonical knowledge helps to explain where multiple literacies come from. The understanding that prior knowledge conditions language use is of the utmost importance. This insight goes far to prevent the "diagnosis" of unsuccessful college writers as cognitively deficient (see Bizzell; Rose). Instead, as David Bartholomae has shown, we can see them as beginners in academic discourse, trying to find a way to use language for their own purposes in a community whose knowledge they do not yet fully share.

But when Hirsch turns to pedagogy, he begins once again to argue prescriptively. He begins his "Cultural Literacy" essay with this implied causal statement: "The national decline in our literacy has accompanied a decline in our use of common, nationwide materials in the subject most closely connected with literacy, 'English' " (159). Hirsch then invokes the turn-of-the-century practice of teaching from lists of authors, first established (although Hirsch does not say so) by Harvard University. While he names them at length, Hirsch denies he wants to recommend a return to the particular texts that made up these lists (159–60). But he returns to the idea of uniform lists in his recommendation for the formation of a "National Curriculum Board" that could establish new lists for contemporary schools (167–68). Indeed, Hirsch has recently established a Cultural Literacy Foundation with the avowed purpose of designing standardized tests of students' knowledge, tests intended to be used to shape school curricula (see Heller).

What exactly is wrong with defining cultural literacy in terms of a common list? Opponents question the social and political biases that would inform the process of choosing works for the list (see Warnock). But Hirsch claims that his list is fair and representative (he developed a list, recently published in book form, with the aid of grants from Exxon and the National Endowment for the Humanities; note that Hirsch's continued success in receiving financial support for his work suggests its potential broad influence). In addition to canonical literature, Hirsch includes nonfiction references such as the Declaration of Independence, minority figures such as Frederick Douglass, and popular culture items such as

Pinocchio. By and large, however, the concessions to popular and minority cultures appear to be few. The core of the list is the core of Western high culture.

Hirsch does not deny that "choosing the contents of cultural literacy" requires a "difficult political decision" (167). Moreover, he seems to rule out any transcendent principles for deciding what works belong on the list—a departure from his habitual practice—admitting instead that selection will proceed by "discussion, argument, and compromise" (167). He does not want to require that every American school teach every work on the list—local selectivity and addition would be allowed, within some limits, presumably. He thus attempts to forestall critics who would argue that his dream for a national curriculum is totalitarian, racist, sexist, and laden with social class prejudice.

Nevertheless, the function of history in Hirsch's argument points to the argument's crucial weakness: his idea of how canonical knowledge gets established. One cannot argue with Hirsch's choices of items for his list without tackling this issue first. Hirsch justifies his concentration on Western high or academic culture on grounds that this is our tradition: "no culture exists that is ignorant of its own traditions" (167). At this point Hirsch turns from the question of how this particular tradition got to be *the* tradition, concentrating instead on the need for *some* tradition to unite an increasingly fragmented society. He hopes that we Americans will decide we want "a broadly literate culture that unites our cultural fragments enough to allow us to write to one another and read what our fellow citizens have written" (167). To want this, as Hirsch himself points out, is to adopt the traditional point of view, "Our traditional, Jeffersonian answer" (167).

History functions at this crucial point in the argument in several ways. First history is depicted as presenting us with the core curriculum of Western academic culture, essentially as a *fait accompli*. We are not now in a position to argue about the canonical status of most of the works on Hirsch's putative list, for they have been established by the impersonal force of history. Hirsch does not depict modern people as completely powerless before the force of history. We can add works to the canon, for instance. But no matter how unfair we now think the processes of history to have been, when we see how history has systematically excluded certain social groups from representation in the high culture, we can do nothing about those injustices now.

More importantly, history blocks our examining the attitudes that compel us to submit to it. One such attitude is that those cultural subgroups not presently represented in the academic canon are "fragmentary" and in need of unification. In short, the academic canon is now performing for Hirsch exactly the same function that Standard English did in *The Philosophy of Composition:* he imagines that it has been granted by history the power to transcend and hence to control local cultural canons. Hirsch detaches the academic canon from its own social origins, which are systematically suppressed—for example, in his forgetting to mention that the turn-of-the-century lists he admires were first promulgated by Harvard, a highly race-, sex-, and class-determined institution.

Moreover, Hirsch assumes that history has granted the academic canon the right to exercise this power over other cultures, through establishing canonical ways of thinking and of using language, canonical values, verbal styles, and mindsets as the "most important" to our national culture. This kind of valorizing of the canon resembles the process whereby humanist literacy scholars establish the importance of literate ways of thinking and of using language. Hirsch links the two arguments when he says: "Estimable cultures exist that are ignorant of Shakespeare and the First Amendment. Indeed, estimable cultures exist that are entirely ignorant of reading and writing" (167). Humanist literacy scholars frequently protest, as Hirsch does here, that their oral/literate dichotomy is not meant to imply any absolute inferiority of oral culture. They simply claim that the cognitive abilities fostered by literate culture are necessary now, the world over. Similarly, Hirsch does not wish to claim that everyone ignorant of his academic canon is inferior. But everyone ignorant of this canon in America is inferior because knowledge of this canon is necessary to enter the national literate forums—as defined by Hirsch.

Hence, "history" in Hirsch's argument becomes a cover term, concealing not only the process whereby certain texts achieve canonical status but also the process whereby attitudes toward the very existence of any canon, and its function in society, become ingrained. Hirsch adopts a determinist view of the power of history. He seems to say that both the content of the academic canon and our attitudes about the rightness of its dominance have been fixed by the past life of the society that has formed us. We may be able to make minor changes, but basically, we must submit. If one believes this, then there is no objection to teaching in the most indoctrinating fashion possible. What students lack is canonical knowledge: let's give it to them.

IV

How can we avoid the "foundationalism" of humanist literacy work and of cultural literacy work such as Hirsch's when we argue about literacy? I would like to suggest a rhetorical view that offers both a better understanding of how to argue and a better understanding of literacy itself. First how to argue: from a rhetorical point of view, one is never able to prove an opponent wrong absolutely, to present evidence that demonstrates the opponent's error and one's own correctness for all times and places. This is the kind of proof sought in "foundationalist" arguments. Rather, from a rhetorical point of view, what one does when arguing is to seek to persuade a particular audience, in a particular time and place. An argument is provisionally correct if it carries the day, but is always subject to dialectical revision.

This rhetorical view of argument means that in framing an argument, what one needs is not absolute truth or unimpeachable evidence, but rather means of persuasion that will move this particular audience. Rhetoric has traditionally been defined as the study of the means of persuasion. "Means" of persuasion can vary from enthymemes to gestures that express a speaker's ethos to tropes that are presumed to have some affect built into them structurally. The study of these means of persuasion has two ends: first, to call them to the communicator's attention, and second, to investigate *what* they mean in a given rhetorical situation. Aristotle notes, for example, that appeals to prudence will move old men, but not young ones. To understand how to use the means of persuasion effectively the rhetorician needs to know the audience well. This can mean knowing the audience's age and social condition, the audience's personal interests, and more, the audience's values.

I would argue that this focus on the means of persuasion implies not only a notion of the provisionality of all arguments but also a view of literacy as something local, something shared in a social context. The rhetorical investigation of audience entails attempting to share the canonical knowledge that constitutes the group as an audience. In other words, it is research into the group's cultural literacy. In classical times, such study appeared to be the study of universal human nature because rhetoricians typically had to do with a single, homogeneous audience. Increasingly since the Renaissance, however, rhetoric has sought to deal with the pluralism of the modern condition. Rhetoricians may very well have to deal with audiences whose shared knowledge seems quite alien at first. Thus the study of contemporary audiences has come to seem like comparative anthropology, while tracing the development of shared knowledge over time calls for discursively sophisticated historical study. In other words, rhetoric's commitment to understanding the means of persuasion has led, especially in modern, pluralistic times, into the historical and comparative study of ideologies.

I do not intend to suggest, however, that such study raises rhetoric above ideology. That would leave me open to a charge rhetoricians have faced ever since Plato, namely that they are fundamentally dishonest because they try to be in a community without being of it—to use some of its shared knowledge to achieve their own purposes while preserving a cynical distance on the world view implied by the knowledge. The best answer to this charge was suggested by the Sophists, namely that rhetoric itself creates all knowledge (see Gronbeck; Engnell). Knowledge is not a content conveyed by rhetoric; knowledge is what ensues when rhetoric is successful, when rhetorician and audience reach agreement. If this is true, then by the same token, rhetoricians cannot share a community's knowledge while remaining unchanged. Rhetoricians' own world views will be influenced to the extent that they assimilate the community's knowledge to their own discourse.

In other words, when you argue with someone, you own thinking is inevitably influenced by what you have to do to persuade the other person. All arguments are not only ideological, but dialectical. Hirsch's approach to the "problem of canon formation" is weakened by ignoring this aspect of argumentation. For him canon formation entails simply figuring out what texts (in the broadest sense) are in fact the most influential. Hirsch rules out any "merely ideological" attack on a work's canonical status. If it is in the canon now, it can be dislodged only if one can "prove" that it has not in fact had such influence. But current debates among literary critics over canon formation have been much more ideological than this. For example, feminist critics have argued that works by women writers should be moved into the canon in order to change the ideological bent of scholarship, to correct its male chauvinism. At the same time, many of these feminist arguments are couched in an argumentative style sanctioned by the male-dominated literary-critical tradition and designed explicitly to appeal to such readers. The feminists have been influenced by the audience with whom they are arguing—as some feminists, in turn, have noted and deplored!

Fundamentally, Hirsch sees ignorance of the canon in terms of a problem in deciphering literary allusions. He does not do justice to the value of his own insight concerning the crucial importance of knowledge to participation in discourse, for he does not consider the possibility that the very ability to count allusions depends on the canonical knowledge one already has. The researchers compiling the common list will be guided in their perceptions of what is frequently cited by what they can recognize on the basis of their own education. The researchers' own cultural assumptions will predetermine what will be perceived as "important." An example of this kind of circular reasoning about influence can be found in Hirsch's "Cultural Literacy" essay, in which, as I noted earlier, he cites Thomas Jefferson as an authority to support his view that a canon including Jefferson's Declaration of Independence should be imposed on all American schools.

If we see the production of literacy as a collaborative effort—if we adopt a rhetorical perspective on literacy, which dialectically relates means of persuasion to audience's canonical knowledge—then we need a pedagogy much less prescriptive than Hirsch's or Farrell's. Teaching academic literacy becomes a process of constructing academic literacy, creating it anew in each class through

the interaction of the professor's and the students' cultural resources. I would argue that this is in fact what happens, very
slowly—hence the increasing pluralism in academic literacy noted
earlier.

But if one wishes to foster this process, to support oppositional
forces as I said I did, then the problem with this model of the
dialectical formation of academic literacy is that professor and students do not appear to be equal partners in the collaboration. The
professor automatically has more persuasive power for what he or
she wants to include in academic literacy, simply by virtue of the
social power his or her position provides over the students. A larger
version of this problem has emerged in connection with the concept of "interpretive communities" in reader-response literary criticism and writing-across-the-curriculum work: when the professor
initiates students into currently acceptable methods of responding
to texts—or into the practices of any other academic discipline—
isn't he or she simply forcing conformity to these practices? Even if
we understand disciplinary practices to be developed by human
beings, the master practitioners in the field, rather than to be
discovered in some absolute form, independent of human agency,
isn't the result for the student the same, namely submission? Can
change occur only when the material world erupts into the academic community and forces an adjustment—but not as a result of
the initiatives of any human newcomers?

I do not know that anyone has yet articulated a truly collaborative
pedagogy of academic literacy, one that successfully integrates the
professor's traditional canonical knowledge and the students' noncanonical cultural resources. Certainly I cannot do so. It is extremely difficult to abrogate in the classroom, by a collective act of
will, the social arrangements that separate professors and students
outside the classroom. Integration has not been achieved if the
students are simply allowed to express affective responses to canonical knowledge as conveyed by the professor; or if the professor
simply abdicates the role of guide to tradition and encourages the
students to define a course agenda from their own interests. For
example, we might expect Richard Rorty to favor a pedagogy that
raises questions about canonical knowledge and opens the academy
to new cultural resources. This has been his project in his own

scholarly work. Yet in discussing pedagogy, even Rorty can find no way around an unequal relation between professor and students.

Rorty argues that we should "give students a chance for intellectual hero-worship" by depicting the "great men" of traditional intellectual history not as geniuses in touch with transcendent truth, but as "fighters against their time" who "were taking on the problems which the community around them had inherited" and "inventing new forms of communal life by inventing new songs, new discourses, new polities" (10). To be sure, this approach historicizes intellectual work and emphasizes its discursive basis. But students are cast very much in a subordinate role, as worshippers, and whom they are worshipping is made clearer later in the same essay, in which Rorty notes with approval: "In practice, the content of core curricula is whatever books the most influential members of the faculty of a given institution all happen to have liked, or all like to teach—the books which give them the greatest pleasure" (12).

In other words, students are to be seduced into cultural literacy by their admiration, first, for the master practitioners who are directing their lives in the classroom, and second, for their masters' intimate friends to be found in great books. Rorty uses the term "eroticism" to characterize the teacher-student relationship he desires. Of course, this is meant as an ironic commentary on Plato, but Rorty's version of cultural literacy itself evokes the homoeroticism of the *Phaedrus*. It seems quite appropriate that throughout his essay, Rorty uses the masculine pronoun exclusively to refer to the masters and their worshippers.

It's not that I wish to inveigh against any pleasure resulting from reciprocal acts of teaching and learning, or, more important, against Plato's vision in the *Phaedrus* of an education that reaches the whole person, not intellect alone. Rather, I simply wish to show how difficult it can be to make education truly reciprocal, and not something done to one person by another. Rorty's model inevitably takes on these instrumental overtones, and typically, they are accompanied by elitist implications such as attend Platonic homoeroticism. The masters, too, learned to love their favorites from their own teachers.

Such a closed system would indeed seem to support the view that only a radical change in historical circumstances, an eruption of the material world, can force changes in the academic canon. Once change has been initiated by impersonal forces, students may find the opportunity to act on their own cultural agendas—some newcomers may find that they are better equipped to deal with the crisis, precisely because they have not yet learned to view the world in the currently traditional academic ways, than are the convention-bound masters. If we are forced to this conclusion about the possibility of change, must we give up trying to be actively oppositional? Must we simply passively await an opportunity that may never come?

We have to be careful here not to fall back into a "foundationalist" way of arguing about change. If the power of an individual to effect change is qualified, if opportunities for oppositionally motivated change are contingent upon historical circumstances "erupting" into the academic community, this does not mean that change is now out of human hands. Rather, we should understand that change is always immanent but becomes evident when the time is right—and when those who wish to effect change are willing and able to engage in the rhetorical processes that make change happen. That is, those who support change must persuade other members of the academic community that the prevailing notion of academic literacy needs revision. We should not expect those with a critical perspective on prevailing notions to be any more able to transcend historical circumstances than the supporters of the dominant culture are—to wish for this power is to fantasize avoiding the rhetorical process.

We also have to be careful not to resurrect a determinist view. The opportunities historical circumstances present for cultural change may be very difficult of access for individuals—but not for groups. You can't act alone, perhaps, but you can act with others with whom you make common cause. Again, this view is congenial to the rhetorical perspective—persuasion is not based on idiosyncratic values but on what is shared. A truism worth repeating is that only through collective effort have changes been effected in the academic canon so far—whether we speak of theoretical shifts such as the rise and fall of New Criticism, or changes in the subject of study such as feminist-motivated revision of the textual canon. I need not advocate, then, the creation of oppositional discourses within the academy—people working out their relations to the changing historical circumstances are creating them all the time. I do advocate, however, the recognition that this process constitutes "normal" intellectual life. The crucial moment in the inculcation of cultural literacy will be finding ways to persuade our students to participate in this life with us.

REFERENCES

Applebee, Arthur N. *Tradition and Reform in the Teaching of English: A History.* Urbana: NCTE, 1974.

Baron, Dennis. *Grammar and Good Taste: Reforming the American Language.* New Haven: Yale University Press, 1982.

Bartholomae, David. "Inventing the University." *When a Writer Can't Write: Studies in Writer's Block and Other Composing Process Problems.* Ed. Mike Rose. New York: Guilford, 1985. 134–65.

Bizzell, Patricia. "Cognition, Convention, and Certainty: What We Need to Know about Writing." This volume.

Bizzell, Patricia, and Bruce Herzberg. " 'Inherent' Ideology, 'Universal' History, 'Empirical' Evidence, and 'Context-Free' Writing: Some Problems in E. D. Hirsch's *The Philosophy of Composition.*" This volume.

Engnell, Richard A. 'Implications for Communication of the Rhetorical Theory of Gorgias of Leontini." *Western Speech* 37 (1973): 175–84.

Farrell, Thomas J. "I.Q. and Standard English." *College Composition and Communication* 34 (1985): 470–84.

Finegan, Edward. *Attitudes Toward English Usage.* New York: Teacher's College, 1980.

Goody, Jack. *The Domestication of the Savage Mind.* Cambridge: Cambridge University Press, 1977.

Gronbeck, Bruce. "Gorgias on Rhetoric and Poetic: A Rehabilitation." *Southern Speech Communication Journal* 38 (1972): 27–38.

Havelock, Eric. *The Literate Revolution in Greece and Its Cultural Consequences.* Princeton: Princeton University Press, 1982.

Heath, Shirley Brice. *Ways With Words: Language, Life, and Work in Communities and Classrooms.* Cambridge: Cambridge University Press, 1983.

Heller, Scott. "Author Sets Up Foundation to Create 'Cultural Literacy' Tests." *The Chronicle of Higher Education* 5 Aug. 1987: 2.

Hirsch, E. D., Jr. "Cultural Literacy." *American Scholar* 52 (1982–83): 159–69.

———. "Culture and Literacy." *Journal of Basic Writing* 3 (Fall/Winter 1980): 27–47.

———. *The Philosophy of Composition.* Chicago: University of Chicago Press, 1977.

Hirsch, E. D., Jr., Joseph Kett, and James Trefil. *Cultural Literacy: What Every American Needs to Know.* Boston: Houghton, 1987.

Ong, Walter J. *Orality and Literacy: The Technologizing of the Word.* New York: Methuen, 1982.

Rorty, Richard. "Hermeneutics, General Studies, and Teaching." *Synergos: Selected Papers from the Synergos Seminars* 2 (1982): 1–15.

Rose, Mike. "The Language of Exclusion: Writing Instruction at the University." *College English* 47 (1985): 341–59.

Scribner, Sylvia, and Michael Cole. *The Psychology of Literacy.* Cambridge: Harvard University Press, 1981.

Tannen, Deborah. "The Oral/Literate Continuum of Discourse." *Spoken and Written Languages: Exploring Orality and Literacy.* Ed. Deborah Tannen. Norwood, N.J.: Ablex, 1982. 1–16.

Warnock, John. "Cultural Literacy: A Worm in the Bud?" *ADE Bulletin* 82 (Winter 1985): 1–7.

Beyond Anti-Foundationalism to Rhetorical Authority: Problems Defining "Cultural Literacy"

When students enter college, it soon becomes apparent that some of them are already comfortable with academic discourse, while other students seem quite unfamiliar with academic discourse and resistant to learning it. This state of affairs might not be considered a problem: the academy might simply expel those who do not share its discourse and welcome and reward those who do. Indeed, this is how the situation is handled in many schools today.

Many writing teachers, however, have not been satisfied with this response to the lack of shared discourse. Many of us have felt that it is unfair, a shirking of our professional responsibility simply to expel from the academy those students who do not share our discourse. The unfairness is exacerbated by the fact that failing to share in academic discourse is often not a personal or idiosyncratic failing but rather seems to be a function of belonging to a social group that has experienced other exclusions and disenfranchisements—that is, other injustices. Writing teachers, then, have seen the lack of a shared discourse as a problem and have tried to remedy the problem by studying ways to initiate all students into academic discourse.

E. D. Hirsch has suggested in his recent work on cultural literacy that Americans have another, larger problem involving the lack of a shared discourse, that there is a national, pubic discourse

Reprinted with permission from *College English* 52, no. 6 (Oct. 1990): 661–75. Copyright 1990 by the National Council of Teachers of English.

community in which issues of grave collective importance are discussed. But, according to Hirsch, not all American citizens can participate in this national discursive forum. Thus there exists a problem of exclusion antithetical to a democracy in which all citizens ought to be able to participate in the national discourse. Hirsch sees education as the solution to this problem and has proposed that the schools should introduce all students to the national political discourse. Hirsch has offered his project of teaching cultural literacy as a means to this end.

In pursuing this project, Hirsch makes some assumptions that are similar to those we writing teachers have made in attempting to introduce students to academic discourse. First, Hirsch assumes that sharing a discourse means more than sharing the ability to encode and decode a particular grammar and syntax. That is, he imagines a situation in which people all know English, or some form of English, but still do not share a discourse. For Hirsch, "sharing a discourse" means not only sharing a tongue but also sharing a mass of contextual knowledge that renders the tongue significant. In its broadest outlines, this is the definition of "literacy" that is identified as "cultural." That is, the ability to read, write, and speak—to use a language—is contingent upon possession of the cultural knowledge that renders the language significant, shapes situations for its appropriate use, and so on. There is, in fact, no such thing as simple literacy at all according to these assumptions; every form of literacy is a particular cultural literacy.

Some of us composition teachers have argued, following similar assumptions, that students who have difficulties with academic discourse are not illiterate but rather lacking in the particular academic cultural literacy. Mina Shaughnessy has pioneered this way of understanding the difficulties of what she calls "basic writers" when she suggests that what they need to know, more than corrections of their English usage, is "how proof is defined in the various situations [they] must think and write in" (271). The student writer must establish a credible academic persona through the method of his or her argument—for example by learning what counts as adequate evidence in various acaemic disciplines—and also through the employment of a transdisciplinary academic vocabulary. In short, a specific cultural content must be supplied to remedy the lack of a discourse shared by students and teachers. Recent discussions of this problem in composition studies (such as my essay "Arguing about Literacy") have focused on adjudicating how much of the cultural content should be supplied by the teacher from the traditional academic store and how much should come from students' knowledge of the treasures of other, nonacademic cultural literacies.

I would agree with Hirsch, then, that in order for people to share language, they must share knowledge. Indeed, this is the general import of the concept of "discourse community." It might be said that a particular cultural literacy is what members of a discourse community share. But I disagree with Hirsch's assumption that there is a relatively stable, definable national discourse community. This assumption allows Hirsch to define our current national problem as one of initiating all citizens into a predetermined or "given" national discourse community by supplying them with the knowledge that will enable them to share this community's language. To frame the problem in this way frames it in terms that appear to make it easily amenable to educational remedy. Let the schools inculcate the requisite knowledge. Such a solution is analogous to the solution some composition specialists have suggested for the academic discourse problem: let the freshman writing class inculcate the knowledge requisite to allow all students to participate in the academic discursive community.

I am coming to suspect, however, that the academic discourse community is not such a stable entity that one can define our teaching problem in terms of how to get student writing to approximate a set of well-known and accepted academic models, as Shaughnessy has suggested (257–73). I now think the academic discourse community is more unstable than this—more fraught with contradiction, more polyvocal—and that this instability is a sign of its health, its ability to adapt to changing historical conditions. I think it would be a mistake to rush closure on a unitary conception of what academic discourse should be and then turn this concept into a Procrustean bed that all students—and professorial—writing must fit.

At the same time, however, I think it is important for students and teachers to work collectively toward achieving consensus on a pluralistic grouping of ways to do academic discourse. Some consensus is needed so that we can share a discourse and get on with our work, while including the greatest possible diversity of participants and remaining open to change in response to the cultural literacies of new groups who want to join in our projects. We may wish to do away with an oppressive academic discourse, but we cannot do without any academic discourse at all.

Similarly, I believe it is of crucial importance for Americans to share a national political discourse. Unlike Hirsch, I do not believe that a relatively stable and unitary form of this discourse presently exists. If a unitary national discourse ever existed, it may have owned its existence to historical circumstances that greatly limited the group of people who had access to it in terms of race, sex, and social class. As with the instability of academic discourse, I would like to regard the present instability of national discourse—or more precisely, the open-endedness of the question of whether we can have a national discourse at all—as an opportunity. Perhaps we Americans have the opportunity now to collaborate on forging a more collective, pluralistic, inclusive national discourse. I certainly believe that such a democratic shared language is needed, in view of the gravity of the political problems that confront us: racial injustice, economic inequality, environmental destruction, and the prospect of nuclear war. Perhaps it is only because I myself am a teacher that I hope a national discourse could contribute substantially to the redress of our national ills—as if there were not pervasive material circumstances preconditioning people's unequal political, and academic, participation. Or perhaps my hope arises from an awareness that intellectuals in other countries—in every other country in the world—play dynamic roles in the shaping of collective political life. Perhaps we should regard this, too, as part of our professional responsibility.

It is the desperate character of our current national political life that dismays me when I contemplate the reaction of scholars in English studies to E. D. Hirsch's cultural literacy proposals, wrongheaded though these proposals are. It seems as if these scholars are denying my hope for the political consequences of a national discourse, denying their own vocation as intellectuals. Hirsch has been almost universally condemned on grounds that he has no legitimate authority on which to base his decisions about what knowledge should comprise the cultural literacy that would enable Americans to share a national discourse. Moreover, it seems that scholars in English studies believe that no one could possess such authority. While I do not want to credit Hirsch's authority, I want to explore the possibility that there is another, legitimate source of authority on which we as scholars of language-in-use could draw to assist in the formation of a national discourse.

I think that Hirsch has been attacked without accompanying suggestion of an alternative to address the lack of a shared discourse because English studies is under the domination of a theoretical orientation I will call the "philosophical." The philosophical orientation as I define it has its origins in a search for truth. This truth is supposed to exist independent of human beings on a plane beyond the material and temporal. Humans do not make truth, they discover it. The human who possesses true knowledge can use it to guide decisions on what is good, whether for personal morality or political ethics. The true knowledge becomes the basis or foundation of the person's entire world view. Hence this kind of knowledge has been termed "foundational" knowledge. A person may have to be convinced by rhetorical means that a particular item of knowledge is true or foundational, but once this conviction is achieved, the necessity of accepting the truth is presumed to be self-evident.

Scientific knowledge is the paradigmatic example of foundational knowledge. In English studies, the search for foundational knowledge has taken the form of a search for truths about human nature, which could be rendered up by close attention to the literary text in which they reside. This is the project of New Criticism. Given the domination of science as a model of foundational knowledge, human nature for the literacy critic has been defined more in psychological or anthropological, rather than in religious or ethical, terms—for example, in the work of Northrop Frye.

In recent years, however, this philosophical orientation has undergone a radical change. Influenced by scholars in the discipline of philosophy, such as Richard Rorty, who believe that there is no transcendent truth, at least none accessible to human beings, many in the academic community assume that everything humans take for truth is made, not discovered, by humans. Thus, according to this reasoning, foundational knowledge is really the product of cultural activity, shaped by ideology and constituted, not merely conveyed, by rhetoric. In short, there is no foundational knowledge, no knowledge that is necessary or self-evident. Whatever we believe, we believe only because we have been persuaded.

There has recently been much talk of a rhetorical turn in English studies, and it arises from the new anti-foundationalism of our philosophical orientation. If all knowledge is nonfoundational, made by people, then the discourse used to frame and promulgate knowledge takes on new importance. Persuasive language is no longer the servant of truth, making it possible for people to understand so that they can believe. Rather, persuasive language creates truth by inducing belief; "truth" results when rhetoric is successful. Hence scholars in English studies, already professionally committed to studying language in use, wish to take rhetoric as their new domain. Work in composition and in literature is converging on rhetoric.

It seems to me, however, that this rhetorical turn is still hampered by our ties to the philosophical orientation. If we are now anti-foundationalists, we are also still philosophers. That is, we are still asking whether foundational knowledge can be achieved, although now we answer that question, no. We are still nostalgically evoking the search for truth, only continually to announce that truth cannot be found. We spend our time exposing truth claims as historically, ideologically, rhetorically constructed; in other words, we spend our time in the activity called deconstruction.

We have not yet taken the next, crucially important step in our rhetorical turn. We have not yet acknowledged that if no unimpeachable authority and transcendent truth exist, this does not mean that no respectable authority and no usable truth exist. Our nostalgia for the self-evident and absolute prevents us from accepting as legitimate the authority created by collective discursive exchange and its truths as provisionally binding. If we could take this next step, we could perhaps find the collective will to collaborate on a pluralistic national discourse that would displace Hirsch's schemes while addressing the same lack he delineates. Indeed, we might imagine the public function of the intellectual as precisely rhetorical: our task is to aid everyone in our academic community, and in our national community, to share a discourse.

We can use the anti-foundationalist philosophical perspective to critique Hirsch and Allan Bloom, another proposer of a scheme for cultural literacy. But such critiques by themselves are inadequate. We must go on to develop a positive or utopian moment in our critique, an alternative to totalizing schemes for national unity. Some Marxist and feminist theorists, as I hope to show, are beginning to indicate the direction in which this further step in our rhetorical turn might lead.

I

To illustrate the weaknesses of the anti-foundationalist philosophical perspective, I would like to examine the Modern Language Association yearbook *Profession 88*. The policy-forming or political function of this journal was underlined by the MLA's unprecedented decision to devote the 1988 yearbook not to reprints but to articles invited to address a single theme: the cultural literacy work of Allan Bloom and E. D. Hirsch. Moreover, seven of the eight articles in this issue condemn schemes for cultural literacy roundly, in similar terms and with similar alternatives. First the promoters of schemes for cultural literacy are attacked on grounds of falsely claiming to possess foundational authority. Then the individual autonomy of each student and teacher is defended against the encroaching demands of schemes specifying a traditional content for cultural literacy. Finally, the curricular pluralism which is presumed to result from such autonomy is praised on grounds that it facilitates the study of difference.

Hirsch and Bloom are accused by their critics of claiming an authority that presumes to transcend historical circumstances, thus giving its possessor the right to range over the history of the entire Western intellectual tradition and select the truly "great" works. As some critics note, Allan Bloom is more vulnerable than Hirsch to charges of claiming to possess such transcendent authority. Kenneth Alan Hovey, for example, describes Bloom as believing that ordinary people, who are caught in the historical circumstances of "nation, race and religion," can produce little more than time-bound, culture-bound work, or what he calls "literary ephemera" (44). But Bloom believes there is also a class of being called the philosopher, who is not caught in historical circumstances, who "ris[es] above time," and who consequently can distinguish, and presumably produce, "great books" (44). Hovey thus indicts Bloom because, from the anti-foundationalist point of view, this special class of being, the philosopher, does not exist. There is no philosopher rendering true judgments of the timeless. Rather, what we think of as the status of being timeless is in fact a judgment that is historically constructed—made by "the times themselves," in Hovey's phrase (44).

Hirsch might be brought under the fire of this critique as well, though Hovey does not discuss him. Although Hirsch sees the content of national cultural literacy as appropriately changing over time, he places the power of deciding what changes to render canonical in the hands of experts such as himself. He has even proposed the creation of a sort of Académie Américaine to determine the content of a national cultural literacy. Hence in practice his national cultural literacy takes on the authority of timeless truth, and his experts function just as Hovey says Bloom's philosophers do. Up to this point I can agree with Hovey's critique as it might be applied to both Bloom and Hirsch.

It is striking, however, that "philosopher" becomes a term of reproach in this critique. In *Profession 88*, William K. Buckley and Helene Moglen also use the term negatively, even bitterly, as in this characterization from Moglen: "Once [Bloom] had himself become a high priest in the exalted order of philosophers, he delivered to awed neophytes the revealed meanings of the sacred texts" (60). The point, of course, is the foolishness of pretending that one can be a traditional philosopher with access to the transcendent truth of timeless texts. Anti-foundationalism makes the pretense pathetic, if not vicious. But what strikes me is the sense of loss conveyed by the emotional tone of these anti-foundationalist critiques. As I have suggested, anti-foundationalist philosophers are preoccupied with the necessity of saying no to foundational knowledge. Hence their concern is simply to knock down any authority claims made by others and to offer instead little more than a presumed individual autonomy.

This point has been made most neatly by an exchange in *The Chronicle of Higher Education* between Lynne Cheney, chair of the National Endowment for the Humanities, and noted anti-foundationalist philosopher Stanley Fish. Cheney is one of the public officials who have been convinced that our schools need schemes for cultural literacy. In support of this position, she writes: "The humanities are about more than politics, more than social power. What gives them their abiding worth are truths that pass beyond time and circumstance—truths that, transcending accidents of class, race, and gender, speak to us all" (A20). In other words, Cheney asserts that there are texts which contain true knowledge. She assumes that everybody has the capability to discern the importance of these texts, simply by virtue of being human—they "speak to us all." Fish later commented on Cheney's remarks as follows: "Once you have subtracted from the accidents of class, race, gender, and political circumstance, what is it that you have left?" (qtd. in Green A16). The correct anti-foundationalist answer to this question is, nothing.

The next step in undermining foundational authority claims is often to suggest that the authority really rests on ideologies that are conditioned by the claimant's personal circumstances. For example, in *Profession 88*, Buckley depicts Bloom as a social climber who longs for a state ruled by an elite group which he could join. Andrew Sledd and James Sledd depict Hirsch as a sycophantic ideologue of the American capitalist "gerontocracy" (38). Moglen argues that at bottom Bloom is anxious about his male potency and seeks to defend it via a reified concept of machismo propped up by the Western intellectual tradition.

Buckley, the Sledds, and Moglen would not themselves claim to be free of historical constraints. But they would see their argumentative position as superior to that of Bloom and Hirsch because at least they admit that they are so constrained. For anti-foundationalists, however, admitting to historical constraints means giving up all claims to an authority that they could hope to get many other people to acknowledge. Hence this line of argument leads to the position that decisions about what to read and write should be left up to individual teachers and students. This position is taken in *Profession 88* by James A. Schultz, reporting on the opinions of the

MLA Committee on Academic Freedom, as well as by Moglen, Buckley, the Sledds, and Paul B. Armstrong.

The anti-foundationalist philosophers are correct to attack any authority that claims to place itself beyond question. The problem is that they still cling, as I noted earlier, to the conviction that the question about foundational knowledge and unimpeachable authority is the single most important question, even if it has to be answered in the negative. Hence, because they must answer no to the all-important question, they feel they have no authority to offer any strong alternatives to the schemes for cultural literacy they debunk. All they feel they can do is to speak up for their own and everyone else's autonomy.

I would argue that the defense of autonomy leads to a dangerous sort of political quietism. In their deconstructive mode, the anti-foundationalist critics do point out the effect of historical circumstances on notions of the true and good which their opponents claim are outside time. In other words, the critics show that these notions consist in ideologies. But once the ideological interest has been pointed out, the anti-foundationalists throw up their hands. And because they have no positive program, the anti-foundationalist critics may end up tacitly supporting the political and cultural status quo.

A striking example of this quietism can be found in Hovey's argument. Like many other critics of schemes for cultural literacy, Hovey attempts to appropriate the overtly political and ostentatiously patriotic language of his opponents, in this case Bloom, and to use it to bolster his own position. But because he is not really recommending any action, the political language becomes denatured and political processes are actually covered over rather than revealed. Hovey argues that "the creed of America since its beginning" has been to oppose designating certain works as "Great Books" (45). Thus he tries to identify his own rather than Bloom's as the truly patriotic position. Then Hovey goes on to explain why our creed rejects "Great Books":

> The settlers and founders of America, while recognizing the need for authority, also saw its dangers and rejected the authority of a canon of books as much as they did a state church and a hereditary king. As a result, in America all books as well as all men are created equal. As

some people, nonetheless, show themselves worthy of higher offices, some books in time gain higher respect. (45)

In this passage, Hovey's first sentence equates rejecting a "canon of books" with overthrowing "a state church and a hereditary king." Presumably this equation is based in the idea that canon, church, and king would all claim to possess authority defined by foundational notions of the true and good. The anti-foundationalist philosopher delegitimates this authority by pointing out that there are no foundational notions, thus exposing the fact that the authority in question is really established by political means. If the authority's claims for respect and obedience are not foundational, then they can be resisted and changed by the same political means that established these claims in the first place.

This is the kind of resistance that Hovey sees people mounting when they created the political entity of the United States. One might suppose, then, that he implies that we should mount a similar kind of resistance when confronted by schemes for cultural literacy, since these schemes, like the political structures overthrown by the American revolutionaries, claim to be defined by foundational knowledge and have the support of powerful political figures. Hovey's first sentence, in other words, equates questioning the canon with not only political but explicitly revolutionary activity. He would seem to open the door to a full consideration of the political functions of schemes for cultural literacy and of the counter-claims their attackers might make, the "revolutionary" curriculum they might set up after the traditional canon is overthrown.

Hovey's next sentence, however, slams the door on any consideration of revolutionary politics. He seems to be arguing that the American Revolution overthrew the power, not of specific political institutions, but of history itself, so that now, "as a result," in America if nowhere else, historical circumstances have no constraining power and "all books as well as all men are created equal." It's as if Hovey has approached a topic so frightening to him—namely, the revolutionary curriculum—that rather than address it, he's willing to throw to the winds his credentials as an anti-foundationalist philosopher. For no anti-foundationalist philosopher could ever think that the power of history had been suspended anywhere. And once Hovey has repressed historical considerations by asserting the initial equality of all people and their books, he cannot give a political explanation of why some people and some books enjoy privileges over others. He is forced into the traditional philosophical position, which he had just been condemning in Bloom, that some inner worth allows particular people to rise to positions of political power and particular books to achieve a higher or canonical status. As he says, "some people . . . show themselves worthy of higher offices" and "some books in time gain higher respect." It would seem that we cannot employ our critical faculties on the processes whereby privilege is acquired, but we must simply wait for the intrinsic worth which justifies privilege to make itself evident. This is quietism.

Fortunately not all anti-foundationalist critiques of schemes for cultural literacy stop here. As I noted earlier, another concluding move is to endorse the curricular pluralism that presumably will issue from the exercise of autonomy by teachers and students. The call for pluralism does imply some positive political action beyond the quietism of the call for autonomy. This is because the call for pluralism implies enlarging the contents of national cultural literacy to include literature of value to social groups whose interests have previously been excluded in the establishment of the canon, excluded precisely because these groups were relatively politically powerless. Given who are included in and excluded from the canon already, to talk of enlarging it would seem to invite talk of the functions of education either to reproduce or to resist political inequalities. Of all the contributors to *Profession 88*, Helene Moglen comes the closest to letting this overtly political kind of discussion concerning the curriculum emerge, when she suggests that models for alternatives to schemes for cultural literacy can be found in programs for feminist studies, ethnic studies, and writing instruction.

Moglen gets caught, however, in the contradiction that besets anti-foundationalist philosophers when they try to articulate positions that require the positive assertion of the good. The contradiction is simply this: to wish to enlarge the canon is to imply that one has some values one is willing to rely on to designate the knowledge that should be added. Moglen speaks of the claims of women and ethnic minorities. But an opponent might ask by what right she presses these claims. If one does not happen to share the interests of these groups, why should one respond to their claims? Anti-foundationalist philosophers cannot answer this question because they cannot without logical inconsistency claim to possess any values to the authority of which anyone else should bow nor any knowledge anyone else should regard as true. Hence although Moglen seems clearly to be speaking out of some sense of social justice to be served, some value that causes her to identify women and ethnic minorities as groups needing more representation, she denies her own authority as a teacher to set a pedagogical agenda that would include these groups, and she endorses only the authority of students' own experiences and judgments. Presumably if Moglen had a class of wealthy white boys, she would have no choice but to grant their autonomy and let them avoid literature by women and ethnic minorities if they so desired.

Anti-foundationalist critics sometimes try to get out of this bind by arguing that they want a pluralistic canon simply so that the nature of difference can be studied. Previously noncanonical works need to be included to provide a contrast with the canon and so facilitate the study of difference. For example, María Rosa Menocal advocates the study of rock music lyrics as an aid to understanding lyric poetry. Andrew Sledd and James Sledd suggest that we can recognize the presence of difference by the difficulty to which it gives rise in interpretation, and they argue:

> All citizens of the USA—students and teachers alike—need constant practice in the reading of just those texts that are hard to read, and essential to read, because they do presuppose knowledge and beliefs that are alien to us. (38)

Apparently it does not matter what we read, so long as it is unfamiliar. By this logic, while white men should be reading work by women and ethnic minorities, women and ethnics should be studying the traditional canon. As with the argument on autonomy, there is a subtle denaturing of potentially political language here. The anti-foundationalist critics may recommend enlarging the canon with works by previously marginalized and politically disenfranchised groups, which would seem to ally the critics with a radical or revolutionary political position. But the critics can retreat safely into philosophy by claiming that they advocate these particular additions only because these happen to be the works missing now, and so are the ones needed for contrast.

I think there is a sort of pedagogical bad faith in this position. We tell the students we are only teaching them about difference. Yet in order to do that, we must deconstruct ideologies the students hold as foundational, a very painful process that students often oppose no matter how egalitarian and nonauthoritarian the teacher tries to be. For example, James Berlin has designed an experimental course to replace traditional freshman composition at Purdue University. His course asks students to deconstruct dominant ideologies on relations between the sexes and between employers and workers. Berlin has found that students hold firmly to the ideologies they are supposed to question. Women and men defend prostitution as a woman's right to make money any way she sees fit; and they explain unjustified pay cuts, unsafe working conditions, and other oppressive job situations which they have experienced as "good lessons" that toughen them and so will help them get ahead in the future.

Berlin's account makes me wonder what he can offer to students to make it worth their while to bear with the painful deconstructive process he asks of them. It seems to me that Berlin, and many of the rest of us who try to make a pluralistic study of difference into a curriculum, are calling students to the service of some higher good which we do not have the courage to name. We exercise authority over them in asking them to give up their foundational beliefs, but we give them nothing to put in the place of these foundational beliefs because we deny the validity of all authority, including, presumably, our own.

This pedagogical failure is illuminated by the critique of current practice offered by Jeff Smith, the only contributor to *Profession 88* who defends schemes for cultural literacy. Smith also appropriates political language for his peroration, and here is how he characterizes the evolution of the anti-foundationalist position:

> The United States was founded by people who believed that popular self-determination was served by empiricism: you could be made free

by attention to "nature" and its "self-evident truths." To many professional humanists today and perhaps, in less articulate ways, to large sectors of the public, democracy seems better served by skepticism. To demand attention to something "objective," to "privilege" some way of knowing or something to know and to give it priority in the classroom, is repressive; human liberation is served by never making such requirements. (28)

Smith plays on the word "liberation" here to suggest that whereas it may once have had political connotations, in the revolutionary days of the founding of the Republic, now all it means is a kind of individual autonomy that is in fact quite vulnerable to control by larger social institutions. "Skepticism" becomes not so much a principled position from which to articulate a political critique, as a philosophical void on which the political status quo can inscribe its dominant ideologies. Smith argues:

[In the 60s, skepticism] was still bound together with a politically healthy distrust of prevailing institutions of power. Today, those institutions and their demands—for instance, the demand that we grade students—are no longer openly resisted. Indeed, now that [skepticism] is an officially recognized doctrine . . . there are students out there being graded on whether they correctly grasp it. (28)

I suspect that Smith is right to see skepticism as a prevailing view not only among academics but also among "large sectors of the public." Jackson Lears has recently suggested that skepticism, or what he calls "pervasive irony" and the hip smirk, infuses the cultural milieu of television. Reviewing a book by Mark Crispin Miller, Lears approves Miller's reading of television's ironic stance as a subtle way of threatening the viewer to abandon belief in anything or else risk becoming the butt of a sit-com joke. Lears says:

So we are left with a form of domination that seems at once archaic and peculiarly modern—one that is dependent not on the imposition of belief but on the *absence* of belief, the creation of a void in which only power matters. . . . The aim of TV irony is not to promote "progressive" political ideals but to discredit all ideals by enlisting viewers in a comprehensive program of subtle self-oppression: urging them . . . to turn themselves into models of blasé self-containment. (60)

Lears's analysis helps us see how Smith has correctly diagnosed the source of students' opposition to Berlin's course and others that seek to teach difference. That is, students oppose being goaded by grades and professorial approval to achieve skepticism or the hip smirk. But it would not be exactly correct to say that this opposition springs from naive foundationalism. I think students oppose the push to skepticism because they've already seen skepticism and they don't like it. The world already looks horribly meaningless to them, and what we take to be their foundationalism is really a pathetic defense erected against this meaninglessness. If we can offer them no better answer to the meaninglessness than television can, then they may as well stay home and watch it instead of listening to us.

II

To take the next step in our rhetorical turn, we will have to be more forthright about the ideologies we support as well as those we attack, and we will have to articulate a positive program legitimated by an authority that is nevertheless nonfoundational. We must help our students, and our fellow citizens, to engage in a rhetorical process that can collectively generate trustworthy knowledge and beliefs conducive to the common good—knowledge and beliefs to displace the repressive ideologies an unjust social order would inscribe in the skeptical void.

Perhaps a way to begin the rhetorical process would be to aver provocatively that we intend to make our students better people, that we believe education should develop civic virtue. Richard Lanham has recently suggested that in the ancient world, such an announcement could be made without embarrassment because the good to be achieved by education was identified with the common good, with standards of civic virtue set by the community in which the education was taking place. In modern times, however, we have assumed that standards of civic virtue, like any other aspect of the transcendent good, can be defined only in terms of foundational knowledge. As a grasp on foundational knowledge has eluded us, we have felt equally disqualified to pronounce on civic virtue. Hence, as Terry Eagleton has argued, the moral scope of education has dwindled to matters of personal virtue only—matters, presumably, of autonomous choice in a morally pluralistic society. As Eagleton says, "Liberal humanism . . . is stronger on adultery than on armaments" (207).

Eagleton would solve this problem by what he calls a "traditionalist" return to rhetoric as the master discourse of English studies (206). A return to rhetoric would mean a return to considerations of the civic virtue classical orators once promoted. Eagleton says that he wants the rhetorical analysis of textual power to "[make] you a better person" (207), and he insists that "better" must be understood to encompass civic as well as personal morality:

> What it means to be a 'better person,' then, . . . must be a question of political and not only of 'moral' argument: that is to say it must be *genuine* moral argument, which sees the relations between individual qualities and values and our whole material conditions of existence. Political argument is not an alternative to moral preoccupations: it is these preoccupations taken seriously in their full implications. (208)

Eagleton argues that we should first ask how to make our students better people, and then decide what to teach and how to teach it on the basis of what best answers the initial question. Moreover, Eagleton takes the truly radical step of specifying his own definition of "better": he promotes a revolutionary civic virtue that must change the social order to foster the common good.

I am suggesting that we must be equally forthright in avowing the ideologies that motivate our teaching and research. For example, in the case of James Berlin's course at Purdue University which I described earlier, Berlin and his fellow instructors might stop trying to be value-neutral and anti-authoritarian in the classroom. Berlin tells his students that he is a Marxist but disavows any intention of persuading them to his point of view. Instead, he might openly state that this course aims to promote values of sexual equality and left-oriented labor relations and that this course will challenge students' values insofar as they conflict with these aims. Berlin and his colleagues might openly exert their authority as teachers to try to persuade students to agree with their values instead of pretending that they are merely investigating the nature of sexism and capitalism and leaving students to draw their own conclusions.

But wouldn't Berlin then be a propagandist? What is the legitimate authority of teachers, or any other orators? I would argue that this authority is derived from ideologies that already have some currency in the community the orators or teachers serve. Not everyone in America is against sexism, for example, but an argument against sexism can make use of values concerning human equality and fair play that even some sexists may hold. In other words, the orator can point out that a contradiction exists among the values that people hold and try to persuade them to rectify it in favor of the values the orator supports. The orator can urge, don't believe in both equality and sexism: give up the sexism. Thus the oratorical exercise of authority does recommend a positive position but does not impose it. The orator tries to achieve a consensus around the change in ideologies he or she advocates, but a consensus can only be achieved through collective participation in the rhetorical process.

Some feminist theorists have been particularly interested in charting the pathway I am indicating here between the personal and the political. They seek to define a rhetorical situation that leaves room for change because none of the parties in the conversation is wholly determined either by material circumstances, such as biological gender, or discursive constructions, such as the current cultural interpretations placed on gender. They seek a situation in which a positive stance, for better conditions as well as against present conditions, can be articulated free from charges of committing foundationalism.

One concise and thorough articulation of this view is Linda Alcoff's definition of "positionality." She argues that the meaning of the concept of "woman" is not defined by inherent, biologically determined characteristics, such as a tendency to nurture. But neither is "woman" constructed discursively of interpretations of gender that have no objective reality. An example of the latter would be to say that the notion that women can't do science is merely an attitude that afflicts women, which they should be able to throw off once they realize its deleterious effects—as if a bad attitude were all that prevented women scholars from achieving

equality in scientific research. Rather, Alcoff argues for an understanding of "woman" as defined, but not totally determined, by
historical circumstances. Alcoff says:

> When the concept "woman" is defined not by a particular set of attri-
> butes but by a particular position, the internal characteristics of the
> person thus identified are not denoted so much as the external context
> within which that person is situated. The external situation determines
> the person's relative position, just as the position of a pawn on a chess-
> board is considered safe or dangerous, powerful or weak, according to
> its relation to the other chess pieces. . . . Seen in this way, being a
> "woman" is to take up a position within a moving historical context and
> to be able to choose what we make of this position and how we alter this
> context. (433)

As I understand Alcoff's argument, the concept of positionality
could as easily be used as a basis for political action by people who
choose to make their race or religion a defining feature of their
identities. For example, under the concept of positionality it would
not make sense to say that being black entails particular innate
characteristics, such as stronger emotions than whites. It would
also not make sense to say that being black is the same as being
white, that color itself is a meaningless category, and anyone who
imagines that differences can be attributed to it is deluded. But one
could choose to work from a position that both acknowledged the
shaping power of current cultural interpretations of ethnicity and
aimed to transform the negative meaning of color differences.

Alcoff, however, may underemphasize the collective nature of
positionality, which would have to be recovered for the concept to
be truly rhetorical. Although I would agree with Alcoff that one's
position has a subjective dimension, positional identity obviously
entails group membership. Group interests hence shape individual
choices for action. Moreover, the collective values of groups or
positions against which one struggles must also be taken into account, as I suggested earlier, as a means to persuasion. Gandhi and
Martin Luther King provide models of how to use contradictions in
the opponents' ideologies to sway them. Feminist theorist Dale M.
Bauer uses Kenneth Burke's notion of identification to further explicate the ways in which rhetorical argument not only deconstructs

opposing views but seeks to win adherents. In a recent essay in *College English,* Bauer boldly associates such an identificatory rhetoric with an appropriate form of feminist classroom authority. She believes feminist teachers should be unembarrassed about seeking to persuade students to accept their analyses in the interests of the common good.

I think it is precisely relevant to our pursuit of a rhetorical turn in English studies that we discuss how our professional identities are shaped by our genders and sexual orientations, religions or secular ethical traditions, racial and ethnic identifications, regional or national origins, and also by the institutional histories of our schools and what is implicated for each of us by teaching where we do. Because we have not yet shared such discussions across the profession, I cannot conclude with a programmatic alternative to schemes for cultural literacy. I can only invite everyone to join seriously in a rhetorical process for articulating an alternative to which many of us can agree. This process will be a risky business; it will require arguing about what we should read and write, arguing about what canon we want to endorse instead of pretending we can will away the power of canons. It will require ideological avowals very uncongenial to anti-foundationalist philosophers. But I'm just not willing to concede yet that the smirk of skepticism is all we academics, or we Americans, can achieve in the face of the present crisis in our communal life. Certainly the last presidential campaign suggested that national discourse is dead, as Michael Halloran prophesied, and that we have no way of sharing views and concerns on the challenges confronting us. Those of us who would like to think of ourselves as humanists, as lovers of language, simply must attempt to create and share utopian rhetoric.

REFERENCES

Alcoff, Linda. "Cultural Feminism versus Post-Structuralism: The Identity Crisis in Feminist Theory." *Signs* 13 (1988): 405–36.

Armstrong, Paul B. "Pluralistic Literacy." Franklin, 29–32.

Bauer, Dale M. "Empathy and Identification." Unpublished ms.

———. "The Other 'F' Word: The Feminist in the Classroom." *College English* 52 (1990): 385–96.

Berlin, James. "A Course in Cultural Studies." MLA Convention. New Orleans, December 1988.

Bizzell, Patricia. "Arguing about Literacy." This volume.

Bloom, Allan. *The Closing of the American Mind: How Higher Education Has Failed Democracy and Impoverished the Souls of Today's Students.* New York: Simon, 1987.

Buckley, William K. "The Good, the Bad, and the Ugly in Amerika's *Akadēmia.*" Franklin, 46–52.

Cheney, Lynne V. "Humanities in America: A Report to the President, the Congress, and the American People." *The Chronicle of Higher Education* 21 Sept. 1988: A17–23.

Eagleton, Terry. *Literary Theory: An Introduction.* Minneapolis: University of Minnesota Press, 1983.

Franklin, Phyllis, ed. *Profession 88.* New York: MLA, 1988.

Green, Elizabeth. "Under Siege, Advocates of a More Diverse Curriculum Prepare for Continued Struggle in the Coming Year." *The Chronicle of Higher Education* 28 Sept. 1988: A13, A16.

Halloran, S. Michael. "Rhetoric in the American College Curriculum: The Decline of Public Discourse." *Pre/Text* 3 (1982): 245–69.

Hirsch, E. D., Jr., Joseph Kett, and James Trefil. *Cultural Literacy: What Every American Needs to Know.* Boston: Houghton, 1987.

Hovey, Kenneth Alan. "The Great Books versus America: Reassessing *The Closing of the American Mind.*" Franklin, 40–45.

Lanham, Richard. "The 'Q' Question." *The South Atlantic Quarterly* 87 (1988): 653–700.

Lears, Jackson. "Deride and Conquer." Rev. of *Boxed In: The Culture of TV,* by Mark Crispin Miller. *The Nation* 9 Jan. 1989: 59–62.

Menocal, María Rosa. " 'We Can't Dance Together.' " Franklin, 52–58.

Moglen, Helene. "Allan Bloom and E. D. Hirsch: Educational Reform as Tragedy and Farce." Franklin, 59–64.

Schultz, James A. "Stick to the Facts: Educational Politics, Academic Freedom, and the MLA." Franklin, 65–69.

Shaughnessy, Mina. *Errors and Expectations.* New York: Oxford University Press, 1977.

Sledd, Andrew, and James Sledd. "Hirsch's Use of His Sources in *Cultural Literacy:* A Critique." Franklin, 33–39.

Smith, Jeff. "Cultural Literacy and the Academic 'Left.' " Franklin, 25–28.

Afterword

Recently I happened to read Max Weber's essay "Science as a Vocation."[1] Weber asserts that science—or perhaps we should translate his term to mean scholarship—is presently thought to be capable of explaining everything in the world. Because of this belief in the power of science, there are no more mysterious forces in the world for modern people, only currently unexplained ones. Human life is rendered meaningless by this belief in the expanding explanatory scope of science, because the individual life cannot be imagined as possessing any satisfying completeness when, whenever one must leave the theater, the unfolding of scientific knowledge is still going on. One always dies too soon.

Hence, says Weber, we modern people are especially susceptible to false prophets—people who claim to be able to put us in touch once again with the mysterious, to speak for mysterious forces. The academic who sets up to promulgate values from his (or her) professorial podium is such a false prophet, for the academic's proper business, science, has nothing to do with values and cannot answer any value questions. Science only explains the world and can say nothing about how people should value what it explains. Hence the academic who claims to have answers to value questions must be implying that he (or she) is getting these answers from some mysterious source.

Weber expresses sympathy for the academic who succumbs to the temptation to set up as a false prophet, or as a "leader"— Weber's equation of these concepts is telling. But he asserts that to give in to this temptation is unmanly (*sic*). Rather, he says, the noble posture for the academic is that of disinterested inquirer, who only analyzes questions of value and poses alternatives to students without, insofar as is possible, indicating his (or her) own preferences in the matter. As a political economist, Weber contends that such concealing of one's own value preferences is particularly desirable when one is teaching about politics. To solace oneself for the moral aridity of one's professional life, Weber suggests that one may turn in private, discreetly, to religion—a choice which should, however, have nothing to do with one's professional life.

Reading Weber's essay, I come easily to the judgment that science does not have the power that he ascribes to it. Postmodern academics do not believe, I take it, that science is capable of explaining everything in the world. Rather, it seems we now believe that our science—again, thinking of that term in the broader sense of all scholarship—does not describe or explain the world so much as it evinces our own perceptual limitations, value systems, prejudices, ideologies. Whereas Weber calls academics to the noble effort of putting aside all value preferences, so far as possible, in our scholarly work, we postmodern academics now believe that the effort of putting aside value preferences is so futile as hardly to be worth engaging.

Yet our loss of faith in science has not revived a belief in mystery. Now that we do not believe we can explain the world, we do not see it as repopulated with mysterious forces. Rather, it seems that we are taking a position similar to Giambattista Vico's, namely that we can, at least, understand what we have made—that is, human artifacts, institutions, civilizations, human history. Our belief in the power of historical and social-constructionist analyses of human activities functions in the same way as Weber's belief in science. What matters is that with the belief in these analyses, it seems that we can still avoid acknowledging any presence of mystery. Thus we are still subject to the same etiology of meaninglessness that Weber diagnosed. We die too soon, because we always die before the course of history is completed.

Moreover, we postmodern academics still regard the profession of values from the academic podium as false prophecy. For where could these values come from? We are no more prepared than Weber to entertain the possibility that they come from some mysterious source. Rather we say with Weber that they must come from the individual's education, group allegiances, ideological indoctrinations, and so on. And we are no more prepared than Weber to sanction the promulgation of such a contingent brew to people who are obliged institutionally to listen to it—students. Instead, we advocate a postmodern version of the moral austerity recommended by Weber—we require that the academic continually point out how one must always see values as screens for material interests.

Weber allows me to see myself as someone who has a great deal of trouble making this intellectual sacrifice, acquiescing in the meaninglessness of human life on behalf of academic inquiry. Perhaps I am beset with the typical modern weakness for false prophets, as Weber warns. But even worse, I can't get rid of the feeling that I ought to be a prophet myself, that my students' desire for a leader is not illegitimate. To put it another way, if I am honest I must say that what I really care about is what my students believe, how they will conduct their lives, and not just whether they have learned to analyze beliefs or lives in correct postmodern fashion. Without fully understanding why I have this concern or how I can legitimate it in postmodern terms, perhaps I am willing to bracket elements of it as mysterious.

This concern seems a bit skew to current trends in composition studies. The field is presently moving from a marginal and disrespected position in the academy to one of greater professionalization and institutionalization. This movement exhibits a strong tendency to pick up what I might call Weberian values about our "science," our research, by way of legitimization. I am willing, however, to refrain from lamenting this tendency if I do not have to regard it as totalizing—if I am allowed to hope we can still engage in discussions of what values we cherish and what values we want to encourage in our students.

I

I suppose it is noncontroversial to assert that composition studies is indeed undergoing professionalization and institutionalization. The proliferation of graduate programs in composition studies and of scholars tenured and promoted for their work in composition studies is no secret. Moreover, this process has tended to privilege the development of scholarly work that can be published and evaluated by traditional means. This tends to privilege activities that are fairly well defined methodologically, so that people can be clear on how to proceed with their projects.

The desire for academic respectability evinced in this process should not be glibly condemned as accommodationist, I think, in view of the insecurity scholars in composition studies have felt in the academy for a long time. People have worked in oppressive conditions that have been justified by lack of intellectual respect for composition work on the part of other academics. With published research, now we can get respect—not everywhere, yet, but the trend is in our favor. The process we are going through now is an unsurprising response to conditions, so long as we remain workers within academic institutions.

If these changes should be seen as consequences of our institutional situation, however, I would not want to say that academic structures have to determine the field of composition studies totally. I think there are special qualities that we can try to preserve as a field. Key here is our commitment to pedagogy. In the interest of meeting student needs as we see them, as John Trimbur has noted, we have always tended to practice intellectual bricolage.[2] We have borrowed freely from other fields if we thought the work could help us teach better.

This tendency might serve us well if we want to avoid becoming locked into a single "normal discourse" paradigm after the fashion of many other academic disciplines. In literary studies, there is much discussion now of how to preserve diverse theoretical viewpoints; Gerald Graff advocates focusing teaching on the conflicts among the positions of various members of the contemporary English department.[3] In "teaching the conflicts," we could be in the "normal" disciplinary discourse and yet question it, a model of activity we might wish our students to practice in other venues after they leave us.

More important to me, though, is composition's link through pedagogy to larger social concerns. In the past, composition studies, unlike literary studies and most other academic disciplines, maintained a very close rapprochement between classrooms and the individual scholar's work. Now our professionalization has legitimated much research that has no immediate classroom application, such as work on histories of premodern rhetoric. Even though we have been hurt in the past by rushing into the classroom with research that doesn't belong there, it is important to maintain what I might call an affective link between our work and the classroom, so that our care for the students, our concern for their struggles, will always be there as a way of informing and checking our scholarly interests.

For me, this affective link to the classroom is also a link to value considerations. I feel the tug of that link not just because I like the students personally, but also because I feel that I have what I can only call moral and political obligations to them in my work with them. This makes it not only legitimate, but imperative for me to relate the scholarly projects I want to do to the kind of person I want to be, trying to help redress economic inequality even though living an economically privileged life in this late twentieth-century global community. This is the lure of the role of prophecy.

Discourse about values may seem to be taboo in our professional forums, but it often comes in through the back door. A word or phrase will become current in the disciplinary discourse precisely because it is morally ambiguous—it could mean a lot or a little. For example, "critical consciousness" could mean little more than self-consciousness about one's writing processes, as Linda Flower has used the term, or it could resonate with all the meanings it has in the pedagogy of Christian and Marxist educator Paulo Freire (see the discussion of Freire in the Introduction to this book). Typically we use these resonant phrases without specifying how far we want them to go. We create a moral ambience that isn't fully accountable to what's spelled out in the discourse. The taboo discussion of values is presumed to be on the table without anyone's having to mention it. Thus it seems I am not the only one who cannot refrain from the temptation Weber condemns.

Perhaps what I am imagining might be characterized as a shift from teaching composition to teaching rhetoric, if "composition" is taken to mean something like instruction in techniques, whereas "rhetoric" denotes education of the whole person in culturally endorsed values, through reading, writing, and speaking. Of course, this is a false dichotomy, in that there can be no instruction in techniques without education in cultural values. But more, I want to promote particular values; I want to feel, with classical rhetoricians such as Isocrates and Quintilian, that I am shaping *good* people by my instruction. Wouldn't this be a version of the classical project of teaching virtue? If so, then one way into the exploration of values would be to ask whether we still think virtue can be taught.

II

If by "virtue" we mean moral values derived from mysterious sources, and if by "teaching" we mean compelling students to live by these values, then for me, the answer to the question of whether virtue can be taught would have to be no. We postmodern skeptical academics say that values from mysterious—transcendent and universal—sources do not exist, or at least are not available to historical beings. I can acknowledge the presence of a mysterious element in my own thinking while at the same time bracketing it off, saying I cannot explain its influence on the rest of my argument. Also, we American democratic academics would have to say that compelling students to do anything is not appropriate pedagogical behavior.

But if I must give up teaching, in this sense, virtue, in this sense, that does not necessarily mean I must give up teaching virtue. I find myself in somewhat the same position as the ancient Greek rhetorician Isocrates. Like postmodern skeptics, he debunked teachers of his day who claimed to be able to foretell the future, that is, who claimed to give their students a set of values guaranteed to apply in all times and places. If one possessed such values, one could foretell how one would have to behave in all times and places. The mysterious sources of such values, Isocrates contended, were not open to our view.[4]

But Isocrates nevertheless set up to teach something that he thought people ought to pay good money for, something that he thought he deserved praise from the community for promulgating. His solution to the problem of where to get values to teach was to say that he would get them not from some transcendent realm, but from the traditions of his community; indeed, this is where all values must come from, according to postmodern skepticism. As for compelling change in his students' characters, Isocrates argued that while he could not guarantee to change them he could attempt to influence them, that is, to persuade them, to adopt the values deemed most praiseworthy in his community. His authority as a teacher of virtue, in other words, would be established rhetorically.

Our situation, of course, is not identical with that of Isocrates. The Athenian community of Isocrates's day could be treated as much more culturally homogeneous than contemporary America, in part because social exclusions were accepted—of women, for example, and of slaves—that we would find unacceptable. Indeed, postmodern skeptical academics are habitually fearful that any talk of teaching virtue will tend to introduce exclusions, as socially privileged groups in our diverse nation will tend to arrogate to themselves the right to define what virtue gets taught.

But my commitment to American democratic values will not let me rest with a skeptical prohibition on any instruction in virtue at all. I feel strongly that American academics are indeed abandoning their responsibility to the community when they allow a theoretical perspective to silence them on questions of grave importance to common security—I mean questions concerning Americans' ability as a nation to learn to appreciate and to negotiate among the differences that characterize this diverse society. I feel strongly that we academics need to find more ways to promote social justice—that is, at least, to work against economic inequality and rampant hatred of difference. If this is false prophecy, so be it. I'm willing to risk looking as if my values come from a mysterious source, while being able to provide explanation only to the effect that they are historically located and communally sanctioned.

As explained in the Introduction to this book, I can no longer feel that I am doing enough to promote social justice simply by helping students to get an education, even if I specify a mission to teach students from groups that have suffered discrimination. This explanation once satisfied me when I could believe that I was giving no direct instruction in values in the classroom, but rather was simply offering students the value-neutral tool of academic discourse. I would have admitted, perhaps, to giving some indirect instruction in values, for example through taking care to assign readings written by members of diverse social groups, but basically I could see myself as the objective scholar that Weber recommends as our role model. I saw my commitment to social justice being served more by the aftereffects or outcomes of my classroom work (through the academic success of previously disenfranchised students, for example) than by the actual content of my interactions with students.

Postmodern skepticism has taught me, however, to view all knowledge, values, and individual subjectivities as possessing no transcendent essence or eternal truth, but rather as emerging endlessly from an interplay of social, cultural, and historical forces. I should now see myself as viewing the world through an unremovable lens of beliefs and values that have been shaped by the ways the people around me have taught me to react to my experience; and I should see that even my sense of who "I" am has been similarly shaped.

Therefore, I must see all my classroom work as deeply imbued with my moral values. I certainly do not go into class and announce that we will now commence indoctrination into the following table of laws. Yet everything I do in the classroom is informed by one or another element in my world view, thus potentially conflicting at every turn with other elements in the students' diverse world views and, because of my institutional position at the head of the class, potentially undercutting their values. Service to my personal morality thus can no longer be seen as an aftereffect or outcome that is neatly separable from the classroom work; in other words, my morality can no longer be regarded as purely private and personal, as Weber would have it. My values take on an ethical dimension because I am always trying to persuade my students to identify with them, whether I always realize I am doing this or not. And my values take on a political dimension because the differences in students' ability or willingness to respond to my persuasive pressure, differences that affect their success in my classroom whether I am always aware of it or not, are differences that tend to spring more from their social group membership than from anything that could still be called personal idiosyncracy.

This conclusion seems to eliminate the option of claiming that I foster social justice precisely by *not* talking about it in class. To disavow my moral agenda is simply to cover over my inevitable persuasive approaches. Thus this conclusion also disturbs me because it seems to make it inevitable that I will contravene my democratic values even as I try to serve them. Insofar as I am pushing these values in the classroom, I am being unfair to the students who can't or won't accept them. I lay myself open to charges of what I might call "vulgar politicization" or ideological tyranny in the classroom, the sort of thing that fuels attacks on so-called "political correctness."

One way out of this dilemma is to attempt to install a debunking or deconstructive method in place of persuasive efforts on behalf of my world view. In other words, I might try to escape by saying, "I will avoid inculcating my world view precisely by focusing the classwork on the study of how world views get inculcated." Among the most interesting recent attempts to explore this solution is Steven Mailloux's in *Rhetorical Power*.[5]

Mailloux begins the book by describing the following interpretive sequence:

> The Space Act of 1958 begins, "The Congress hereby declares that it is the policy of the United States that activities in space should be devoted to peaceful purposes for the benefit of all mankind." In March 1982, a Defense Department official commented on a phrase used in this statute: "We interpret the right to use space for peaceful purposes to include military uses of space to promote peace in the world." (3)

Mailloux tells us that he posed this reading as a problem to his students in order to lead them to see that the meaning this official claims to have extracted from the statute comes neither from the text alone nor from any commonly held conventions for interpreting such texts, but rather from other elements in the official's world view, such as a moral commitment to militarization. Thus Mailloux attempts to debunk or deconstruct the official's interpretation by showing it to be self-serving.

Mailloux tells us, however, that one of his students persisted in defending the official's interpretation. Mailloux says that this opposition awakened in him a "theoretical urge," the desire for an argument that could somehow compel the student's assent to Mailloux's critique. In the grip of the theoretical urge, Mailloux longs for what he calls a "general theory of interpretation that could supply rules outlawing my student's misreading" (4). But Mailloux finds that he cannot believe in any of the contenders for the role of general theory. Hence it seems that Mailloux must acknowledge that his preference for a reading different from that of his student stems from a clash of his and the student's values.

Just at this point, however, Mailloux shies away from concluding that he is theorizing or creating interpretations on the basis of his own admittedly contingent world view. Rather he attempts to hold a fig leaf of method before the nakedness of his moral commitments, presumably because he has been trained, as we academics all have, to view the open professing of moral commitments with embarrassment. Mailloux calls his method "rhetorical hermeneutics." This method supports postmodern skepticism when, as Mailloux says, it "gives up the goals of Theory [to supply compelling rules for interpretation] and continues to theorize about interpretation only therapeutically, exposing the problems with foundationalism" (17).

But when Mailloux explains what rhetorical hermeneutics has to do besides this critiquing and debunking, we find that it is little more than providing documentation of just how socially, culturally, and historically determined the interpretations in question are: rhetorical hermeneutics "should also provide histories of how particular theoretical and critical discourses have evolved" (17). The "hermeneutics" part of this method is its "exposing" of problems, while the "rhetorical" part is its historical research on the evolution of discourses. Mailloux characterizes rhetoric as the study of "historical sets of topics, arguments, tropes, ideologies, and so forth which determine how texts are established as meaningful through rhetorical exchanges" (15).

Because he purports to be offering no more than a method here, Mailloux can only speak wryly about his own moral commitments. For example, when describing his posing of the Space Act interpretation problem to his students, Mailloux says self-deprecatingly that he spoke "with just the right touch of moral indignation" (3). Mailloux is not arguing for quietism, however. He insists in several places that one need not await the advent of transcendently ratified values before making arguments against specific moral positions (see 169, 180). He asserts, "Our beliefs and commitments are no less real because they are historical" (181). Moreover, the exemplary histories Mailloux gives in his book are deeply imbued with his moral values and derive much of their persuasive power from these values. But it seems Mailloux cannot allow himself to talk directly about the moral commitments that inform his work.

A case in point is a sentence that occurs near the end of the book, in Mailloux's history of interpretations of the ABM Treaty: "I am certainly not saying that it is impossible to disagree effectively with the Reagan administration's absurd reinterpretation of the ABM Treaty" (180). This sentence bespeaks Mailloux's opposition to quietism, and he goes on to mention several rhetorical strategies for disagreeing effectively, even while bearing in mind, as he says in good postmodern skeptical fashion, that "the resulting interpretation is, of course, just as contingent as the militaristic reading" (180).

But Mailloux focuses in this sentence on the method of arguing, not on the moral position he takes. Having made this statement, Mailloux is allowed by the terms of his own argument to go on to talk about how to disagree, but he is not allowed to talk about what he means by dropping into this sentence the judgment that the Reagan reinterpretation is "absurd." He is not allowed to talk about the moral position he is taking by using that word. The word "absurd" becomes a sort of wistful signal to those readers out there who agree with Mailloux, not about interpretation, but about militarism.

Perhaps Mailloux hopes that the practice of rhetorical hermeneutics will lead us to his positive beliefs (e.g. racial equality not white supremacy, common security not national security) without his having to be embarrassed by stating them. Mailloux's attitude here seems similar to mine when I thought I could foster social justice by teaching academic discourse as a morally netural tool. Stanley Fish has condemned this attitude as what he calls "antifoundationalist theory hope," and I have been persuaded to Fish's point of view.[6] To return to my earlier metaphor, I reject the possibility that rhetorical hermeneutics can budge our world-view lenses.

At the same time, it may well be worth while to study lens-fixing processes. A better metaphor than "lens" for world views might be instead the machine the optometrist uses to find what lens works best for you, a machine that flips various lenses in succession before your eyes. Perhaps by studying the processes of lens-fixing, we can get our hands on the control knobs of this machine, can affect the procession of lenses before our eyes, even if it is impossible ever to remove the device from before our faces. I think rhetorical hermeneutics and other such historical and social-constructionist forms of analysis might be a way to help us get our hands on this mechanism.

At the same time, I recognize an impulse to do more than study world views and hope that increased tolerance emerges. I recognize the impulse to teach one's values forthrightly, since it seems inevitable that one's teaching will be value-laden. This impulse urges me to seek another way out of the dilemma of the postmodern skeptic who wants to promote social justice.

I might take my stand forthrightly on values that I acknowledge as constructed by my social, cultural, and historical circumstances, and, in effect, warn students in advance that if they come to me, this is what they will be getting. Thus at least I cannot be accused of imposing so-called "political correctness" on hapless students or of duping them into exposing themselves unawares to my persuasive approaches. Representatives of this solution can be found among academics who announce that they are speaking "as a woman," for example, or "as an African-American." This approach has much in common with Linda Alcoff's concept of "positionality."[7]

Alcoff rejects both essentialist or cultural feminism and a deconstructive or radically skeptical view which would disallow any assertions at all about gender-based power relations. Positionality has a material base in its assumption that we can say that embodied differences among people do exist, for example differences of gender or race. The meaning of these differences, however, is to be understood as defined, but not totally determined, by social, cultural, and historical circumstances.

If one is biologically female, for example, one has to contend with the constructed meanings of the category "woman"; but Alcoff also argues that such categories are fluid and dynamic, changing with changing circumstances. As she says, "Seen in this way, being a 'woman' is to take up a position within a moving historical context and to be able to choose what we make of this position and how we alter the context" (433). Although Alcoff is primarily concerned with constructions of the female, she notes that her analysis could apply as well to individuals who feel constructed most saliently in other categories such as race, ethnicity, or sexual orientation.

In effect, what I gain by the argument is the right to present my body as my justification. It's as if I am saying, "Because I am embodied in a form that is interpreted in particular ways in the present moment, I am allowed not only to study the processes of interpretation but also to take exception to those meanings I find threatening to my physical and mental well-being and to fight for the promulgation of meanings more conducive to my self-interest." Furthermore, I presumably save my self-interested position from seeming selfish by identifying my own efforts with those of other members of what I take to be my "kind" or group, in this case others who are constructed as "women."

I now suspect, however, that this theoretical view leads to what I might call a sort of group selfishness. The teacher who announces her or his Alcoffian position will probably tend to attract students who already have some affinity for the announced position— indeed, it is on this presumed tendency that the defense against imposed "political correctness" rests. But such preaching to the converted, I fear, conduces to a group identification that has an in-built tendency to become more insular and intense the more the group is threatened, or perceives itself to be threatened, from the outside. The group tends to insist ever more strongly on its own victim role and its unmet needs, and concomitantly to reduce the chances of working with other groups against common sources of oppression. I think we see here the fulfillment of Weber's most telling warning against false prophecy from the academic podium, when he contends that it can lead to group fanaticism.

One example of such negative synergy comes in Elizabeth Ellsworth's account of her graduate education course at the University of Wisconsin, the announced aim of which was to design materials to combat the white-supremacist racism evinced in recent incidents on the campus.[8] She attracted to the course diverse students all morally committed against racism, and also seemingly eager to participate in her announced collaborative, critical-pedagogical approach. Nevertheless, Ellsworth tells us, the course was a failure. The students sorted themselves along lines of race, gender, sexual preference, religion, social class, and other categories. Finally unable to do any work together, they formed what Ellsworth calls "affinity groups" to meet outside of class time; two of these groups did manage to complete their separate anti-white-supremacist projects.

Reading Ellsworth's account of what happened in this course, I found myself wondering whether her practice of encouraging students to speak about their positional or group self-interests actually worked to create mistrust and an unwillingness to cooperate, contrary to her best intentions. It's as if students fell into a habit of constantly reminding themselves, in terms of their own victimage and unmet needs, of the many reasons why they should suspect and avoid other groups of students in the course. They thus made it impossible for themselves to look past these admittedly very significant differences to the commonalities that all groups might share—such as a moral commitment to oppose white-supremacist racism, and a sense that every group's well-being, even if the group is not defined in terms of race, might be enhanced by the defeat of racism. Would the various groups indeed share these commonalities? I do not know. But I want to advocate a pedagogy informed by the hope that common or related historical circumstances among the groups may have induced them to arrive at moral positions that are indeed similar.

Another version of this negative synergy is played out at Holy Cross College, where the overwhelming majority of my students are middle- and upper-class white Roman Catholics. Many enter college in possession of some contradictory beliefs: on the one hand they hold racist, sexist, anti-Semitic, and other discriminatory views; but on the other hand, they believe in democratic social justice, or what they tend to think of as the right to equal opportunity. This contradiction could be pedagogically fruitful if one wished—as I do—to strengthen and refine their commitment to social justice, for one could point out the contradiction and create a cognitive dissonance that one could attempt to nudge toward resolution in favor of democratic values. In fact, I try to do this.

But my pedagogical process is sometimes interrupted by another value contradiction. When students begin to see the first contradiction, and to give up discriminatory views in favor of more egalitarian ones, they become more open to hearing testimony about victimization and unmet needs from members of groups that have suffered discrimination—African-American students, for example. The so-called "majority" students even recover testimony of their own suffering, in some cases—white women students, for example, find they have much to say about sexism in the Catholic Church.

But my students also strongly hold a value that it is selfish to speak up for one's own interests, that one should always seek to subordinate one's own interests to those of the more needy; indeed, the school's motto is that we form "men and women for others." I might add that this value of self-abnegation has been pressed particularly upon the women students. So any student who begins to testify about his or her own victimization and unmet needs will be discrediting himself or herself with other students who are unable to hear more than that someone is selfishly complaining. Perhaps this negative synergy would be interrupted more effectively not only by pointing out that the testifier is speaking for group grievances, but also by indicating the extent to which this particular set of group grievances touches on the concerns of groups to which the listening students might belong—common concerns and value responses growing out of shared or similar historical circumstances.

This cross-referencing of interests might be facilitated if we could get beyond what I might call simple positionality, that is, the assumption that an individual will be significantly constructed by only one aspect of her or his embodiment. As I read about the groups into which Ellsworth's students fragmented, I found myself wondering which group the homosexual Jew joined, or the African-American woman. Most of us, I suspect, find ourselves being constructed differently in different times and places—here our race is salient, for example, and there our sexual orientation. Positionality tends to function more as essentialism, I suspect, when only one position is considered to be normative. But if our multiple allegiances are acknowledged, perhaps we thereby increase the chances for making common cause across group boundaries to address the social evils that afflict us all.

III

What is to be done? As a teacher, I would like to try, on the one hand, to encourage students to explore the historical rootedness of their own *several* Alcoffian positions; in this project Mailloux's rhetorical hermeneutics would be very valuable, for example in tracing the evolution of moral discourses the students hold as normative. Students can be encouraged to see themselves as moral agents whose authority to make judgments of their own and others' actions is historically contingent, but as Mailloux says, no less real for all that.

On the other hand, in the process of pursuing these historical researches and examining their own positions, I want to help students discover heretofor unrealized points of contact with the interests of groups to which they do not belong, and moral commonalities with other positions. As Henry Giroux has argued, it is possible for the teacher to point students toward materials that show not only that difference and dissent have been significant in American life in the past, but also that movements toward greater social equality and toleration of difference have sometimes met with success.[9]

What takes this project beyond a sort of historically oriented values-clarification approach is the exercise of rhetorical authority on the part of the teacher. I want to range over the values my students are exploring and try to find those that could be used persuasively to turn students to my egalitarian values. As I suggested earlier, one example of this process in action would be the posing to students of the contradiction between their discriminatory views and American social justice. I see my authority as contingent not only upon the circumstances that give rise to my own commitments, but also upon my ability as rhetor to recognize and incorporate into my persuasive arguments the values and circumstances of my students.

Moreover, after the fashion of Isocrates, I want to encourage my students to imitate my exercise of rhetorical authority. I have to allow them to try to persuade me, a move I think academics seldom make with students some of whose values are radically different from their own, and to persuade other members of the class (indeed, I could now cite values of mine that have been modified by students' persuasion). I have to devise pedagogical mechanisms whereby everyone's access to rhetorical authority could be realized in our work together, for example, through finding ways for students to change the agenda of a course in progress or to take its lessons out into nonacademic contexts.

I am now working on collecting materials that might help us move toward these pedagogical goals. These materials will, I hope, reflect my perception that Americans are united as a national community by few of the commonalities that obtain in other lands—we do not have much in the way of a common ethnic culture, religion, or even a common native tongue. But Americans may be said to be united by a common experiment in negotiating difference, in living with people who are very different from ourselves, whoever we take "ourselves" to be, and in recognizing the humanity of these others. Different groups in America have seldom had the "comfort" of cultural isolation.

Negotiations of difference have taken place in many ways in American experience, and I want to indicate the range of these actions, but my study will focus on negotiations that have occurred through language. I want to focus on moments in American history when different groups were vying for the right to interpret what was going on. I am particularly interested in moments when the situation did not resolve itself neatly into two opposing sides, but rather when there was a plurality of contending voices. I am also particularly interested in situations in which my values of social justice were at issue, perhaps painfully threatened, but also not totally defeated and even perhaps prevailing. The kinds of materials I am collecting include materials traditionally part of canonical "American literature," and also forgotten historical narratives, political documents, personal papers, transcripts of oratory, visual images—the possibilities are open.

For example, I am assembling materials concerning interactions between English immigrants and native Algonquians in colonial New England, which I hope to use both in American literature courses and in first-year composition. I am including canonical accounts of the period such as William Bradford's, but also alternative views by non-Puritans, such as the Pequot War narrative of Lion

Gardener. I am gathering Algonquian testimony from such sources as John Eliot's dramatic rendition of Algonquian arguments against accepting Christianity; Thomas Shepard's transcripts of religious confessions and of speeches against white-supremacist racism by so-called "Praying Indians" who had converted to Christianity; and Benjamin Church's sympathetic eyewitness account of the statements and actions of Algonquians who tried to remain neutral during King Philip's War or who fought fiercely against the English. I am collecting documents for case studies of two Algonquian groups' successful struggles to preserve some autonomy during the colonial period—documents such as treaties, land deeds, petitions by English-literate Algonquians to colonial governments, etc. I want to add an early-nineteenth-century Pequot minister's revisionist history of the seventeenth-century period, a history which cites and contests many of the earlier sources. I am collecting visual images such as maps and drawings by early English settlers, illustrations from captivity narratives, portraits of Native American leaders, etc.

I also want my students to participate in collecting and selecting materials for study, to demonstrate the way cultural archives are always shaped by human agency. Therefore I hope to direct students to assemble their own collections of materials on other instances of situations similar to the one my materials sketch—for example, to explore early relations between European-Americans and Native Americans in their home regions (if they are not from New England) or to trace the history of New England tribes mentioned in my colonial materials up through the nineteenth and twentieth centuries.

I don't think American negotiations of difference have always favored values of social justice. Indeed, I realize that it will be difficult to recover marginalized voices without prejudice (e.g., on the difficulties of representing Native American expressive traditions, see Martin).[10] But I hope materials can be selected to show that Americans have very often been concerned about social justice, that if we do not always achieve it, neither can we forget about it. Studying these American materials thus might begin to inspire by association an attachment to values of social justice. As Isocrates suggests, even the orator who studies noble examples only to manipulate the gullible comes to be influenced in social habits by these examples, especially when the orator's mentor responds encouragingly to this identification. But for such attention to civic virtue to occur in our teaching, we as teachers of rhetoric would have to be willing to say what pleases us, and what we believe. We would have to be willing to prophesy for social justice.

NOTES

1. Max Weber, "Science as a Vocation," in *Max Weber: Essays in Sociology*, eds. H. H. Gerth and C. Wright Mills (New York: Oxford University Press, 1958).

2. John Trimbur, "Composition Studies: Postmodern and/or Popular" (unpublished ms.).

3. Gerald Graff, "How to Deal with the Humanities Crisis: Organize It," *ADE Bulletin* 95 (Spring 1990): 4–10.

4. See "Against the Sophists," trans. George Norlin, in *The Rhetorical Tradition*, eds. Patricia Bizzell and Bruce Herzberg (Boston: Bedford Books, 1990).

5. Steven Mailloux, *Rhetorical Power* (Ithaca, N.Y.: Cornell University Press, 1989). All further references to this work appear in the text.

6. Stanley Fish, "Consequences," *Critical Inquiry* 11 (1985): 433–58.

7. Linda Alcoff, "Cultural Feminism versus Post-Structuralism: The Identity Crisis in Feminist Theory," *Signs* 13 (1988): 405–36.

8. Elizabeth Ellsworth, "Why Doesn't This Feel Empowering? Working through the Repressive Myths of Critical Pedagogy," *Harvard Educational Review* 59 (1989): 297–324.

9. Henry Giroux, *Schooling and the Struggle for Public Life* (Minneapolis: University of Minnesota Press, 1988).

10. Calvin Martin, ed., *American Indians and the Problems of History* (New York: Oxford University Press, 1987).

Pittsburgh Series in Composition, Literacy, and Culture

ACADEMIC DISCOURSE AND CRITICAL CONSCIOUSNESS
Patricia Bizzell

FRAGMENTS OF RATIONALITY: POSTMODERNITY AND THE
SUBJECT OF COMPOSITION
Lester Faigley

LITERACY ONLINE: THE PROMISE (AND PERIL) OF READING
AND WRITING WITH COMPUTERS
Myron C. Tuman, Editor

WORD PERFECT: LITERACY IN THE COMPUTER AGE
Myron C. Tuman